WE REMEMBER

WE REMEMBER

The Child Survivors' Association of Great Britain – AJR

Third Edition. Reprinted 2016

Matador
9 Priory Business Park
Kibworth Beauchamp
Leicestershire LE8 0RX, UK
Tel: (+44) 116 279 2299
Email: books@troubador.co.uk
Web: www.troubador.co.uk/matador

Cover photo: Crying Child Monument in Tarnow Poland. Photo: Joan Salter

British Library Cataloguing in Publication Data.
A catalogue record for this book is available from the British Library.

Typeset in 11ptt Bembo by Troubador Publishing Ltd, Leicester, UK
Printed and bound in the UK by TJ International Ltd, Padstow, Cornwall

Matador is an imprint of Troubador Publishing Ltd

Contents

Foreword to "**WE REMEMBER**"

This anthology is based on the memories of individual contributors and, as such, is not designed as historical texts. It represents the range of experiences, upheaval and trauma suffered by children who survived the Holocaust.

Originally published under the title "Zachor" in 2005, it was intended as a memorial to our families who perished. Due to the great demand, it was decided to produce it as a book to reach a wider audience. The Association has grown and several chapters have been added. The original introductions are included in this new publication.

Foreword (2005)

It reads like fiction.

Surely, real life is not so cruel, so devastating, so extreme. Real life does not threaten death every day, split families, dehumanise the dignity of the elderly, or make children, yes, children, the specific target of people bent on their painful and frightening destruction. Real life does not demand that people be so resilient, so creative, so courageous and inventive. Who would possibly hit a grandfather in the face with a rifle butt in front of his grandchild? Who would shoot a pregnant woman with a machine gun at close range? Who would send children to their deaths because they were 'hampering the productivity' of their parents? What real-life story could possibly include stripping thirteen-year-old girls and checking their orifices in front of half a dozen men?

It was not fiction.

But it was another world. It was a world in which the daughter of the family who was hiding Janine brought home an SS officer who buried her brother alive. It was a world in which a simple 'Guten Morgen' from Tom was the difference between life and death. It was a world in which Heidi changed her identity at the age of fourteen and then had to stick to her shaky story with steely determination under the threat of certain deportation. It was a world in which fifteen-year-old Edyta had to organise her own *Ausweis* (identity card) in order to prevent the threat to her own life and to try to complement the pitiful food ration allocated to what was left of her family.

What is so amazing about these testimonies is that they are *all* the experiences of children. It is generally assumed that society will look after its young people, that they will be protected and nurtured by adults whose only wish is to ensure their well-being during the vulnerable years of growing up. It was not so for these children who experienced the adult world as their enemy, creating uncertainty, fear and terror. Their lives were threatened, their security taken away; they were introduced to the most destructive excesses of human behaviour and then left alone to fend for themselves and make sense of a senseless, destructive and murderous world.

These children grew up very quickly. Gina was passed through a window to a pair of outstretched hands and that was all she knew about her future; Lili had to run the gauntlet through a street guarded by soldiers knowing that being caught meant certain death; Edyta rearranged her family in the queue to make sure that they did not end up in the same line to be picked together. They had to think faster than many of the adults around them and adapt to rapidly changing situations in order to survive.

These testimonies not only tell a story, but also provide us with a moving analysis of the moral, spiritual and personal predicament of each individual. One author observes the 'agony of our parents'; another asks, 'Did I hasten anyone's final moment?' We hear about 'unsung heroes', 'murderous fantasies', 'numbed feelings', 'wounded souls', and 'late consequences'. These authors grapple with some of the most demanding and disorientating experiences that human beings have had to go through. In their struggle to convey the magnitude of that confrontation they discuss frankly and openly the huge dilemmas that accompanied such confusing experiences and their long-term consequences. These honest accounts open our eyes to the realisation that the Holocaust did not end in 1945. Far from it.

As I read through these heartbreaking stories, I became increasingly aware of the degree to which whole families were torn apart. These few testimonies recount the same experiences as those of every Jewish family in Nazi-occupied territory. Each one of these stories is extremely powerful in itself, and yet this volume provides only a tiny insight into the scale of the Holocaust as a whole. The same fears, the same dilemmas, the same despair and tragedy, the same resilience and creativeness were repeated time and again, hundreds of thousands of times. The collected words of this volume remind us of both the intimate side of the victims' experience and the scale of the Holocaust.

Maybe it is the mosaic of these short insights which makes this text so powerful; maybe it is because we are afforded deeply personal and heartfelt glimpses into each of these people's troubled lives; maybe because they all tell a similar story of pain and torment, we begin to understand just how complex, how individual, how precise, how intentional the murderous regime of the Nazis and their collaborators (many of whom are mentioned) was; maybe it is because each person tells a story which is representative of all of the other stories which have never been told and can never be told. Whatever the reason, you will not fail to be moved by the sincerity and struggle of each one of these survivors.

The history of the Holocaust can never be told in one volume, nor in a whole library of books for that matter. But if you have to start somewhere, it is in pages such as these that you will find the key. We all know that the Nazis did not murder six million Jews collectively: they murdered one and then another and then another. These people died alone, together.

Each survivor has his or her story to tell, and these should be read one at a time, with care and with contemplation.

In this book you can read them one at a time – together.

Dr Stephen D Smith, MBE
Director, Beth Shalom, Holocaust Memorial Centre, Laxton, Notts

Yiskor (2005)

"Earth, hide not the blood shed on thee"

I feel a deep sense of honour in being asked to write the introduction to this Yiskor book of remembrance, created by the members of The Child Survivor's Association of Great Britain. We, child survivors, have suffered too many losses and still feel them today. It was because of these losses that we came together.

Our child survivor group has now enjoyed many years of success and has brought pleasure and comfort to so many of our fellow child survivors of the Holocaust. I too, have benefited from these for which I will always be grateful. As I watch the Association grow in number and strength, it gives me the pleasure of a father enjoying his child grow, blossom and develop its individuality and independence.

The purpose of remembrance is to prevent the forgetting of the past. For this reason I will return to the events that led to our Association's foundation and some of the events that shaped its growth.

This particular journey began with my struggle to overcome my Holocaust childhood. By the early 1980s I had rebuilt my life with the help of an English accent, a happy marriage, two lovely daughters and a fulfilling professional life. Our social life was full of intellectual friends, music and culture. I believed I had managed to put my survivor past behind me. I thought I had escaped into English middle class life. But this was an unsafe refuge. By 1988 my wife was dying from a cruel form of multiple sclerosis and, despite being a doctor, I was helpless to prevent its painful progress and unable to protect my two young daughters from the effects of watching their mother's prolonged suffering and death. Watching her wasting away, paralysed, mute and blind was like watching the musselmen in Bergen-Belsen. I had not escaped. My past had returned. Taking stock of my life and looking at my aging survivor parents and sister, I was struck by how isolated I was becoming. My many friends, unable to face the sight of my disabled wife, with few exceptions, avoided us. The old saying 'in times of trouble you discover who your true friends are' was only too true.

My father had some surviving family in France, but had avoided and obstructed contact with them for forty-five years due to some perceived insult that he could not forgive. I was thus cut off from them. My wife was an only child. That meant that with her death my family would dwindle away to almost nothing. I began to fear that once my parents had died I would be condemned to a lonely life of isolation.

At that time I thought of myself as the child of survivors more than a child survivor. I had always been told I was too young to understand what was happening in Belsen. I had escaped the effects of the Holocaust trauma suffered by my mother, father and sister because I was so young. My father was a man of action. Perhaps it rubbed off on me. I could not suffer this fate passively. I resolved to face rather than run away from my past. I contacted Ben Helfgott of the 45 Aid Society for advice. He encouraged me to attend the first International Gathering of Children of Survivors in Jerusalem.

The gathering in Jerusalem, a city I love, where I could be a Jew without looking over my shoulder, surrounded by hundreds of fellow children of survivors, was profoundly transforming. The films and presentations were so powerful that they became almost overwhelming. They focussed on so many issues I had avoided that I now had to face. I no longer felt alone. I felt understood and uplifted. In the workshops run by Eva Fogelman I began to examine my Holocaust experience. She put me in touch with the late Dr Judith Kestenberg, the psychoanalyst, who was probably the first psychoanalyst to recognise the suffering of children in the Holocaust.

Returning to England I heard Jack Santcross on radio LBC's 'You Don't have to be Jewish' programme describing his Belsen experiences and his liberation from the transport by Russian cavalry. This was my family's experience. I had never before heard anyone who had so closely shared our experiences. When I contacted him he could not have been more helpful. I explained our shared past and my current struggle. He told me of large gatherings of child survivors who had formed groups, in the USA. I attended my first in 1989. I joined the British table for the Lingfield children who had been the subject of Sarah Moskowitz's book "Love Despite Hate", some of whom are now our members.

I did not believe it possible that any experience could surpass the Jerusalem gathering, but it did. I met other child survivors of Belsen as well as infant Holocaust survivors. The experience was almost indescribably uplifting and healing. For the first time in my life I was able to discuss in the workshops and over coffee so many of my personal struggles with those that had truly understood through having shared my Holocaust experiences. Simply being in each others company seemed to be healing. On my returned to London I felt both immensely uplifted and frustrated. I could not wait for next year's gathering and found myself thinking that if groups for child survivors were so beneficial and special, why did we not have one in London? Spurred on by my own need as well as wishing to help other child survivors, I discussed this with Jack Santcross who first introduced me to John Fransman. With Judith Hassan's offer of the use of Shalvata's premises I arranged the first gathering of The Child Survivors Group in September 1990. Jack Santcross was then driven by his vision of a Survivor Centre and I joined the organising committee, becoming treasurer and editor of the newsletter when Jack resigned.

At the time the 45 Aid Society was a thriving organisation with Ben Helfgott its chairman and Hugo Gryn, its figurehead. It was primarily a child camp survivors' society who met for annual reunions and represented survivors on the Board of Deputies of British Jews. My vision was of a group for social contact, for all child survivors which would include hidden children and Kindertransport. I also harboured the hope that a specialist psychotherapy group for child survivors could be formed one day.

We met monthly and grew steadily. We were filled with hope when the Holocaust Survivors Centre opened, having been promised a full say in the management. The founding groups of the Centre were the Camp Survivors Group, a mixed group of mainly adult camp survivors, the Child Survivor Group and an assorted group of refugees and survivors who had not previously joined any group or organisation. I continued to edit the newsletter. The honeymoon period was full of optimism. The Child Survivor Group was growing. Child survivors were providing much of the energy and creativity that helped the Centre develop, and a psychotherapy group conducted by Earl Hopper, was begun.

However, sadly the honeymoon period ended as the charities' promised say in the management of the Centre by the survivors, began to be eroded. By this time the Child Survivor Group had grown and John Fransman whose great commitment to the group was self evident, having been vice-chairman, took over the helm. John and I felt fiercely protective of the Child Survivor Group and felt we had played a significant part in making the Centre a great success. When the Centre's membership rules were changed which would have meant that the Child Survivor Group would have been disbanded, we chose to remain independent rather than be absorbed by the Centre, and to keep our chosen officers. We were thus obliged to leave the Centre. The group then renewed and renamed itself The Child Survivors' Association of Great Britain.

These experiences have given us greater strength and confidence. In order to avoid being exploited in the future John and I founded a charity, The Foundation for Holocaust Survivors. We also attempted to form a counsel of representatives of survivor groups so that survivors would have a voice, and it would be a survivor's voice. Our attempts floundered after a few meetings, but a committee of this kind now exists, called the 'Umbrella Group'. However, there has been sadness and loss. Reputations have been damaged and our Association's position in the survivor and Jewish community does not command the position it deserves. Let us hope the future will rectify this.

I have benefited immensely from my friendships with child survivors and through founding, building and running the group. These benefits continue now that I am only a humble member.

Having briefly reviewed our history I wish to return to the present, this special volume, and to the future. It is a sign of maturity and courage that we have been able to create this special volume of memories and memorials and to face and retrace our painful pasts. As I read the accounts I am both uplifted by the miracle of our survival and weighed down by the pain of our losses. These histories echo and resurrect so many of my own painful memories, experiences and particularly the pain of my losses. To share our memories and losses in this book is a testament to the creative and constructive use we, child survivors, have made of our experiences. This has been facilitated and supported by being part of the healing processes generated by the continued existence of the Association and the sensitivity of the way it has been run. We have opened our homes and our hearts to each other. We have fed and been fed in this healing environment. Our child survivor group does us all credit and we can be proud of its existence and achievements.

This special volume addresses a concern that my late father expressed when he asked me to say Kaddish for him. Who, in years to come, will speak the names of our loved ones, mothers, fathers, brothers, sisters, sons, daughters, grandfathers and grandmothers, our murdered families who were so dreadfully torn from life? So many fought to survive to bear witness. Most did not succeed. Who will ensure they are not forgotten?

These testimonies describe those experiences and the suffering that we are able to share. There are many memories that are too painful to share. The long lists of our murdered relatives in this volume, are a painful reminder of the extent of our losses. They are more than the losses of the Jewish people. These were our families.

They would have formed the communities that we would and should have enjoyed. Our group, and now our Association, have recreated our own small community. It is special and precious. It brings comfort and joy and as with any family, the usual stresses and frictions. It is a testimony to our Association's health that the joy and comfort it brings is great enough to contain these stresses and frictions. By surviving, rebuilding our lives and by creating this book of Yiskor, of remembrance, we have in part ensured that our martyred families will not be forgotten. This book gives some permanency to their painfully foreshortened lives. May they rest in peace.

Alfred Garwood [formerly Garfinkle]

Preface (2005)

We have written these stories, the memories of our childhood, as adults some sixty years after the events recalled. At that time, we were young children, we had no special skills and little or no education. We were considered to be worthless Jews, vermin, fit only for extermination by the governing powers under which we were living. When we look back, it is remarkable that, despite little if any family or other means of support, so many of us have achieved so much. It is as though we had to prove to the world, and especially to ourselves, that we really were worthwhile citizens who could contribute to society; we needed to show that the Nazi ideology had been totally wrong and was to be abhorred.

So, we went to school and were diligent students. Many of us continued our education to university and graduated with honours; some continued to masters and even to doctorates. We became medical doctors and consultants, school teachers, college lecturers and professors, some worked in industry and some started their own businesses. Thus, we became upright citizens, worthy contributors to our adopted host country's economic wellbeing.

In the compilation of this book we decided to refrain from adding our individual qualifications to our contributions, for we dedicate this book to the memory of our murdered families and to those former members of our Association who have died. They, too, were all worthy citizens of their host countries, whether as bankers, lawyers, doctors, teachers, seamstresses, cobblers or tailors. Then, we were all as they were, despised Jews. Today, in our Association, each of us is important and a valued members.

Since retirement or even before, many of us have taken on the task of educating by telling our story of the Holocaust in schools, colleges and other places, in the hope that it will contribute to a better, more tolerant world. Likewise, we hope this book will also help to make a contribution to that endeavour.

John Fransman
Chairman, The Child Survivors' Association of Great Britain

A Lament as Introduction (2005)

When people come to talk with you about "the war", the Second World War, and discover that you, a Jew, spent that period on the Continent of Europe, they usually ask a series of questions. These include: where were you born, how did you survive, what happened to your parents, and how old were you at the time? Some of us, Child Survivors of the Shoah / Holocaust, were only babies in arms, others were toddlers, some already ten years old, or even a few years older. Too frequently, these people, older survivors included, will then say "Oh, you were too young to remember anything about it" implying that the whole matter had just passed you by. In all honesty, I must admit that I used to say that of myself.

Everybody was trying to reconstruct their own life, after a devastating war. Gentiles had read or heard horror stories from or about survivors, and about people who had been murdered by the Nazi war machine. Most could not understand, could not grasp what had happened, what inhuman acts had been committed during their lifetime. They did not want to be reminded about that turbulent and often painful period. However, the media frequently referred to this period, came up with new 'discoveries'. You could not escape from being reminded.

I grew up in the Netherlands and came to England, to study in 1961. In England, neither Jews nor gentiles could grasp what had happened, could not cope with Survivors, did not know how to speak to them about this difficult subject and, therefore, avoided talking about it. There was then and even now a complete lack of understanding. I recall part of a conversation in 1962, with my landlady, a very well-educated gentile, who was married to a high-ranking Jewish civil servant. We had talked about the winter of 1944/45 which was severe and long. I mentioned that we had so little to eat when I was in hiding, that my foster parents took me with them on journeys on foot in the snow, along farmhouses, begging or bartering for food. Her reply was: "I always managed to give my family butter." I was left speechless at her insensitive response.

This is one of the reasons why Survivors kept quiet, something they had learned in camps or in hiding. Besides, they, too, were busy trying to build a new life, trying to forget, suppress what they had experienced, because remembering was unbearable.

In the 1980s Child Survivors started meeting and forming groups. In 1994 I was introduced to a group of Child Survivors in London. Some had been in hiding, others had been in concentration camps, in ghettoes, on the run for long periods of time, or had come as Kindertransporte. All of us had ended up in Britain, and we had in common our wartime experiences, however diverse these had been.

It was around that period that I started to realise that some unremarkable events in my life resulted in very strong emotional reactions that would last – sometimes for days. I also found that this was, and is, not uncommon amongst my fellow-survivors. Having looked back at my life, I have now realised that these emotions had probably commenced with a very memorable event, namely the arrival of our firstborn, and had again occurred when our second child was born. The arrival of each grandchild, had the same effect. I feel that this is because these children would not have been born – if the Nazis had had their way.

Several years ago, members of the Group, now called the 'The Child Survivors' Association of Great Britain' wanted to provide a Memorial for members who had died. During a discussion in October 2000, the idea of a book was put forward. This suggestion met with general agreement. Susan Pollack volunteered to act as co-ordinator of a working party consisting of Alfred Garwood, Harvey Millan and Gina Schwarzmann. They produced a document which set out the details and time scale for the production of this book. Once the contributions from members started to arrive, an editorial committee consisting of Susan Pollack, Halina Sand and myself, as co-ordinator, began the task. At a regular meeting, the membership made it clear that only 'minimal editorial changes' should be made. The result lies before you.

Sadly, during the preparation of this book, Harvey Millan passed away. He had provided the main input and inspiration to the working party, and had been a wise councillor to our Association on numerous occasions. His advice and help is sorely missed. It is for this reason that we dedicate this book to his memory.

We also want this book to be a memorial for the 1½ million Jewish children who were murdered during the Shoah. Moreover, we wanted to provide our own children and others, with a lasting record.

The illustrations on the front cover and between the sections, are the artwork of Lucienne Pszenica-Morrison, one of our members.

It is said that "redemption is supposed to come with the narration of memory." May this book, a narration of our separate memories, help us who still grieve, to find salvation.

Henri Obstfeld

WE REMEMBER

HENRY ABRAHAM

My Account: Holland 1940-45

I was born, like Anne Frank, in Germany, in the city of Hamburg and came to the Netherlands as a child of two. We settled in the city of Amsterdam in 1935. My father was a stockbroker. Stockbrokers were the first on a list of Hitler's favourite people to be expelled from Germany as he held, what he called, "International Finance Jewry" responsible for Germany losing the First World War. Hitler had fought in that war with great ardour as a common soldier. It was "International Finance Jewry", those parasites on the body politic, who by financial international manipulations had succeeded in snatching victory from what would otherwise have been the victorious German army. The Germans, he taught, were a superior race, normally destined to win, but unfortunately infiltrated by these Jewish leeches and blood-suckers who were only interested in lining their own pockets. "Jews, oh Jews, you're bloodsuckers, toads, every vile and bloody beast, vampires flying to a feast." Thus sang Heinrich Heine, the great German poet, in the 1840's in a satire on a medieval disputation between a rabbi and a Capuchin monk. Prophetically, he was also the man who said: "There where one burns books, one will in the end burn human beings" And, of course, it all came true.

Our family had to flee Germany, from one day to the next. How my father managed to survive in Holland in those days, I cannot understand. In Holland it was very difficult to get a work permit at that time, due to mass unemployment. Without a work permit one could not get a residence permit, a typical Catch 22 situation. But he started to do business without an office or staff or anything else, from street telephones, with America, Germany and Holland. Soon he had an office in Amsterdam again, literally on the same block as the father of Anne Frank.

Holland was a very pleasant country in those days, especially for children, and in spite of all that happened there, shortly after the Germans marched in on 10 May 1940, we children had a very nice time. The Nazi occupiers promised the Dutch people to rule with reason and consent, and great understanding and morality. The Dutch, after all, were a kindred people, racially similar to the Germans themselves. But not so the Jews. The latter were Untermenschen or a racial subspecies of humanity. Against us, they began to pass one law after another, very slowly, but with German thoroughness and very systematically. First, they started with the bicycles. We had to hand them in to the German authorities. The bicycle was the chief mode of transport. Then they forbade the Jews to take any form of transport which included the buses, trams, trains, cars, or anything that moved. All Jews had to be registered, with a Registration Card, bearing a huge letter J for 'Jood' (Jew) on it. This was done, we have now learned, at the suggestion of the Swiss government. They wanted to be sure that if any Jewish person came knocking on their gates, seeking to flee, they would immediately know whom they were dealing with.

On 1 May 1941 came the requirement to wear a large yellow Jewish star, sewn on all clothing for immediate identification. For instance, if one were caught on a tram wearing such a star, this meant instant arrest and deportation. However, not wearing a Jewish star had exactly the same result. Caught without a Jewish star, if the Nazis thought you looked Jewish, also led to immediate arrest. These laws meant identification, isolation from the larger society, humiliation and constant anxiety, as so many people were picked up. It was forbidden to sit on any park bench; those had a sign 'Forbidden for Jews and dogs'. It was forbidden to shop in an 'Aryan shop' (non-Jewish shop) and in Jewish ones only between the hours of 3 and 5. A curfew was instituted for all Jewish persons, and we kids had to be home by 7:00 p.m. Any-one caught after 7:00 p.m. could be arrested and deported, and that without parents. This was one way of learning to be punctual. All public places of entertainment were forbidden, almost from the beginning. No bars, no cafés, no restaurants, no theatres or movie houses; nothing was allowed. As for 'Aryan' children, with some of whom we played on the street, they were allowed to visit us in our homes, but not vice versa. One has to remember at this point that Jews had been living in Holland as relatively free citizens for some 600 years.

By 1942, we were required to move into a ghetto. The neighbourhood, the Transvaal *buurt* with streets named after people and towns in South Africa, in the Eastern part of Amsterdam, was inhabited by lower middle class people. This was very convenient for the Germans, for we were not allowed to leave this ghetto. In 1943, the Germans marched in an entire army subdivision of the Wehrmacht, and arrested 99 % of the people they found there. After that morning there were only three Jewish families living legally in Amsterdam. We were one of the three because we had acquired South American passports, from Haiti. The Germans, of course, knew these to be phony. Haiti, indeed!

We children had long ago been expelled from Dutch schools, and put into Jewish schools, until they deported all our Jewish teachers, and schooling of whatever kind ended. I missed school for a total of four years.

On 8 May 1944, even we were arrested, and thrown into a large Dutch prison, and thence taken to Gestapo headquarters. After five days in a dark cellar, we were interviewed by an SS Obersturmbahnführer who wanted to know how come we were still in Amsterdam. My father explained that we were debarred from transportation due to the fact that we were Haitian citizens. This the Obersturmbahnführer found so funny, he nearly fell from his chair laughing. He said: "I know you think we Germans are dumb, but that dumb we are not. Haiti is a black republic, and you are not exactly black." But my father insisted we were, indeed, Haitians and said that his mother was in Haiti. She was long dead, deported to Theresienstadt from an old-age home. He said: let them prove where she is. Finally, they decided to ship us to Bergen-Belsen, a great privilege, for Belsen was a 'preferential' camp reserved for Jews earmarked by the Nazis for possible exchange against money or goods or against German nationals interned in hostile territories. The Germans could hold such people as hostages, later to be exchanged for German spies and collaborators whom the Americans had incarcerated in the U.S. And that is exactly what happened.

Thus, by virtue of the strength of our so-called "South American" (Haitian) passports we were shipped via Westerbork, the transit camp in Holland, to the 'Vorzugslager' Bergen-Belsen. For that is what the Nazis called it – a 'preferential camp'. I have often since those days asked myself: "Was this, indeed, a preferential camp?" Yes, it is true that they had no gas chambers there like in Auschwitz, that they kept the family together, that they permitted us to wear our own clothes. In that sense, in the eyes of the Germans, and perhaps even in our own eyes, it was a 'preferential camp'. But let us make no mistake about this. The Germans did not really want us to live in a preferential way – at least not all of us. They only wanted to keep us barely alive, so that one day they might have a few people to 'exchange' against Germans held in American internment camps.

Herzberg, the great chronicler and the first to write a book, *Amor Fati,* about Belsen after the war, asked: "Was this, indeed, a privileged camp or was it not?" The Germans even referred to it as a recuperation centre. But the only recuperation there was working oneself to exhaustion and being left to die, slowly, oh so slowly, and living in such filth and muck, with so little to eat, that the lice, which cause typhus, would destroy you within five days, if you caught that dreaded disease. In the last 3 months, nearly everyone caught it. Little Anne Frank died of typhus, a horrible disease, not to be confused with typhoid fever which is mild in comparison. Yet during the war, Bergen-Belsen was regarded by many as a veritable Mecca. Jews doomed for deportation to Auschwitz offered thousands of guilders to go there, instead. Things were much better here than in Sobibor, Majdanek, Treblinka and Belzec, to name but a few besides Auschwitz.

But yet, as time went on, especially after Josef Kramer became Commandant of Belsen in December 1944, it was turned into a real concentration camp, a Vernichtungslager, an extermination camp. There you were to starve to death helped along by disease and decay. As I said, as I remember it, things went from bad to worse. The food rations got increasingly smaller, until they were nearly nothing. People froze by day, and they froze by night. There was no heating of any kind. One was surrounded by almost total darkness in the winter. Today, psychologists believe that some people get depressed by lack of sunlight during winter, and have invented the term SAD (Seasonal Affective Disorder) for a type of depression that is caused by this.

In Belsen, there were lots of things to get depressed about. In fact, it was abnormal not to get depressed. Though the authorities in Bergen-Belsen eschewed extermination as such, conditions were harsh in the extreme. The work commandos were set to the hardest of labour, sometimes for nineteen hours at a stretch, guarded by merciless SS men, accompanied by vicious dogs. The dogs were followed up by blows. Old people had to work. And then there were Jewish Kapos (Kamp-Polizei), followed later by Polish Kapos. These people were Polish civilians, but also murderers, bank robbers, etc. One of them beat my father with a truncheon, because his commando did not march fast enough carrying the very heavy 'Gamellen', or food containers.

People were constantly moved, from one barrack to another. For old people, already sick with starvation and dysentery, this proved frequently fatal. They could do nothing for themselves, lay down in the dirt and died. In addition, in all this filth where no one could wash properly and nearly everyone had dysentery, it stank to high heaven. My mother, sister and myself had to sleep in a bunk, right next to the toilets, and on a bad night, with bad dreams, I can still smell those aromas. Then, there were the murderous roll-calls, for every morning we had to be counted, and the Germans insisted that everything be correct. So, if one was missing, and one was always missing (they had thrown him into solitary confinement in a bunker, and forgot to count him), we could stand there for hours and hours in the cold.

To quote Herzberg, a lawyer, again: 'Time and again we were taken aback by the spiritual and moral decline, indeed ruin, all round us. Everyone stole, not only those from the poorer classes, but leading businessmen and bank directors. And yet – and yet – there was something the Germans could not destroy, try as they might.' Loden Vogel (pen-name for a leading Dutch psychoanalyst, still living in Amsterdam) wrote on 15 February, 1945: 'I am dead tired, hungry and at the end of my tether – but somewhere, a part of myself, the most important part, remains untouched, at peace – something within us remains forever immutable'. Viktor Frankl, a survivor from Auschwitz, an eminent psychiatrist, who lost his father, his mother, his brother and his wife in the Holocaust, says exactly the same thing: 'Something remains, forever immutable.' He is fond of quoting Nietzsche: 'He who knows the why, will always know the what'. That is what, as a psychologist, I always taught my students – they can take away from you everything – everything, except one thing – your mind, your thoughts, your integrity, your faith. And then, if you are so fortunate as to survive physically, you will also survive mentally and psychologically. That is the difference between those who become psychotic, and those who never do.

Quoting Herzberg again: 'We salute you, little boy, caring for your lonely baby sister, combing her hair every morning, sharing with her the few good things that come your way. We salute you, mothers, who – come what may – yet find the heart to keep your children clean and healthy. We salute you, all who have remained steadfast, who refuse to give in or to surrender, who have held high your heads, in this unspeakable vale of tears.'

Miraculously, some of these children emerged undamaged from this pit of hell, and I have the great fortune to be one of them.

Undamaged in body, but what of the mind? One can spend a lifetime trying to repress these images, these emotions and these feelings, but as Freud would say, they linger on in the unconscious, and are never, ever really forgotten. For so many people, it all comes back, when they get older, and are retired. It is like Sisyphus who, having rolled the rock back up to the top of the mountain from whence it will fall again into the valley. He has to trudge down and pick up the rock once more, to again roll it up the mountain, and suddenly becomes conscious, as he walks down, of the absurdity and the meaninglessness of his life – it is that which constitutes the tragedy of his life. So the existentialist psychoanalysts teach us. But they are the atheistic existentialists, for whom life no longer has any meaning. But for me, who has faith, there is the Almighty, and he will always be there to help you – even in the darkest hour. Perhaps not for the millions of other people whose lives were extinguished eternally – but for me, yes. No one will ever be able to explain the Holocaust – it is something holy. As Arthur Koestler put it: "A faith is not acquired – it grows like a tree. Reason may defend an act of faith – but only after the act has been committed, and the man committed to his act."

Three months before the liberation of the camp, the Commandant, Josef Kramer, announced on the Appellplatz. 'We have decided to select 301 of you, out of 5,000 with foreign passports, and to put you on a Red Cross train and to send you to Switzerland, there to be exchanged for German civilians whom the Americans have locked up in prison.' But which 301? He said to his adjutant, 'Give me a list.' The adjutant pulled out Uruguay. 'How many?' '250, Herr Commandant!' Kramer eyed it with suspicion and tore it up. Next, Paraguay. 'How many?' – '150, Herr Commandant.' Again he took the list and tore it up. Next, Peru. 'How many?' '75, Herr Commandant.' Once again he took the list and tore it into shreds. He said, 'Do you think, I am mad, that I am going to stand here in this cold, and go through hundreds of names? Give me a short list, a very short one.' 'Here it is,' shouted the Adjutant. 'I have found one!' 'What is it?' 'Haiti'. 'How many on that list?' 'Four, Herr Commandant.' 'That is the right number. Put them on the List.'

That was me, my father, my mother and my sister. The next morning we were on our way to Switzerland. But when we got to Biberach, a German town on the border of Switzerland, the Zugführer (official in charge of the train), SS Hauptsturmführer Schmidt, suddenly announced: 'Do you think, we Germans are crazy, to let 301 of you out of a concentration camp? 175 out!' In the end there were only 126 Bergen-Belsen inmates left who traversed the border into Switzerland. The Swiss border police welcomed us with drawn bayonets. They demanded to know who was a Jew and who was not. 'Jews, to the left, Aryans to the right'. I thought to myself, this is not possible. It is not possible that in Switzerland, that neutral country, that has not had a war in 250 years, where food is plentiful, which has every luxury in the world which we had forgotten, all this would start all over again. But it did. Instead of a nice comfortable Swiss hotel with white sheets and bedding, we were marched off to a stable where we had to bed down on straw, reserved only for pigs. We were not allowed to receive any phone calls or make any. And, of course, no visitors. For food they gave us, starved people who should have had porridge at most, oily sardines in cans. But the hungry people gulped down the sardines, and six died instantly. All this under the aegis of Swiss military doctors. About 15 of us remained in Swiss hospitals, and now we were only about 105.

Then came the next announcement: 'Five more days, and in five days, if you are not out of here, out of Switzerland, you shall see what happens to you!' And so they put us on another train, through just liberated Vichy France, to the port of Marseille onto an American hospital ship, reserved for wounded US soldiers, amid a luxurious splendour we had not seen for years. We thought we were veritably in seventh heaven. Clean white sheets, nurses, doctors, wonderful food, for us who were almost all sick with lice, typhus and dysentery. When the American captain learned from his adjutant that we were only refugees from a concentration camp, and in no way wounded American soldiers, he ordered us off his ship within five minutes. And so they put us back onto the quay, and loaded us on a very old, just about to sink, Italian schooner. A few people were flown from Marseille to New York.

Instead of going to America, as arranged in the American-German exchange agreement, they took the remaining 90 of us to North Africa, to the province of Algeria, then a Department of France, and into an UNRRA camp set up for post-war refugees. But that was the most wonderful year we had in the entire post-war period. No-one had to work, only if they wanted to, and only doing what they wanted to. We children had only one obligation: to study English from 10-12 in the mornings; after that we were free the whole day. We spent it swimming on a gorgeous beach, better than at the Riviera. These beaches were not yet commercialized. The sunshine was glorious, and the fruits we bought from the Arabs delicious.

After a year of this, waiting for our American visas, we were taken in the middle of the winter on a completely empty Liberty Ship to the port of Baltimore in the USA, and from there to New York. From 1946 till 1972, I lived in New York City. I went through public school and high school, and studied at Columbia University where I obtained my Ph.D. In 1972, we decided to move to London, to return to Europe where our roots were.

JACK BILD

Jack and Manfred

The following is my attempt to set out as faithfully as I can all the
wartime events as they affected my mother, my father and me, Jack,
between March 1943 and May 1948 (date of our departure from
Belgium). I have to admit from the outset that for the war years this
account is based not on personal memory, as I was only 2 years old
when the war ended, but on the information I received from my
mother while she was alive (she died in 1977) and from my brother
Manfred who is still alive and recalls all of the war years quite clearly.
Though, like me, my brother was placed in hiding (late '43 to end '44),
he was with my mother when my father was arrested and then
deported. She and my brother went underground. Manfred has total
recall of all events from then on, including my birth in clandestinity in
Brussels and the arrangements subsequently made for my being placed
in hiding. At the time of my father's deportation my mother was three
months pregnant with me.

My parents and brother left Germany shortly after the fateful
Kristallnacht, the November 9, 1938. Through a series of hired
smugglers they were able to cross into the Netherlands and then into
Belgium, arriving as refugees in Antwerp with just a few personal
belongings. They lived for a short time in very rudimentary
accommodation on Leeuwerikstraat and were subsequently interned
in a refugee camp at Marneffe, Namur Province. They stayed there
until the German invasion of Belgium. After a vain attempt at fleeing

to France before the advancing German troops, they retraced their steps after several weeks. Eventually they returned to Antwerp, where they settled in a flat at No 13, Statiestraat. In January 1941 all three were placed in "sejour forcé et surveillé" (under house arrest) for several months at Diepenbeek, Limbourg Province.

After they were allowed to leave the confines of Diepenbeek, my parents decided to move to Brussels where they occupied a small room at No.33 Rue de la Poste, near the Gare du Nord, from summer 1941 to August 1942 when my father was deported to Malines and then to Auschwitz.

From here onwards in this account, my brother Manfred describes my family's situation in Brussels prior to my father's deportation and up to my birth and immediately thereafter.

I don't know how we found this room on Rue de la Poste, nor how we moved our stuff there, but I remember that this was where I would become aware that my mother was pregnant. Of course, I could not suspect then that from here on our two lives, my brother's and mine, would be forever intertwined and several times put at serious risk. It was summer, people sat on their doorsteps in the evening and chatted, falling quiet as they watched German soldiers march by singing in boisterous tones their famous Heimat songs. For several months our mother was the breadwinner. She had got wholesale access in Antwerp to a line of men's and women's undergarments and peddled them to people she knew. She even made so bold, for a short while, to sell to the German military.

The first year of the occupation was quite benign in some ways. The Germans sought to have all local commerce continue as before and did not hassle the Jewish community excessively. They were, I suppose, organising themselves for the raids, detentions and deportations that were to follow later. Papa took care of me. I remember well with what compassion he would draw me, asleep, out of the crib every morning and comforted me softly "here, sleep some more on my shoulder", before he set me down to get me dressed. It made waking a bit more bearable, I suppose, but not enough to reconcile me to my fate of early risings year after year for a long school career that was just beginning. He showed every concern for my well being and my schooling. He helped me with my home work, took care of my meals and my clothes and liked to horse around when he was in a good mood. On his birthday, February 29, 1942, mum bought him a wristwatch. He was very proud of it and asked me every two minutes to ask him what time it was.

There were other events to make the year interesting. Our dear mama got arrested in Antwerp for staying out past the hour of curfew (which was, I believe, 9:00pm for anyone without special authorization). Indeed, some days she stayed overnight in Antwerp where she had kept a small room on Statiestraat. One evening, in the spring of 1942, going back late with her wares, she was stopped in the street and clamped in jail. I was horrified to think of my mother in jail and I kept asking my father when she would come home. It won't be long, he reassured me. In fact, she was gone for six weeks!

The certificate issued in 1980 by the Administration for War Victims states she was incarcerated in the Prison d'Anvers for only two weeks, from May 16 to 31, 1942, but I know that's wrong, for she often talked about those hellish six weeks in Antwerp, remarking that, had she been detained two weeks longer she would probably have been shipped off on one of the first transports to Auschwitz. Indeed, that's what happened to two other Jewish women with her in that prison. It may be that the short period mentioned in the document before me refers only to the initial or final period of her imprisonment, because I believe she was moved from one jail to another.

After mum was finally released, I thought life would return to what I had begun to consider as normal. It was, however, not to be. As I've said before, it was an eventful year. It was around that time, that the subject of my having a baby brother or sister came into the conversation, indeed, one night after a doctor came to make a house call on my mother. Until that day in the summer of 1942, doctors had only ever been summoned for me, this time I was sent out of the room while he examined my mother.

It was also around this time that we were issued with our "Judenstern" badges and there was much discussion about when, where and how to wear them, and the risks involved. If the police stopped you and asked for your papers, you could be arrested for not wearing your badge. Looking back on it now, I can't believe that people could be so blind as not to see what this was leading up to. Individuals had regularly been disappearing or been asked to register for labour camps. Every week the police and the Wehrmacht were coming out with new regulations on the treatment of Jews. And now, just because those lame Jewish committees were distributing the badges, some people thought it might actually be safe to wear them!

My mum was the first to see the looming danger. She stopped her trips to Antwerp and stayed home while dad tinkered with various part-time jobs here and there. One job almost got him into serious trouble. I was completely unaware of it at the time. After the war was over and our mum told me what he'd been up to, I recalled that there was indeed a period on Rue de la Poste when he took to sleeping in late in the mornings. This had not been his habit until then. It made it even more difficult for mum to prepare breakfast and caused her to keep me quiet so as to let him sleep. It turned out that for some weeks my dad had been working nights helping with a clandestine printing operation run by the newly formed Brussels resistance. I was extremely proud of him when I found out, but shared retrospectively some of mum's anguish when I learned that it was as a result of that night work that he once got stopped in the street (I know not by what sort of police) and only succeeded in avoiding arrest because the intercepting officer took pity on him.

This incident, in effect, marks the beginnings of the severest part of what mum called "die Verfolgung" (the persecution). Up till then, and in her mind, the special treatment reserved for Jews had to do with discrimination and limitation of movement and activities. Bad enough, but now we were being hunted. She made sure we limited our movements as much as possible and she curtailed my attendance at an urban summer camp. I can't say exactly when this was, but it had to have been between June, the month of Jack's conception, and August when the deportations and the roundups of Jews began in earnest.

I shall now try to recount that fateful day when my father was captured in a raid in our neighbourhood. It was a pleasant summer day. It may have been just after my birthday or a week or two before. I had received a new suit in anticipation of my birthday. I remember mum announcing it with glee quite some time before. It was an item she had acquired in the course of her 'handeln" and I had insisted my Judenstern be sewn onto it. They considered that, as a child, I was exempt from wearing it. However, after my pleading it was sown on anyway while they insisted that I could wear it only in their presence.

The first organized street raids happened soon thereafter and neither mum nor dad wore the badge of capture from then on. So I assume our dad wasn't wearing it that day. Unbeknown to them though, I was wearing it and, ironically, it may have saved my life that day. I had been allowed to go and visit a friend who lived not too far away. I clearly remember taking my jacket out of the box under my bed, without my parents knowing it, to show off my new suit and star. Later in the afternoon I wore it as I marched home passing by the Rue Verte where our cousin Ruth lived. I called out to them on the third floor "Taaante Behhrtehhl" so that our aunt Bertel would, as usual, throw down the key. I received no answer which I could not understand as I had been told to go there that afternoon. I yelled a few more times, but no one came to the window. At that point, a woman approached me and told me to hurry home because bad things were happening in the neighborhood. She took off my jacket and folded it, star inside, over my arm. As I made my way home, within the two or three blocks that separated our houses, I saw cars and some uniformed men gathered in front of a house, and a number of bystanders staring warily at what was going on.

When I got home I found my uncle, aunt and cousin there … and my mother in tears. I learned there had been a raid in the Rue Verte.

Dad had been visiting the other Bilds and probably expected to pick me up there. They had all been watching the raid from the third floor window. When it seemed all over, Papa went downstairs, opened the front door briefly and was whisked away in a passing Gestapo car. That was the last any of us saw of him. Our cousin Ruth told me subsequently that when this episode is retold in her family, one always stresses the fact that our father, just before they dragged him away, took care to slam the front door after him. It locked automatically on the inside so that no one could enter the house he had just left and search for further victims.

Did any of this affect my brother? He had been conceived only a couple of months earlier. It is hard to imagine that his prenatal environment had not been placed under serious stress. From that moment on, until well after the war, I never knew my mother to have an anxiety-free moment. Her first move that day was to abandon our dwelling. She was determined that we would not spend another night in our little room. If, in a subsequent interrogation, Papa was forced or tricked into giving his address we would not be safe there. She went across the street and begged the neighbours, people we had never met, to let us spend the night with them. They knew what had happened and agreed without hesitation. In the following days we moved twice more in this fashion, staying with perfect strangers who fed us, watched over me as mum busied herself with a) finding us new lodgings in a different neighbourhood, b) trying to find some authority who might be able to release my father, c) agreeing with my uncle to break all contact from then on, in case either of our families had been placed on an arrest list as a result of dad's capture, d) arranging with a mover to pick up our effects at Rue de La Poste without giving him any indication of where to take them. We subsequently met the driver at a distant street corner and had him deliver us to a small room at 59, Rue de L'Etang in Etterbeek. Weeks later we moved everything ourselves into a place nearby on the Place Jourdan (3, Rue Froissart). In this way mum hoped she had wiped out all our traces. She then proceeded to register herself at a hospital for the time she was to give birth. The address she gave for that purpose was the one in the Rue de l'Etang.

Before long our tante Bella and little baby Colette arrived in Brussels and moved in with us into this quite decent two-room flat. It was bright, fairly spacious, had a balcony and a separate small bedroom. There was a coal burning stove and not much else. A cold-water tap and a toilet just outside the door at our end of the hall, completed all the mod cons. The landlord was a small, elderly gentleman with a thin grey goatee. He let us have an ancient large clothes closet and a few kitchen items, all for 270 francs per month. Cheap as it was, I could never figure out how mum managed to pay the rent. Her "Unterstützung" (financial assistance) came to only about 50 francs per week.

I do know, however, that when the persecution neared its most dangerous peak and our Mum hardly dared leave the house, she sometimes went for months without paying the rent. Whenever I expressed concern about it, she just shushed me and tried to reassure me, while the worry in her eyes never left her. In many ways, however, this did turn out to be a lucky find. While it was not entirely outside the area inhabited by Jewish refugees, it was not in the heart of the more central area where they tended to congregate. Though the building afforded nothing like hiding places or an emergency escape, its landlord was sympathetic to our plight and would never denounce us. However, the most valuable part of it was the fact that the address was never entered anywhere near our name. This didn't mean that we were never bothered, but at least never by a knock on the door with the command "Aufmachen" (open up), as so many of their contemporaries had to experience.

I do remember frequently our sitting around in the evening trying to figure out how we could hide ourselves in the small bedroom if someone came looking for us, or climb from one balcony to another, to seek refuge at the neighbours. It was a situation which was clearly impossible, and yet, no one panicked. I guess we realised only much later that our lives hung on a thread and that it was a matter of mere chance that we didn't all perish even before the birth of my little brother. Yes, 3, Rue Froissart, was a kind of shaky haven and it was the place where Jack Bild was first received into the family.

What was much more trying for our mum during these terrible days, were her experiences outside the home. She was thirty-two years old and a quite striking looking blonde who made more than the occasional male turn to look at her. In those days women were not overly bothered by the attentions of lecherous men. Those were trivial worries compared with a gaze that might be coming from a plainclothed Gestapo officer or collaborator. Many were the times when Mum came home an hour later than she'd planned, simply because she'd had to take a long detour to shake off some stranger she imagined was following her. She'd walk miles to ensure no-one knew where she lived. I can only guess at the stresses such scares produced in Jack's intra-uterine environment in the last few months of her pregnancy. On a couple of occasions she had to jump off a streetcar before the next stop, when she noticed plainclothes men checking passengers' papers. Such checks were, of course, sometimes aimed at the underground resistance, but they usually ended up with Jews and other undesirables being arrested at the same time.

Nor was that sort of tension always of a nervous or emotional kind. One purely physical event occurred in her eighth month when a military truck rammed a streetcar she was on. The window next to her was smashed and, as she made her way out the rear exit she twisted her ankle and fell in the roadway. She was able to pick herself up and hobble home. I remember the incident well; I noticed how shaken up she was when she came through the door. She was wearing a greenish winter coat with a hood at the back. After she'd taken it off and shook it out, she discovered the hood was filled with shards of glass that fell all over the floor.

I know our Mum worried constantly about the effects all these events must have had on the baby she was carrying. She didn't say so to me then in so many words, but after the war, when I was older, she confirmed to me the tremendous strain she had been under. Quite apart from the fact that she was also poor, husbandless, persecuted and without enough to eat!

We all looked forward, however, to the day of the birth. Much was made of the fact that she had a suitcase ready to take with her to the hospital. After moving to the Place Jourdan, she had kept the little room on Rue de l'Etang. As the days for the birth approached, she'd take her little hospital suitcase with her and spent the night at her official address.

So, as Mum made her way each of those several evenings to spend the night at Rue de l'Etang, she knew she was taking a risk that could be fatal to her ... but not for the rest of us. I guess the idea of giving birth anywhere but in a hospital, never occurred to her. I have no idea how many there were of these lonely nights — what I do remember clearly is the day I woke up and tante Bella announced: "You have a baby brother!' I was overjoyed. The main thing was she would be bringing home a little brother; a playmate I had a great need for, now that my recreational activities were ever more restricted.

Within a matter of days I gathered from my eavesdropping on her chatter with tante Bella a fairly complete account of the trip to the hospital and most of the details of the birth itself. When she felt the moment to be close, sometime after 11 pm, she got dressed, took her suitcase and flashlight (no-one went outside after dark without a flashlight) and walked alone to the hospital. I gather the doctors and nurses were not unfamiliar with her type of predicament. She kept recounting the indelible impression left on her by one of the nurses who cried bitter tears throughout the birth. Moreover, it turned out to be a breach birth. I can't imagine a more distressing situation: bringing a child into the world with nothing but the certainty of life threatening danger for him in the foreseeable future.

New problems arose almost immediately after their return to Rue Froissart. It now became virtually impossible to go outside. On Sundays I would sometimes be allowed to take the baby in his carriage into the Parc Leopold which was just one block away from our house. But I could not be put in charge of such walks on weekdays, for my not being at school would raise questions.

From the above it should be clear how close my brother Jack came to never seeing his first birthday. Disaster could have struck through any number of missteps, snares or fatal coincidences. Any one of us, including the dairy shopkeeper, the barman downstairs or the nosy concierge next door, could have let something slip. As I go over these events I can see our Mum coping in her natural practical way trying to keep focused on the task at hand and determined never to stop striving for the maximum invisibility. Having her sister with her was, I'm sure, a support that made some of the hardships more bearable. What I can't describe is how she bore the anguish of every moment lived under that sword of Damocles.

That summer was the first time when Jack and I were separated. He was barely six months old and I had just turned eight. While we had an understanding landlord who went out of his way to keep suspicion about us at bay, we had no protectors or helpers who could do the shopping or other external chores for us, to prevent our having to hazard the out of doors which became ever more dangerous. It became clearer by the day that the immobility imposed on those two women by the two infants and a very visible boy like me, would before long lead to the capture of all five of us. Two acquaintances of theirs, women in much the same situation, found themselves dragged out of their flat one Sunday while the neighbours who were hiding them, were at church. They were deported with their five children.

Not long thereafter my mother took me with her to a bureau of the Belgian Red Cross. She had been told that they would be able to place me in a safe hiding place. She explained to me that quite probably neither of us would know where I would be taken and that she would never know until the persecution has ended. By that time I had learned not to ask foolish questions anymore, such as how long this could take. All I understood was that hiding was the most important thing for as long as it was needed, and that there were many good Belgians who were prepared to help us. I was being taken to the Red Cross as an interpreter, since there wouldn't be anyone there who spoke anything but French. Where did Mum get all this information? How did she know exactly what the interview would involve? These were the mysteries that children lived with all the time when they had to share the predicaments of the adult world without being involved in every step of confronting them.

A couple of weeks later, the three young women who came to fetch me, found me ready and willing to go. They were kind and lively and took me in a streetcar to Louvain. About an hour or so later we arrived at the Chateau Rouge in Linden, a children's home run by l'Oeuvre nationale de l'Enfance where Jack was to be sent a few months later. Two or three weeks later I was fetched from this very competently-run home and taken by a very kind young man to my next destination, a convent in a town called Klein Willebroek. My departure from there, several weeks later, followed a long and circuitous route via a short stay with an abbé (abbot) in Malines and a convent in Tirlemont, before I finally arrived at the farm in Lubbeek where I was to stay until after the liberation of Belgium.

I think it was in about December 1943 that my mother and her sister decided to put their remaining children into hiding as well. They addressed themselves to the same organisation which had taken care of me. According to what my mother told me later, several people came to fetch our cousin Colette, 1½ years old, and my brother Jack who was nine months younger. They were brought to Linden where they remained under the care of Mlle Madeleine Sorel. I learned later, both from my mother and from a priest who was regularly in touch with Mlle Sorel, that the entire home in Linden had had to be evacuated at a moment's notice one day in early 1944 when a local official had slipped word to them that a garrison of German soldiers was about to be billeted there. Mlle Sorel, her staff and some 75 children thus took off, moving across the country for several weeks in search of another haven. One can only guess at the level of anxiety all those children and their protectors must have felt during that period.

Soon after the liberation, our mother and aunt started out on foot in search of their little ones. The clandestine network had worked well: not even the Red Cross was able to trace the many moves the

Linden institution had made in 1944. After more than one month's searching our mother and her sister finally came upon a home near Namur, the Chateau de Bonesse, where they found their beloved little children. Both were apparently in fair health physically, but neither could speak, not even a word. Our cousin Colette was by then more than two and Jack exactly 18 months old. He could not walk either. Our mother and aunt were both able to get temporary work and lodgings at the place where they found their children and were thus able to recover their strength somewhat, before returning with them to Brussels. The Germans were gone.

There was no longer any need to feel afraid. However, daily life and the feeding and caring for infants were still far from easy for two widows with no resources. I rejoined them all in the spring of 1945. By that time my brother Jack was able to walk, but spoke not yet a word. Whenever my mother left the house, he shrieked and screamed inconsolably until she came home. I remember saying to my mother that such incessant crying could cause some sort of damage. Even so, it wasn't until he was five years old that my mother came to the conclusion that the wartime experience had indeed left some marks on Jack. Though he could by then make all his wants known quite well, he still had difficulty speaking intelligibly at all times. His physical development seemed good although he had a serious problem of bowel and bladder control, the latter lasted into his ninth year. Mum sought at all times to minimize Jack's problems and to encourage him to live as normal a life as possible. When in his teens, however, he began to show signs of extremely serious shyness and an abnormal reluctance to be with people. She realized then that the marks that had been left on him from their separation during his infancy, were deeper than any of us had suspected.

I hope that the foregoing account will serve to provide some of the setting of my brother Jack's earliest years.

Montreal, Quebec, November 24, 2003.
Manfred Bild

BETTY BLOOM

Remembering the Years
1930 – 1945

I was born in Berlin on the 18th January 1930, the second daughter of a young Orthodox Jewish couple who had settled in Germany shortly after the First World War. My father, Josef Schütz came from *Dukla,* a small village in the Carpathian area of Poland. My mother, Bertha, was born in *Korczina,* near *Jazlo,* some twenty miles from *Dukla.* Unfortunately I never asked her, before it was too late, where or how they met, or many other questions. Having lost her mother when she was only fourteen years old and being left to look after her father and two-year old twin brother and sister, she found it difficult to talk about her early life in Poland

I grew up, as any normal Jewish child, believing the rituals of our quiet family life were the norm: going to Synagogue in our best Shabbat clothes; *Seder* nights with my father dressed in a *kittel*; the kindling of the *Chanukah* candles; my first school day with a big '*Zuckertüte*' filled with sweets. Remaining forever with me are other memories of this time: the smell of my mother's baking and of the bales of leather which my father cut up for his shoemaker clients; tobogganing in the local park; outings to the zoo and the botanical gardens; being taken by my father to see the Olympic flags flying on the *Kurfürstendamm*; my excitement at the birth of my younger sister, Bronia, in 1935; learning to read and crying over "Uncle Tom's Cabin"; listening to my older sister, Ruth, reciting poems by Schiller and Goethe; watching my first Shirley Temple film; a holiday with my mother in *Ziegenort* on the Baltic sea. I thought this life would go on forever.

Gradually, however, the atmosphere in our home was becoming tense and things were changing: no more outings; no birthday parties; my eldest cousin, Batya, leaving for Palestine; the SA marching down our street singing about Jewish blood dripping from their knives; a large sign painted on our shop saying *"kauft nicht bei Juden"* (do not buy from Jews); being told that I was no longer welcome in my non-Jewish school. But my childhood came to an abrupt end when, at dawn on the 28th October 1938, three men in SS uniform banged on our front door and gave my father five minutes to pack a few belongings. They did not even give him time to kiss us good-bye. It was to be the last time I saw my beloved father.

On that day, *Heydrich* the *Reichsführer* and Chief of the German Police ordered seventeen thousand Polish Jews to be rounded up and deported to the Polish border. The Poles refused to admit them, so they remained in no-man's land, in inhuman conditions, without adequate clothing, heat or food. The Germans eventually forced them at gunpoint to flee to the nearby Polish town of *Zbaszyn* where they were incarcerated in a hastily erected camp, before eventually being allowed to leave for other parts of Poland. This, being the first organised Nazi pogrom, was the actual precursor of *Kristallnacht* which led to the Nazi's so-called "final solution" and the Holocaust.

Soon after my father's deportation, my mother was forced to hand over our shop to a non-Jew and strangers came to our apartment to look at and offer ridiculous prices for the beautiful cherry-wood dining room furniture which she had looked after so carefully. On my ninth birthday, instead of a party, I accompanied my mother to the station to say good-bye to my cousins, Susi and Paula, the daughters of my mother's brother, Uncle Markus, who were leaving for England on a *Kindertransport*. I had spent many happy hours with them in their lovely flat, being very impressed by their piano, typewriter and especially their sunken bath.

On the 22nd February 1939, it was our turn to leave Berlin. As the German Jewish Community felt that they had to give priority to their own children first, we were unable to get onto a *Kindertransport*. At Ruth's instigation, my mother took the extremely courageous decision to put us on a train with other "*Kinder*" leaving for Belgium, without papers and without a foster family to receive us. I cried bitterly as I did not want to leave her and my little sister Bronia. My mother even managed to follow the train to the next station so that she could wave to us again. It is a sight that I will never forget.

In Cologne, all the children, except us, were issued with identification tags, which on arrival in *Aachen*, were checked by the Belgian border guards. Noticing that we did not have the necessary passes, a *gendarme* abruptly told us to get off the train; thus "*decendez*" was the first word of French I learned. Being a well brought up, obedient little girl, I started to get up, but Ruth, at not quite fourteen, already showing the maturity and courage which she later displayed in her work for the Resistance, told me to sit still and wait. In what seemed an eternity, the same *gendarme* came through the compartment, looked at us and said "*continuez*" – carry on – my second word of French. On reflection, I realise that this probably saved our lives. Had we not been allowed into Belgium, we would have returned to Berlin and would certainly have perished together with my mother and Bronia.

It was early evening by the time we reached the Jewish Refugees Committee's assembly rooms in Brussels where the "*Kinder*" were being met by their foster families, but the welcome extended to us was far from friendly. We were told in no uncertain terms by one of the people in charge that "they had enough legal children, so did not need any 'illegals'." Belgium had restricted the intake of *Kindertransport* children to six hundred, therefore we were an added burden and I hope and pray that Ruth and I did not deprive two other children of an escape.

Slowly the hall was emptying and we were told that we would be taken to a Salvation Army hostel. To us, coming from a religious home, this was the last calamity which could befall us on this dreadful day. However, as luck would have it, Ruth recognised a school friend amongst the few children who had not yet been collected. She implored her foster parents to take us also to which they readily agreed. We spent two weeks with the warm and welcoming family *Padawer* in their beautiful villa in *Uccle* whilst they made arrangements for the Jewish Refugee Committee to take us to the Home, *General Bernheim*, where we joined some forty-five girls from Germany and Austria aged between seven and sixteen who, like us, had no relatives in Belgium. We were delighted to learn recently, that the *Padawer* family, who had welcomed us into their home, had survived the Holocaust by escaping to America.

The Home was led by a young Jewish couple, Alex and Elka Frank. Life there was monotonous with few lessons and walks along endless fields of sugar beet, relieved only by very occasional outings to Brussels with one of the Committee ladies who plied us with "*frites*" and "*gaufres*", which resulted in my being carsick on the return journey. We learned to play dodge ball which became a passion. Letters from my mother made me more homesick than ever.

I had a short spell in hospital to have my tonsils removed. Being small for my age and not a good eater, the Committee ladies decided that a spell in the countryside would help me. To my horror the fortnight they chose for my stay with a Flemish family coincided with Passover and I refused to eat until a packet of Matzos was sent to me half-way through the Festival.

In August 1939, just three weeks before the outbreak of war, my mother, who by chance had kept her Czech passport in her maiden name, obtained an English visa as a domestic servant and, on the way to England with Bronia, spent two days with us in the Home. It was wonderful to see her, but hard to say good-bye yet again. Imagine her distress when the Committee told her that she could not take Bronia, then only four years old, with her to England, as they would both be sent back.

Being too young for our hostel, Bronia was sent to an orphanage near Waterloo. Ruth and I were allowed to visit her once. We found her absolutely desolate and unable to speak a word of her native German. We were heart broken to leave her there, but had no alternative. On the brink of deportation, she was rescued by a wonderful Belgian couple who saved her life at the risk of their own.

On the 10th of May 1940 Belgium was invaded and being near the border, we could hear gunfire in the distance. Five days later we were told by Elka Frank to pack a few belongings and to get ready to leave. I cannot remember how we got to Brussels where we were joined by a group of fifty Jewish refugee boys from a nearby hostel. Together we left for the station which was chaotic with crowds of people trying to escape from Belgium. At last, late at night, someone – we don't know who – managed to get two goods' wagons for us, one for the boys and one for the girls, and the train slowly left Brussels.

Of the journey, some traumatic memories remain: the train being bombed; my sister Ruth, with another older girl, getting off at a station in order to use the toilet and the train suddenly starting to move and my panic at the thought that I would never see her again; being passed by train-loads of soldiers, some wounded, coming back from the front. But for me the most distressing moment came when I had to use a beautiful leather shoulder bag which my mother had bought me as a going away present, to relieve myself. Whenever the train stopped in a village, the local population turned out to bring us water or milk. We had no food, other than what the boys had brought with them and they forever held it against us that we girls brought clothes, whilst they provided the food.

Four long days and nights later, the train finally came to a stop near the tiny village of *Seyre*, in South-West France, where we had been allocated an old barn belonging to the local squire. It had no electricity, heat or sanitation and the boys' first job was to fetch tables and benches from the nearby church so that we could at least sit down. The winter of 1940 was particularly severe and Alex Frank with some of the older boys walked for miles through the snow to find some food for us, but, as I could never get used to the cold, the hardest thing for me was sleeping on straw covered only by a thin blanket. Water for cooking, cleaning and washing had to be brought from a nearby pump, which froze up. Due to poor nutrition, illnesses broke out and my sister's legs were covered in large boils.

Conditions improved somewhat in May 1941 when we were 'adopted' by the *Croix Rouge Suisse Secours aux Enfants* –the Swiss Red Cross Children's Rescue- who found a disused *château* for us on the outskirts of a village called *Montégut Plantaurel*, in the *Basse Pyrénées*, about two hours from Toulouse. Although still without running water, toilets and heating, apart from a wood-burning stove in the beautiful wood-panelled dining room, *Château de la Hille*, at least had beds and the unbelievable luxury of a piano. Amongst the older boys there were two very gifted musicians, a pianist and a violinist who, instead of food, had brought his violin from Belgium. They gave us recitals and instilled in me a lasting love of classical music. For me, the greatest gift was a supply of books sent from Switzerland, which allowed me to hide away somewhere to read and read – forgetting my surroundings, longings for my parents and a normal life.

Slowly our life assumed a routine. We were divided into groups, the youngest children going to the local village school. My group was taught French, literature, history and geography by Alex Frank's mother who had joined us in Brussels and Peter, one of the older boys, who taught us arithmetic. I shall be forever indebted to both "teachers" as this is the only real schooling I have had and my knowledge of French has been of great help to me throughout my working life up to the present time.

The afternoons were spent working in the vegetable garden which we had planted, cleaning our rooms, helping in the kitchen, or doing the laundry in the nearby river. Food was scarce and consisted mainly of maize cooked with water, the occasional eggs which Alex Frank insisted we should eat raw for additional nutritional benefit, powdered milk sent by the Swiss Red Cross and *topinambour*, a type of sweet potato planted for cattle and the only food which I have sworn never to eat again! Ruth and I developed jaundice, a very debilitating and lengthy illness. Walking in the countryside, we gathered blackberries and chestnuts and once, to our delight we found a potato which we presented to Ruth, our group leader, as a birthday present. Eventually, the older boys and girls found work with the local farmers. Ruth went to work for a Swiss family at some distance from the *Château*, which meant that I only saw her very occasionally when she had an afternoon off.

News of the war came via Radio Andorra and I can still see us huddled around the wireless and hear the voice of the announcer saying "*Aqui Radio Andorra*". At times we even heard the cryptic messages broadcast by the BBC to warn the Resistance of parachute drops. While we had no news at all from my father, contact with my mother in London was restricted to the occasional twenty-five word messages which we were allowed to send via the Red Cross and she did not know, until much later, that Bronia had been left behind in Belgium. On going through her papers after her death, I found all of these "letters" which she had carefully kept and no doubt re-read many times.

In spite of all the hardship, the spirit of comradeship, morale and self-discipline in the *Château* was exceptionally high, with the older boys and girls looking after the younger ones. This sense of communal responsibility and belonging helped us to overcome many of the problems we had to face.

Memories have many facets, good and bad. Chief amongst the good ones is learning to swim in the nearby river, much to the horror of the locals who, used to washing once a year, said that we would catch our death by going into the water; an excursion to the nearby *Maz d'Azil* stalagmite caves; putting on plays for visiting Red Cross officials; but best of all, a fountain pen which Ruth gave me on my twelfth birthday which was to be my most treasured possession for years to come. Bad memories include having my hair shaved off completely due to an infestation of lice and being punished for uttering a word of German on waking one morning, which was forbidden and resulted in my being locked up in a room for a week with only bread and water, although Ruth managed to smuggle some food in to me, as well as being woken up at dawn to pick frozen Colorado beetles off our plants. Worst of all was having to get up many times a night in the freezing cold to use the latrines.

Alex Frank left us to join the Free French Forces in London. The Red Cross sent us two "educators", one of whom was *Mlle Rosie Naef* a spinster of about thirty years of age, with no experience of dealing with children or young people. Having spent the previous years working with Albert Schweitzer in *Lambarene*, she thought that we were shamming when feeling ill and was intent on making us work as much as possible to overcome what she thought was idleness. We were more fortunate with their second choice, *Eugen Lyrer*, a middle-aged bachelor who travelled to Toulouse to buy books for us and, even more important, showed us some understanding and kindness.

Even this modicum of normality ceased when on the 14th August 1942 we were awoken by the sound of lorries being driven into the courtyard of the *Château* and found ourselves surrounded by a group of *gendarmes* who, collaborating with the Germans, had come to arrest all our boys and girls over fifteen years old. They were taken to the *Camp de Vernet*, a concentration camp previously set up for political escapees from Franco's Spain. Although Ruth was not in the *Château* at the time, they knew her whereabouts and much to the Swiss family's distress she was also arrested and taken to the camp.

Mlle Naef, to her credit, immediately went to the Commander of the camp to demand the release of all her charges, but meeting with total indifference and even threats for her own safety, she contacted the Director of the Swiss Red Cross in France, Mr *Maurice Dubois*. Without consulting his superiors in Bern, he went straight to René Bousquet, the Chief of Police of the Free French Zone in *Vichy* and threatened to withdraw all Swiss Red Cross aid to children in France if the *La Hille* youngsters were not immediately set free. Thus, at the very last moment, Mr *Dubois* succeeded in saving them from deportation and certain death. He was honoured by *Yad Vashem* as a

"Righteous Gentile" for his efforts on their behalf.

Our relief on our comrades' return, although great, was of short duration. We realised that we were in danger and that it was only a question of time when the *Milices* would return to arrest us all. Small groups of the older boys and girls left *La Hille* to try and escape into Switzerland or Spain. Some were successful, whilst others, being over the age of sixteen, were either sent back by the Swiss or betrayed by their Spanish guides and thus, sadly, we lost twelve of our comrades who were caught and perished in Auschwitz. Amongst these was *Inge Helft* whose mother had made contact with my mother in London. I met her after the war and she greeted me with the words which I will never forget: "Why did you survive and not my Inge"? How could I answer her?

At nightfall, on the 31st December 1942, Ruth came to say good bye to me. She and her friend Lixie had decided to try and get to Lyon where Mr *Lyrer* had given them the address of someone who would help them to obtain false documents and food coupons. Needless to say, knowing the danger they were facing, I was extremely anxious, but felt that they had made the right decision as life *in La Hille* was becoming extremely difficult. The older boys and girls spent every night hiding in an onion cellar which could not be seen from the outside. We, younger ones, took turns to look out for the *gendarmes* who we were sure would return at any time, so that we could warn them.

After sleeping rough for two nights, Ruth and her friend finally reached *Lyon* only to find that the person they were to contact had been arrested. They found refuge in a convent and eventually made their way to *Annecy* to be closer to the Swiss border. As Ruth could not contact me, I had no news of her whereabouts and only found out much later that she had moved to *Grenoble*, realising that, being over sixteen, she would be sent back if she tried to cross into Switzerland. Eventually, she made contact with members of the MJS, a Zionist Jewish Youth Movement, who provided her with false papers in the name of *Renée Sorel*. The MJS' main activity was to try and save as many Jewish children as possible by smuggling them into Switzerland and Ruth's role was to act as a courier. One of their members, Marianne, was caught near the Swiss border after having successfully arranged the crossing of several groups of children. She was tortured by the Gestapo and died without denouncing her comrades.

One day the MJS heard that the Germans had discovered that a Jewish baby, named Corinne, had been hidden in an orphanage prior to her parents being arrested. Being frightened, the matron of the orphanage had refused to hand the baby over to an MJS member and was waiting for the arrival of a Gestapo officer who was to pick up the infant that afternoon. As there was no time to lose in order to save the child, Ruth volunteered to dress up to look like a German officer, call at the orphanage and demand that the matron hand over the child to her. The matron, threatened by Ruth with the closure of the orphanage if she refused to do so, readily complied with her request. Ruth took the baby to a safe house and she survived the war. Many years later, Corinne who had immigrated to Israel, found Ruth's address. She knocked on her door one evening and when Ruth opened, simply said: "*Je suis Corinne*". In the Talmud it is written that "*whoever saves a single life, saves the entire world*" – Ruth has certainly earned this accolade.

After this daring rescue under the noses of the Germans, it became obvious that the Gestapo would be looking for Ruth and that it was not safe for her to remain in France. It was decided that she should try and escape to Spain via the *Pyrénées*. However, she would not leave without making sure that I was in safety in Switzerland and on the 12th September 1943 sent a note to Mr *Lyrer*, asking him to bring me to *Annecy*. I left the *Château* without being able to say good bye to my comrades. Mr *Lyrer* took me on his bicycle and without any problems we arrived in *Pamiers*, the nearest town to *La Hille* and from there took the train to *Annecy*. Whereas I remember very little of the long journey, I very clearly remember arriving at the station in *Annecy* which was full of Germans who were checking the papers of all the passengers getting off the train. To my great relief we passed the control without difficulty as Mr *Lyrer* had documents to say that I was going to a Red Cross hostel near *Annecy*.

I cannot describe my joy at seeing Ruth again, which was only spoilt when she told me that I would be leaving for *Annemasse*, a small town on the Swiss border, as the MJS had arranged with a guide to try and get me to Switzerland that night together with the family of one of their members. The afternoon passed very quickly. After taking leave of Mr *Lyrer,* who had to return to *La Hille*, we walked through the beautiful little town down to the lake, had an ice cream in a small café and then it was time to say good bye once again. I did not want to leave Ruth, but realised that there was no alternative. Little did I know at the time that it would be twelve years before we would see each other again!

Towards midnight the guide told us that it was not safe for us to leave for the border that night. The Germans, having caught a group trying to cross into Switzerland the previous night, had intensified their patrol of the border. So we spent the day in hiding in the guide's home. Just before dawn the following day, the guide took us to the border and told us that he could not accompany us any further and that we would have to cross over three barbed wire fences to reach Switzerland.

He gave us only vague directions and after negotiating the second fence we were not sure whether to go straight ahead or turn to the right. The family, consisting of a mother, father, young boy of about seven and a girl of my age, thought that the guide had indicated one way, whereas I thought it was the other. Finally it was decided that the parents would stay with the boy whilst their daughter and I would go ahead to "spy out" the land. After only a few minutes' walk, to our horror, we heard German voices. Very quickly and quietly we retraced our steps and, following the other path, found the third barbed wire fence which we managed to climb under. We were in Switzerland! Immediately we were surrounded by Swiss border guards who told us that they had seen us almost walking into the arms of the German patrol, but had no way of warning us. We had escaped by the skin of our teeth.

It was six o'clock in the morning by the time we arrived at the border police station where, without so much as offering us a drink, they proceeded to interrogate us. After having taken a note of my name, place and date of birth, they asked me how and why I had come to Switzerland. I replied that I did not know how I had come (obviously I was not allowed to tell anyone) and was asking myself "why"? Some time later, we were loaded onto a police vehicle and taken to the Refugee Camp of *Charmilles*, on the outskirts of Geneva, which I saw, to my dismay, was surrounded by a barbed wire fence and was policed by armed guards with dogs. Were we refugees such a danger to Switzerland's security that we had to be treated like criminals? Life in the camp was hard, without adequate food or sanitation, but what upset me most of all was that, contrary to *La Hille*, there was absolutely no cooperation between the detainees. No one bothered about the children like myself, not even the family I had crossed the border with, no schooling or medical attention.

I became ill, with bouts of high fever and many years later when trying to conceive, the doctor diagnosed that I had contracted tuberculosis in the Fallopian tubes during that time, which left me unable to have children. One of my greatest problems was that I only had the clothes I had come with from *La Hille* and in order to wash my underwear I had to stay in bed while it was drying. Luckily, at the border, I had given my nationality as Polish (in Germany one had the nationality of one's father) and received the bountiful sum of five Swiss francs a month from the Polish consulate which allowed me at least to buy stamps so that I could write to my mother.

I spent nearly five months in various internment camps near Geneva, all equally as badly run and disorganised; the last one being appropriately named *"Le Bout du Monde"*. Eventually, the Red Cross sent me to live with the Swiss-German family *Mäder* in *Schaffhausen* just before my fourteenth birthday, which meant that I was no longer of compulsory school age. I asked if I could be trained to become a nursery teacher, but was sent to a "Household" school, where I was taught to cook, clean and run a proper "Swiss" household. I was allowed to practise my newly acquired skills by helping *Frau Mäder* in the afternoons and in my spare time. I was readily accepted by my "school mates" as I had made great efforts to learn *Schweitzerdeutch*, which they said I spoke "like a native" thus adding another, but soon to be forgotten, language to my repertoire.

Having entered Switzerland illegally, I had a police record, which necessitated a weekly call at the local police station. There were about a dozen young Jewish refugees in *Schaffhausen*, but we had no contact with each other, except for a visit of a rabbi every two months, which the Zurich community paid for in their generosity. One of these visits took place during *Chanukah* and we, in all innocence, thought we might be given a doughnut or some special treat – but all we got was an apple and a couple of walnuts – this has also remained a memory. My adoptive family asked why the Jewish families in *Schaffhausen*, of which there were a few, had not taken in any Jewish children – I could not answer them.

Schaffhausen had no synagogue. Being close to the German border town of *Rheinhausen*, which had a larger Jewish community, they held joint High Holiday Services before the war. This proximity to Germany cost *Schaffhausen* dearly, as one day the American Airforce mistook one for the other and released some bombs which were intended for Germany, causing considerable damage and some panic amongst the local population. Thus I had a chance to find out how it felt to be in a bombing raid and thought of what my mother had endured in London for years.

I was not unhappy in *Schaffhausen*, but very lonely and missed the comradeship and intellectual stimulation which *La Hille* had provided. Therefore, I was delighted when, at the beginning of 1945, I was asked whether I would like to move to Bern in order to look after a distant member of the *Mäder* family who was desperately ill and needed day and night care.

Before leaving *Schaffhausen*, on a bitterly cold day in January 1944 when the washing I was hanging out froze under my fingers, I received a postcard from Ruth sent from *Cadiz* saying that she had succeeded in making the extremely difficult journey across the *Pyrénées* to Spain and was in sunny *Cadiz* awaiting a ship which would take her to Palestine. I was very jealous!

In Bern, I stayed with this lady for the next six months, cooked and cleaned for her and gave her frequent pain killing injections (much to the amazement of her doctor when it was time for me to leave). I became very fond of her and I believe that this feeling was mutual.

I was in Bern when the war in Europe ended on the 8th May and I was at last able to make contact with some other *La Hillers* and also joined a local young Zionist group where I met my first boyfriend who took me to see "The Tales of Hoffmann", my first opera. I formed a lifelong friendship with another, Didi (who is now a member of my sister's Kibbutz). On *Rosh Hashanah* 1945, Didi and I went to look for the synagogue which we found with some difficulty, having followed a man wearing a hat who turned out not to be Jewish. This was the first time after six long, difficult and hazardous years that I entered a synagogue. The feeling was indescribable.

During my stay in Bern I was given permission to spend a weekend in Zurich with Mr *Lyrer* and was able to thank him personally for taking the risk of accompanying me to *Annecy* in defiance of Swiss Red Cross regulations. He certainly had a hand in my escape and survival.

Soon after her arrival in London, my mother had applied to the Home Office for permits for us to join her in the UK. Her application was refused on the grounds that being in Belgium we were not in danger! She re-applied in 1942, was asked to send £60, a fortune in those days, and was told that, provided we could get to Portugal, arrangements would be made for our onward journey to England. This, in 1942, was as likely as a trip to the moon.

Finally, in October 1945, the Home Office granted her request for a visa for me and on the 22nd October I received a letter from the Red Cross instructing me to proceed to Zurich where I was to meet one of their representatives who would provide me with the ticket for my train journey to London. In the instructions, which I still have, I was told not to bring more than one suitcase which I could carry myself. I found this hilarious as all my worldly possession would have fitted into a small hold-all.

Strange as it might seem, whereas I can remember the overnight journey via Paris and my arrival at Victoria Station which I found dark and gloomy after Switzerland, I seem to have blanked out the reunion with my mother completely. I had last seen her when I was barely nine years old and was returning as a nearly sixteen year old and, through force of circumstances, a very independent adolescent.

Our roles became almost reversed. I felt that I had to make up to her for all the hardship she had lived through during the long war years on her own in London, with the bombs falling and not knowing whether her husband and three children were alive and would survive the endless war. She told me later that it was only her faith in the Almighty which kept her going and, having arrived in England with only the ten marks which she was allowed to take out of Germany, she worked day and night in order to earn enough to make a home for us in London.

To conclude my story, I took English lessons, got lost in the fog, and saw my first English film, 'Brief Encounter'. With the help of a dictionary, and whilst ironing, I worked my way through my first English book, "Gone With The Wind".

At Pitman's College in London, I learnt shorthand and typing so that I could earn my own living and help my mother as soon as possible. It was through my work and knowing French that I met my husband Alan. I was working for a French watch importer who shared an office building with the *Mizrachi* Federation. Alan, a qualified electronics engineer, had volunteered for the Israeli Air force after completing his military service with the RAF. He had returned to the UK for his brother's bar mitzvah and was asked by a friend, who worked for *Mizrachi*, to rewire the building. We have been happily married for fifty-eight years. Another defeat for Hitler's Holocaust!

Ruth, on arrival in Palestine, was interned by the British in *Atlit*, but my aunt Betty who had immigrated to Palestine in 1937 and was living in Haifa, managed to obtain her release. She joined a kibbutz where she met her future husband, David, called Dadi for short, who also came from Berlin. They married in 1947 and became founding members of Kibbutz *Lehavot Habashan* in Upper Galilee. Whilst having four sons, she still managed to train as a nurse and worked in this capacity on the kibbutz before retiring a few years ago. Her sons, all officers in the Israel Defence Forces – one reaching the rank of colonel in the Air Force – are all married and together have given Ruth sixteen grandchildren. They are an exceptionally warm and close-knit family – a credit to Ruth and my late brother in law who unfortunately died in a tractor accident and are a living proof that Hitler's "final solution" did not completely succeed. In the words of the Hebrew song: *"AM YISRAEL CHAI"* – *"THE PEOPLE OF ISRAEL LIVE"*!

After the war, we made many attempts to search for my father, including a trip to Auschwitz in 1989, but without success and it was only some six years ago that I found out, through the Red Cross, that according to their records, my father must have perished in Bergen Belsen in January 1945, as after that date there is no further trace of him. This is the worst news we could have had, as the thought of what he must have endured to survive for so long in the camps, only to die a few months before the liberation, will haunt me forever.

My mother did not remarry. She did not enjoy good health and spent her last years divided between her home in London and Israel where she had her own little place on Ruth's kibbutz. I visited her several times in hospital in *Safad* and she eventually died in Ruth's arms, in her eighty-first year, on Memorial Day, the day before *Yom Ha'atzmaut* 1983. She is buried in the kibbutz cemetery, a peaceful site, surrounded by the green hills of the Galilee and on her grave we have placed a plaque in memory of my father who has no known grave.

The feeling of kinship engendered in the *Château de la Hille* has remained over the years and we have had several reunions of the surviving "children" in Israel, France and the States. Following a reunion of the "Children of *La Hille*" at the *Château* which took place in 2000 with the participation of over thirty surviving "children" coming from all over the world, even Australia, the Mayor and community of the tiny village of *Montégut Plantaurel* decided to create a museum in our memory. *LE MUSÉE DES ENFANTS DU CHÂTEAU DE LA HILLE* was inaugurated in 2007 and is frequently visited by groups of school children and young people in order not only to show them what happened in the past, but to instil in them a sense of pride and an openness to all who might need their help, wherever they may be in the world.

EVA CLARKE

Born in a Concentration Camp

I was born in Mauthausen concentration camp on 29th April 1945. My mother, Anka Bergman, and I are the only survivors of our family; all the others were killed in Auschwitz including three grandparents, my father, Bernd Nathan, uncles, aunts and my seven year old cousin, Peter.

In 1933 my father had left Berlin for Prague where he eventually met and married my mother, on 15th May 1940. In December 1941 my parents were sent to Terezin (Theresienstadt) where they stayed for three years. During this time my mother became pregnant with my brother, Jiri (Hebrew name: Dan) When the Nazis discovered this fact my parents were forced to sign a document stating that when the baby was born, he would have to be handed over to the Nazis – to be killed! It was the first time my mother had heard the word 'euthanasia'. However, my brother died of pneumonia at the age of two months. His death meant my life! Had my mother arrived in Auschwitz-Birkenau holding a baby, she would have been sent immediately to the gas chambers. But because she arrived there without a baby and yet pregnant again with me (but not visibly), she survived.

My mother was in Auschwitz-Birkenau from the 1st to the 10th of October 1944. Following his sudden deportation from Terezin and ignorant of his destination, my mother had volunteered to follow my father. Tragically, she never saw him again and he never knew that she was pregnant. After the war my mother was told by an eyewitness that he had been shot on 18th January 1945, less than a week before the Russian army liberated the camp (27th January 1945).

As my mother's pregnancy was not obvious and as she was deemed fit for work, she was sent out of Auschwitz to work as a slave labourer in an armaments factory in Freiberg, Saxony, near Dresden. My mother was to remain there for six months, getting weaker while becoming more visibly pregnant.

At the end of March/beginning of April 1945, the Nazis were retreating and evacuating the concentration and slave labour camps. My mother was not on a death march; she was forced on a train. This time it was not a cattle truck, but a coal truck: open to the skies and filthy. What followed, was a three-weeks' nightmare journey around the Czech countryside, without any food and hardly any water. The Nazis did not know what to do with their 'dying cargo'. Under 'normal' circumstances the train would have been sent back to Auschwitz, but this was now April 1945 and Auschwitz had been liberated in January.

The train eventually arrived at Mauthausen concentration camp. My mother had such a shock when she saw that name at the station, that labour began. I was born on a cart, in the open, without any assistance. My mother weighed about 5 stone (35 kg). She had the appearance of a scarcely living pregnant skeleton. I weighed about 3 lbs. (1½ kg)! And we both survived the experience! This was mainly due to the fact that the gas chambers had been blown up the day before my birth and that the American army had liberated the camp three days after my birth.

My mother is alive, reasonably well and was 94 on 20th April 2011.

STEVEN FRANK

The Young Gardener

I was born into a secular Jewish Dutch family in Amsterdam, in July 1935, as one of three sons. My older brother is three years older and my younger brother 20 months younger than I am.

My father was born in Zwolle, eastern Holland, in 1903. He was a highly regarded and successful lawyer in Amsterdam, a member of many national committees, and a founder-member of the first 'legal aid' organisation, 'Ons Huis', giving free legal advice to the poor of Amsterdam.

My mother was born in Eastbourne, England, in 1910, but came to Holland when she was eighteen, to attend a domestic-science college, to finish her education. It was at this time that she met my father.

They were married in 1931 and briefly resided at Merwedeplein 36, not far from that other, well known Frank family. By the time they had three sons we lived in a lovely large house in the then new part of Amsterdam Zuid (South).

With the invasion of Holland in May 1940 my parents discussed the possibility of fleeing to England where my mother's family lived. At that time my father who was the legal adviser on the board of 'Het Apeldoornse Bos', a well-known Jewish mental hospital, refused to leave the mentally handicapped patients to the evil intentions of the Nazis. Someone had to speak for them. And so we remained in Holland. My father joined the Dutch resistance and was involved in issuing false papers to escaping Dutch Jews en route to Switzerland.

The anti-Jewish measures in Holland are well documented. I particularly recall the wearing of the star, and the banning of my visits to such places as our local park, the zoo, and most of all, my local primary school. I remember going to the all-Jewish Dalton school where, from time to time, classmates and even teachers would disappear. It was in January 1943 that I last saw my father, when he left home and walked to his office in the centre of Amsterdam. The Gestapo raided the office and took my father away to prison in Amersfoort where he was interrogated, tortured, and finally taken to Westerbork and then on to Auschwitz, where he arrived in very poor physical condition. He was sent to the gas chambers, where he was murdered on around January 21st 1943, aged only 39 years. He had achieved so much in such a short life.

My mother was now alone, and started to show the courage and ingenuity which were to help her so much in the camps later. She changed places with a cleaner in the prison and saw my father briefly two or three times. With no money coming into the household, she started a school for Jewish children in our large house, cut men's hair, as Jews had difficulty finding Jewish barbers, and sought the help of friends to get her husband out of prison.

Three good friends of my father's petitioned the German authorities for clemency describing the good things my father had done during his short life. Although the Germans would not relent, they did allow my mother and us to be placed on the 'Barneveld List'. This list contained Dutch Jews who were at the top of their professions, the upper echelon of Dutch Jewish society. And being on this list definitely saved our lives in the end.

In March 1943 we were ordered to report to the railway station, to travel to Barneveld. We were housed in a castle called the 'Schaffelaar'. Our stay there was on the whole a happy one. No one was hungry, and the grounds were beautiful, with a lily pond in the centre of woodland. Some schooling was available, although being taught as an infant by a professor was not ideal, but I learned all my tables and knew all the provinces of the Netherlands and their capitals! To be more realistic, medical services were very basic. I caught a bad dose of impetigo, and although we had the best dermatologists, we had no medicine. I had to lie in the sun by the pond all day and was bandaged up at sunset with bandages made of sheets. It was in Barneveld that I learned the love of gardening. Many children had their own little plot to weed and to sow with flowers and vegetables.

In September 1943 the German army entered the camp and we all had to leave for Westerbork. This brought pandemonium to the inmates, as everyone knew that after Westerbork it was Poland. In Westerbork we were housed in one barrack, No. 85, with men at one end and women and children at the other end for sleeping. One could move freely around the barrack during the day. It was grossly overcrowded, with bunk beds two high near the window sides and three high in the centre, all jammed together, so that one had to crawl over other people's beds to get to one's own. Although we were not hungry there, the sanitary conditions were appalling. Like most of the inmates I had dysentery, and also jaundice, and a worm infestation of the bowels. We were there for a year, during which time we saw friends and family being deported weekly on Tuesdays to the east, to Auschwitz, Sobibor, Bergen–Belsen and Theresienstadt. Our barrack was attacked by the Royal Air Force in the spring of 1944, killing one of my much loved friends whom we had adopted as our surrogate grandfather. The tragedy was that this old man loved England and everything English, and would speak at great length in English with my mother. Our barrack was destroyed and we moved into barrack No. 72, where I met a man who was growing tomatoes outside his barrack window, and as I had gained an interest in growing plants in Barneveld, I used to help him. One day he said to me: 'I have to go, look after the tomatoes.' I am still growing them today, for him.

We were transported to Theresienstadt on the penultimate transport to leave Westerbork, in September 1944. After a thirty-nine hour journey in cattle trucks with no food or water, we arrived. Much has been written about this place. We survived because my mother, realising the difficulties ahead, got work in the camp hospital laundry where she had access to hot water. This allowed her to wash our clothes when no one was looking, and also to wash other people's clothes: this labour she bartered for food, mainly a bitter bread, which she mixed with the hot water to make a thick consistency which she called 'broodpap', bread porridge. She dispensed this from an old aluminium saucepan with one spoon, at the children's home where we now were. She gave a spoonful to each child. I never saw her take a spoonful for herself.

As children we collected razor blades and swapped them like stamps. We made torches from old batteries, torch bulbs and wire. We would 'regenerate' the worn-out batteries by sleeping with them between our legs at night. This gave enough light for a short while the following evening. Hunger and how to alleviate it, was our overall concern. My mother must have sunk to her lowest ebb when in January 1945 many of the Barneveld group were transported to Switzerland, in exchange for ambulances and medicines. We were liberated by the Russians on May 9th 1945, a day I shall never forget. After a month in quarantine we were allowed to go and we had an unusual journey to England, but that is another story.

HEDI FISCHER FRANKL

My Memories of the Holocaust

I was born in the Hungarian town of Balassagyarat in 1930. The town is situated 80 km north of Budapest, on the former Slovak-Hungarian border, and had 28000 inhabitants including 2000 Jews. My father, Geza Baruch Fischer, was a District Chief Rabbi. We belonged to the orthodox Jewish community. My mother, Rozalia, was born in Vac, near Budapest. Her maiden name was Herzfeld and she was one of 13 siblings. My late father died of cancer in 1941, thus he was not alive when men were sent to labour camps. My mother was a widow aged 39 when she was taken to Auschwitz. There my two younger sisters, Judit and Györgyi, and my younger brother Andor (Shloimi) were also murdered.

In 1940, Hitler had formed an alliance with the Hungarian Government of Horthy. While life seemed to be normal for most of the Jewish population, all Jewish males aged between 18 and 45 were called up for Labour Service. They were gathered in Labour Camps and sent to work in mines, building roads and to help the Hungarian military where casualties were the heaviest. Jews in the Labour Service were ordered to wear yellow armbands. In these Labour Camps conditions were awful. Twice daily they were given some kind of soup and 400 gram of bread for the whole day. They had to walk five to ten kilometres to work and be doing the hardest menial work for about 12 hours in the greatest heat and in the worst freezing, rainy weather. Many got ill and many died.

Others were transported to the Ukraine from where only ten percent came back alive. My uncles Laci and Yenkele Herzfeld managed to escape from such a Camp, by bribing the guards. They went to Palestine on an illegal ship and survived. My aunt Kato and Yakob Rosenberg were already living in Tel Aviv since 1938. Only four members of my mother's family of 13 survived the Holocaust, three in Palestine and uncle Hashi in London. The others were victims of the Nazi genocide.

The Nazis occupied Hungary on March 19th 1944. The next day new laws were brought in. First, all Jewish shops were closed and blocked up with big notices saying 'Jew Dog' or 'Jew Pig', or just the word 'JUDE' (Jew) and a big swastika. Then big posters on public walls announced that all Jews must relinquish their vehicles. Next came the order that Jews had to bring all their gold, silver and precious jewellery to the town hall, to help the German war effort. Withholding any such articles would be severely punished. We did not possess a car, but my bicycle had to be given up. It really upset me as I was quite attached to it, and used to go everywhere on my bicycle. One could see in the synagogue courtyard huge piles of bicycles, motorbikes, etc.

The next announcement decreed: All Jews, including children and infants, must wear a yellow star on their outer garments in the shape of the Star of David, its size to be 8 x 8 cm. From that day on Jewish persons who were caught not wearing a yellow star, were arrested and imprisoned. The Christians of our town watched us with glee, glad that their Jews were being humiliated. Our usually peaceful town had changed fast into a menacing place.

One night there was a knock on our door. When my mother opened it she saw two strange men. They begged my mother to let them in and hide them. They were Jewish refugees from Czechoslovakia. Of course my mother agreed. I was in the next room and overheard the conversation between my mother and the two strangers. 'Mrs Fischer, don't stay in the ghetto. It will mean certain death to you and your children. They will deport you and kill you. You are a young woman and do not look Jewish. Go to Budapest with false identity papers, save yourself and your children.' I heard my mother respond: 'I don't believe God would allow it to happen. We are innocent, God-fearing people; so why should they want to harm us?' 'But they do! Because if you do not believe us who have seen our own families taken to death-camps, you will live to regret it and pay with your lives.' My mother then said: 'I don't care about myself, but I do want to save my children.'

The ghetto was to be set up and closed off within the next few days. My mother began to realise how dangerous our situation was, thanks to those two Jewish refugees who did their best to open her eyes and to advise her. It was then that she went to a washer woman and bought the identity papers of her daughter, Borishka. She paid plenty for it, but the woman was poor and needed the money. Similarly, identity papers were bought for my eldest brother, Henrik Erwin, who went off immediately. Unfortunately, he was recognised and imprisoned, tortured and deported to Auschwitz. We did not know what happened to him until after the war.

On the 7th May 1944 I was put on the local train by my mother, to go to Miskolc and pose as a Christian girl. Before undertaking this journey, my mother cut my long black hair, put a permanent waive in it and dressed me in peasant clothes so that no-one should recognise me. Later I found out that Mrs Melegh, our good Christian neighbour had been approached and agreed to hide my two young sisters and young brother at her parents' farm. Mrs Melegh assured my mother that her peasant family would take good care of the children and that they would be united with my mother after the war. But the children would not stay at the farm without their mother. They cried so much that my soft-hearted and devoted mum took her children back into the ghetto from where they were deported to Auschwitz, to be murdered in the gas chambers.

As for me, I was taught what to say and how to behave, so that people would not become suspicious of my real origin. I was to tell my new hosts that the doctors considered it important for me to have a change of air. I was given much money to pay for my board and lodging. Mother also gave me some golden rings and necklaces. In case I should run short, I would have these to sell. The family in Miskolc lived in a very modest flat. The man was a cobbler. There was a daughter of about my age.

When I said goodbye to my little sisters and brother, I kissed and hugged them with great sorrow in my heart. I did not know that I would never see them again. The problem was that until that day, I had never been away from my family and I felt terribly homesick. I started roaming the streets and walked into music and book shops. It was in one of these shops that two girls who were also living with false papers, recognised me as 'one of us'. In Hungarian we said: 'You too a musician!' I saw a lot of these girls, to ease my loneliness. We knew that if they found out, the Hungarians would denounce us and would give us over to the Gestapo.

So we lived in fear, but also in hope. Ignorant as to what was happening to our families, we believed that at the end of the war, we would be reunited with them.

Only days after my arrival, I had to watch the pitiful procession of the local Jewish people being taken to a station from where they were deported. I had suppressed my emotions, for I was supposed to behave like the rest of them: glad to get rid of the Jews. Inwardly I suffered greatly. Little did I imagine what was in store for me. I could not get out of my mind the picture of the Jewish people of Miskolc, each holding a bundle of belongings, walking towards an unknown destination. It was like a scene from 'Fiddler on the Roof', as they were leaving Anatevka after the progrom. It was such a sad sight, the old and infirm carried on a man-drawn cart, little children holding on to their mother's hand. I wonder how many of them knew that death was awaiting them at the end of the journey.

At night I covered my head with the blanket and cried. After only a month of hiding I wished I could turn the clock back and be in the warmth of my beloved family. It was not easy for me to live a double life, pretend to be Borishka, a good catholic girl, when inside me I was still the Jewish Hedi.

One day I decided to go and visit a Turkish bath which was in another part of the town. Having lived without a bathroom, I enjoyed it and felt refreshed. My skin was shining from the steam. I forgot to ruffle my hair or to use any makeup, and looked more like my old self. Maybe I looked even a bit more Jewish. As I stepped out into the street, a tall young man stared at me and followed me. I was worried and wondered what he was up to when he stepped in front of me and said 'Excuse me! May I see your identity card.' With this he produced a card which informed me that he was a detective of the local police. I kept my cool. 'Why are you not wearing a yellow star?', he asked. I put on my most innocent smile: 'Why should I? Are Christian girls supposed to wear one?' He said: 'You look Jewish. I still would like to see your papers.' He was about 25 , and I decided to flirt with him – an automatic reflex, to save time, to save myself. 'Come on, what would a Jewish girl be doing in a Turkish bath? You can't be serious.' He seemed to enter into the spirit of my game and remarked: 'You have a nice face, but you do not convince me. Here is the address of my office and I want you to come along tomorrow at 9 am and bring your papers. If you have nothing to hide, you will appear there.'

I told my Jewish friends what had happened to me. They strongly advised me to get on the next train and disappear from Miskolc, otherwise I would be doomed. But I thought it over: if I go, I may be caught; if I don't go, I could be caught. I was suddenly filled with courage and confidence. The next morning my friends said goodbye to me, expecting never to see me again.

Promptly at 9 o'clock I arrived at the police station. The handsome young detective ushered me into his office and with a surprised look on his face, he said: 'So, you came after all!' He scrutinised my birth certificate, then asked what my mother's maiden name was, where was my grandfather? I could answer his questions as I had been thoroughly briefed by the washer woman. 'Where is your grandmother buried?' 'She is alive', I replied. I could see he was testing me, hoping that I would fail. I gave him my most feminine look and as I was standing there acting confidently, inside I was very scared. He handed me back my papers and said: 'Well, I still think you look like a Jewess, but I suppose I had better let you go, Borishka.' As we shook hands, I said with my best acting voice: 'I hope to see you again.' Once out in the fresh air, I sighed with great relief. I was free.

My friends could not believe their eyes when they saw me again. However, my freedom did not last long. The older of the two girls had a Jewish boyfriend who had false identity papers. He was caught for some black market business. The policeman made him drop his trousers, and his circumcision told them what they wanted to know. He was never seen again. Detectives kept a watch outside his flat and when the Jewish girl, my friend, arrived there to collect his valuables, they arrested her too. At her lodgings, they found the second girl and they questioned the landlady. She told them that a slim, dark haired girl called Borishka, came to visit the girls. They proceeded to torture and threatened to kill the girls unless they revealed who and where Borishka was. At 3 am the girls led the detectives to where I lived. Suddenly, there was loud banging on our windows: 'Open up, Police!', they bellowed. The cobbler confronted the two policemen: 'There is no Jewish girl here!', he protested. But the police overpowered him and entered the home. 'We want Borishka Kovacs.' The two females of the household looked frightened, wondering what was happening. The detectives entered my bedroom. 'Get up, get dressed, you are coming with us', they urged me. Afraid, I tried to avert disaster. 'I am a good practicing Christian. I proved my identity at the police station only the other day', I pleaded. 'You are Hedi Fischer, and don't try to fool us. We know that you are Jewish. Your landlord will be punished for harbouring a Jew.' 'No, please not him. He did not know anything!', I cried. 'They are innocent, please leave them alone,' I sobbed and packed my belongings, and apologised to my host and hostess for deceiving them. They were very distressed, especially the man who, I believe, was secretly sympathetic to the Jews.

The three of us were taken to the local prison, and we spent the night in a cell with hardened prostitutes. I learned everything about sex and four letter words that night.

The next day I was handed over to the Gestapo. About 30 Jewish people of both sexes and various ages, were kept in a room which had the lights on all night. We could only sleep on the floor, without any sleeping bags or blankets. One by one we taken into another room and interrogated. Mostly they wanted us to give information about who else we knew to be hiding. Also, they were looking for hidden diamonds or other valuables. So they ordered me to undress. There were six adult males present, mainly Hungarians. As I had never been seen naked other than by my parents, I refused to undress. Next, two hefty men got hold of me and forcibly removed my clothes. I put me hands in front of my genitals and cried: 'Leave me alone, I am a virgin!' They all laughed out loud. 'Open your legs,' one shouted at me. I was so scared that I felt faint. Next they demanded: 'Bend down so we can examine your bottom.' They looked into all my crevices. But could not find anything there. So they let me put on my clothes I wanted the earth to swallow me; I felt so humiliated, and my dignity had been trampled on, my self-respect in ruins.

From the Gestapo quarters we were taken to a camp where all the Jews who tried to hide, were herded together. I felt so lonely and so sick with fear, I could not stop crying. We all were there like animals, waiting to be slaughtered. Suddenly a girl, a few years older than I, came up to me, and said: 'What is the matter? Why are you weeping?' 'I am alone in the world, and scared.' 'You are not alone, I am here with you. From now on you will be my little sister', she said and put her arms around me. Alice Hersh became my best friend and my only moral support during the ensuing, hard to bear, year.

In June 1944, together with a few thousand other Jews from the Debrecen area, we were loaded into cattle trucks which were then sealed. The temperature in the Hungarian summer was nearly 100 degrees and we were given no water or bread, only a bucket to be used as toilet. Soldiers with dogs and bayonets were guarding us all the way on a horrific journey which lasted five days and nights. The stench in our wagon was unbearable. There were 80 people, old and young, some sick, but none of us had enough space to lie down. The constant heat, hunger, thirst and lack of sleep, made us quite delirious. We had no idea where they were taking us and were convinced that they would kill us when we would get there. I must have been very dehydrated because my whole body had swollen up and I felt ill.

Finally, we reached Strasshof, in Austria, where I was carried out by two inmates and put down on the grass. In the wagon two women of about 40, had committed suicide by swallowing poison, three others lost their mind and two older persons died of suffocation. It is hard to describe how we felt after that humiliating trip. We could breathe fresh air and then we were taken into a place to shower with real water. Our clothes were taken into another room, to be disinfected. After another day's hunger we were given a piece of bread and bacon. As I was brought up on kosher food, I refused to eat the pig product.

More humiliation followed. We had to line up naked in front of several male doctors who examined us for fitness to work. They also looked for lice and other undesirable conditions. Those of us who were declared healthy, were then photographed and given a prisoner number. We were once again herded into a train and transported to Vienna where we were selected for forced labour. In our group there were two friends of Alice who happened to be trained electricians. Together with Alice and me, they volunteered to work in an electronics factory. This was Siemens and Schuckert, situated at Pischelsdorf-Zwentendorf, near Tulln. Our Jewish contingent consisted of only 30 people who were amongst many hundreds of Polish, Ukrainian and Yugoslav workers.

Our barracks were bare; our bed had only straw on it and was full of bedbugs. They kept us awake at night. We had to walk 5 km to our work place and lived on black coffee, a small piece of bread and a kind of soup. Needless to say, we were very hungry all the time and could not think of anything else except of getting hold of some real food. One day, the Germans who were in charge, discovered sabotaged work. They lined up all the Jewish people and demanded that the saboteurs step forward. Nobody did. The Nazi then shouted that unless someone takes the blame, all of us would suffer terrible consequences. They would shoot us indiscriminately. The two friends of Alice then stepped forward, saying that they were the guilty ones. The two men were taken away to the forest where they were shot. What a waste of two more young lives. We were very upset and the old anxiety returned. When the Germans would have no more use for us, they would surely kill us. Added to our constant hunger, we had to live with fear as well.

Alice was working next to the foreman. This middle-aged Austrian Christian was secretly sympathetic to Jews. He told Alice that when the Russians would come to free Austria, the Nazis would evacuate this camp and take us, prisoners, into Germany to an unknown, perilous fate. He advised her to hide in the forest in a bunker and then go to Vienna where he and his wife would be willing to hide her. Alice told him that she would only accept his help if I could come with her too. To this he agreed.

In April 1945 Russian occupying troops had entered Vienna and as foretold, the Nazis prepared to take all prisoners of our camp into Germany. Alice and I walked out of the camp in just the clothes we had on. There was such chaos that nobody noticed us. We found a shelter in the forest and stayed there undetected until the whole camp had left which took more than a day.

When all was quiet, we walked to the next village and posing as Hungarian refugees, we asked for work and food. The peasants gave us both and we slept in the hay of a barn. The next day we walked ten kilometres to the town of Tulln. On the way we saw many Nazis and SS soldiers on motorbikes, rushing in the opposite direction, fleeing from the Russians. Fortunately, they were so intent on saving themselves that they did not take any notice of us.

In Tulln, we tried to find a train to Vienna, but the only train going in that direction, was carrying Hitler Youth. We were determined to go to the safe house offered to us by Herr Mayer and so, not thinking of the danger, we did travel in one wagon with the young soldiers who were going to fight for The Fatherland till their last drop of blood. Actually, we were feeling sorry for them for they were only our aged, 15 or 16, and were going to their certain death. As we sat in the corner of the train, we tried to make ourselves invisible. All the way when the train stopped at stations, we were at risk of being found. But we managed to get to Vienna and to the Family Mayer in Hitzing, the 14th district. For three weeks we were hiding under the beds. This time we were in danger of being raped by the young Russian soldiers of the occupying army. Thanks to the caring kindness of the Mayers, Alice and I were safe.

It was time to return to Hungary. However, there were no train going there from Vienna. We walked to every railway station, but in vain. One day in the beginning of May 1945, we were at the Eastern Railway station, looking for a train to Hungary. There was a Russian officer in charge of the railway traffic. Alice spoke to him in Slovak and told him that we were two Jewish girls who wanted to travel back home. When he heard the word "Jewish", the officer's face lit up and he exclaimed: 'I am Jewish too!'. He hugged both of us with tears in his eyes. He said he did not know there were Jewish girl survivors in Austria. Soon he was able to put us on a very full train which, very slowly, somehow reached Budapest.

We went straight away to the Jewish Communal Office in Ship street where we were given a hot meal, some clothes and an address where we could sleep. We were asked to come back the next day as they were going to find out what had happened with our families, and where they could possibly be located. The JOINT organisation also gave us some money so that we could manage for a few days. On the second day of my visit there, I met two older cousins, Mendy Netzer and Mayer Buchinger. We were overjoyed to find each other and they promptly invited Alice and me to come and stay in their elegant, big apartment. This was a good, temporary arrangement. Alice was determined to make aliyah to Palestine and I wanted to see my family return from the camps.

Every day I went to see the list on the wall of the Ship street office, filled with hope, hungrily reading through the names appearing in alphabetical order. But alas, when my eyes got riveted on the letter

F, there were no Fischers listed. After weeks of daily searching I ran into Mr Ungar, a married man who was from my home town, and who knew my family well. 'Have you heard any news of my mother?', I queried eagerly, full of optimism. 'Don't you know they died in the gas chambers in Auschwitz? Your family together with my wife and two children, murdered in cold blood.' He showed no emotions. I stood there speechless from shock and felt as if the whole world was disappearing beneath me. It was too much to bear, and I fainted. Alice was with me and she suggested to get some fresh air. We went for a walk along the banks of the river Danube.

We were orphans of the Holocaust, claimed by no-one, belonging nowhere, wandering aimlessly, not knowing where to go or what to do. The year spent in the German concentration camp left its mark on us. My body was puffed up from the watery soup and stolen potatoes. I felt the desolation of having lost everything and everyone, and I had no goals in my life. As I looked into the river on that grey spring day, I was immobilised by despair. Heavy, thick fog filled my eyes, invaded my lungs, my whole body. Faces of people passing by seemed to be decked with black veils, black mist covered the houses and filled the air.

I had a vision of my naked mother with soap and towel in one hand and my little five years old sister, Madike, hanging on her other arm. I saw them entering the gas chamber amid a row of Jewish women and children. Then as they were inside, an automatic door closed behind them. Trapped thus, they started inhaling poisonous gas, and gasping for air. I saw it so clearly, my mother's face showing horror and shock as she realised what was happening to them. She held her child close to her body, trying to protect her from the cruel, relentless fumes. Screaming, she tore through the terror-ridden crowd and with her fist she began pounding on the door, shouting: 'Open the door! Let us out! We are innocent! Open up, you murderers!!' Her efforts were interrupted by frequent coughing as her lungs were filling up with poison … She kept her eyes on her little girl, the weaker she felt, the stronger she tried to hold the doomed child … I could see them, hear them and as they slumped to the floor, one by one, I heard my mother reciting 'Shemah Yisrael…' As she uttered these few words of prayer, she fell lifeless burying her half-dead child beneath her ever protective body. A good wife, five times mother, helper of the poor, believing in the One God, she lay there, murdered in cold blood. I saw the darkened sky open up and receive her gentle soul, rising to meet the Maker.

At that moment all the black fog had disappeared and I found myself looking into the even flowing river. I thought: Where was God in 1944? If He did exist, how could He allow six million innocent people to be murdered? But on that gloomy evening in Budapest nothing existed for me except the realisation that I was left alone, the only survivor of a warm, loving family. How could I go on, how could I face life without them? My eyes became misty from an unstoppable flow of tears. I seem to melt into the river, I felt myself sink, becoming part of the water … Yes, I thought, here lay the answer to my misery, the logic of my problem. I will escape into the waves and the Danube will be my redeemer and my tomb. Like a mother its child, the river's waves will enfold me, hold me and I, too, shall be buried with my little sister and brother. I saw nothing but the dark river beckoning me, holding out its invisible arms, ready to enfold me. Filled with the desire to die, I bent over the rail ready for the water to envelope my entire being and felt myself falling, my spirits rising … The words of the old Hungarian ballad on my lips: 'The bottom of the Danube, the bottom of my coffin / The waves of the Danube, my burial shroud / The little fishes of the river, my mourners, the little birds, my choir / Fishermen, fishermen of the Danube, fish me out by Thursday noon / Fish me out and bury me too!' Then, instead of the water, Alice's two strong hands held me, shook me, kept me in life's prison and sentenced me to survival…

Some time after this event, my older brother, Henrik Erwin, returned from Auschwitz, Mauthausen, and Gunskirchen where he had been found near-dead, by the Allied army. He had been put in a hospital, nursed back to health, but not in spirit and mind. We met in out birth place, Balassagyarmat. It was a very emotional experience for both of us.

I had arrived in Balassagyarmat on the 8th May 1945 which was the day the war ended. But we, the orphans of the Holocaust, could not rejoice. We were wounded souls; our inner scars found no healing for a long time. How could we come to terms with our terrible losses? Who or what could replace our former family, our security, the loving arms of mother and the lively presence of Jucika, Bandika and Madike? It felt wrong to continue to look into the faces of our former neighbours who were partly responsible for our families' tragic fate. The same people who had robbed our homes and had taken our hidden heirlooms and when confronted, pretended to know nothing. Antisemitism had not ended with the war. The good Catholics of Hungary were taught by their priests that we, the Jews, killed their Lord. Hatred towards the Jews was written on their faces. And we dared to come back – we who, contrary to their Christian souls' desire, managed to have stayed alive!

Most camp survivors left Hungary either for Palestine or for a western country. Alice who had been raised on Zionist idealism, decided to go to Palestine where she later met her husband, Moshe Bernstein. Her two daughters, Rachelle and Yael, were born there.

On a dismal November evening in 1947, after a turbulent Channel crossing, a trans-European express train brought my brother Hanoch and me to London's Victoria station. We were very disappointed with the cold reception we received from our cousin Bandi Herzfeld who was lucky enough to have spent the war years in London with his parents. My uncle Hashi was overjoyed to see us alive and away from the Communist-ruled country of Hungary. His wife, aunt Mancie or Margaret, on the other hand, hated the sight of us. She did not wish to share her wealth or good fortune with simple, teenage refugees. The same cold indifference met me everywhere in London during the first year of my stay. On the whole, English Jews did not want to know us or help us. We were neither in command of the English language nor accustomed to the local culture and way of life. We were merely an embarrassment to them. Nobody enlightened us about the existence of Jewish Welfare organisations to which we could turn for financial and moral assistance.

We were enrolled into a Cambridge Efficiency School which was designed for foreign students and where we acquired a reasonably good knowledge of the language and local customs. Uncle Hashi paid for our schooling and gave us food and shelter. Unfortunately, at the age of 48 he was already suffering from a serious heart condition. In 1947 heart bypass operations were not done in the hospitals, and he was doomed to die an early death. He travelled to Zurich, Switzerland, to the greatest heart specialist. Alas, it was too late: he could not be saved. He is buried in a Zurich Jewish cemetery.

With his demise our life-line was cut off: aunt Margaret flatly refused to let us stay with her or to give us any financial assistance. So, my brother and I were forced to take a full-time job, to pay for our rent, food and general upkeep. Hanoch became a Hebrew teacher in an East End cheder (a young children's Sunday school) and I worked as a machine embroiderer in a factory in Brick Lane. We both continued our education at Evening Institutes. I took English literature, philosophy and later short hand typing and bookkeeping. My diligence paid its dividends: I became a short hand typist for a carpet import firm in the City. The work was very hard, especially since I had to make an hour's journey by buses. When at home, I had to cook, serve and wash up.

In 1948, Imre Rosenthal and I were married. He, too, was a survivor of the Holocaust having lost his parents in Auschwitz. We lived in two furnished rooms in Stoke Newington. Many Jewish people lived there and synagogues were in abundance. Imre, also know as Tibor, worked in a handbag and leather goods workshop. Later he opened his own handbag factory with a partner, Erwin Schwarz. We lived as observant Jews, kept a kosher home and attended a local shul on Shabbath and High Holy days. My only daughter, Judi Rachel, was born in the Jewish Bearstead Memorial Hospital in Lordship Lane, N.16 . She was a very happy and healthy baby, a bundle of joy. She had curly blond hair and green eyes. However, during the first two years she cried a great deal at night. At the age of four she was enrolled in a Jewish nursery and I could go back to working part-time in an office. Both my husband and I worked hard and saved one income so that within two years we could put down a deposit on a modest house in Durlston Road, Clapton. Hanoch lived with us, in our spare bedroom, and he also had his meals with us. He was teaching Hebrew having graduated with a BA degree from Jews College.

JOHN FRANSMAN

A Jewish Child Survivor's recollections of the Holocaust

I was born in Amsterdam three weeks before the outbreak of the Second World War, as the only child of my English-born mother, Anna Rabbie, and Dutch father, Samuel Fransman. My mother's mother, Rebecca Klok, had been born in Holland and emigrated to England with her husband, Moses Rabbie, at the turn of the century and raised a family of five children, three girls and two boys. These children had often visited their cousins in Holland in the intervening years.

The two eldest children, my aunt Cissie and my mother Anna, both married Dutch Jewish men and settled in Amsterdam. My Grandmother Rebecca had come from London on a visit in August 1939 to help at my mother's confinement. Conscious of the tensions and threatening atmosphere in Europe she suggested that we should immediately return with her to England. My father refused the offer, since he did not consider Holland to be in danger: it was a neutral country and had avoided involvement in the First World War. Moreover, he did not wish to leave his elderly mother or his brothers, sisters and their families. We lived in the south of Amsterdam in a modern apartment, where my father had a workshop and repaired shoes, the trade of his late father, and he had established a comfortable settled married life.

My first memory of wartime under Nazi occupation is a vague recollection of seeing German soldiers marching along the nearby main road sometime after they had entered Amsterdam in 1940. I found this very exciting. I must have been about three years old and I ran with other young children alongside them, they looked so powerful with rifles on their shoulders and singing their marching songs as they passed by. I also remember that my parents became more fearful as time went on, with more and more restrictions being imposed on the Jewish population, including curfews and having to wear the yellow Star of David with the word "JOOD" (Jew) on it. They started to see the roundups of Jews for deportation in what were called "razzias" from mid-1942 onwards. One day my father took me with my moneybox, which contained silver rijksdaalders (crowns) they had saved for me and together we hid it at the bottom of our garden, where we had a coal shed. I had no idea why we were doing this, but I was excited and happy to go along with my dad. By now my parents were realising that the net was closing in. They had also given some precious items and some jewellery to different neighbours for safekeeping. I only found out about this after the war when my mother told me about it and I saw some of the items. One of them was a Persian lamb fur coat which one day we saw being worn by the neighbour, Mrs Hendricks, whom she had trusted to look after it. She had lied to my mother on our return telling her that she had had to sell it for food during the war. She had not expected us to return.

The inevitable day came when the roundups were in our area and then in our street. How did they know who was Jewish and where the Jewish people lived? Did the neighbours inform or were the synagogue membership lists passed to the SD (the German Sicherheid Dienst-Secret Service Police)? There was a knock on the door, and the Dutch "groene politie" (green was the colour of their special police uniform) accompanied by "NSBers" (Dutch National Socialist party members) and German soldiers with rifles, forced us to pack some belongings and to leave in a very short time. We were taken by lorry to the train station and transported in normal passenger carriages to camp Westerbork, in the east of Holland, close to the border with Germany. The camp had been established in the late 1930s as a temporary holding camp to house Jewish refugees fleeing from Nazi persecution in Germany who could not immediately find accommodation or work in the Netherlands. I did not know this at the time but learned about it well after the war.

At this time, June 1943, the camp worked in reverse and was the transit camp from where every Tuesday about one thousand Dutch Jews were transported East in the notorious cattle wagons, to either Sobibor or Auschwitz/Birkenau, most for immediate extermination by gassing. The Germans used the refugee German Jews (who spoke their own language) to administer the weekly transports of Jews, thereby saving themselves from the same fate, at least for the time being. These refugees had been housed there originally by the Dutch Government, and now carried out orders with seemingly typical German efficiency. When my mother talked about these events years later, I realised it had caused tremendous resentment among the Dutch Jews.

As most Jewish people arrived in Westerbork, they were housed in the wooden barracks and usually stayed for no more than one or two weeks before being listed on the following Tuesday's transport. They did not know where they were going to, but they expected to be sent to work camps in the East to help the German war effort. Had they known of their ultimate destination and their fate they would no doubt have rebelled. However, deception was maintained and easier to accept and to believe by the victims than the harsh, bitter truth. In this manner my elderly Grandmother and her sons and daughters together with their families passed through this camp and were soon murdered in Sobibor or Auschwitz, from May 1943 onwards. At that time, for unknown reasons, my parents and my mother's sister's family were not listed for transport East and we remained in the camp until January 1944. During our seven-months' stay we received occasional Red

Cross food parcels and letters from my Grandmother in London. The letters were censored and allowed only a minimum, censored reply. However, these contacts with the outside world were a Godsend and made us feel that we were not forgotten. The letters were as important spiritually as the food-parcels physically, despite our starvation rations.

I have come to learn that great efforts were made in Westerbork to maintain "normal" Jewish life, and some children attended lessons. Many years after the war when I heard the singing of Moaz Tzur during a Chanukah celebration, I was aware that I knew the music. I realised that I could only have heard and learned this song in camp Westerbork during the Chanukah of 1943. However, I cannot admit to remembering much else specifically about Westerbork, as a four year old.

In the middle of January 1944 we found ourselves on the list for the next transport out. We were transported this time in the infamous cattle wagons, to a camp named Bergen Belsen about five or six miles from Celle, the administrative town of the province of Lower Saxony in North West Germany and about 50 miles north of Hannover. The camp consisted of a large number of wooden barracks within a barbed-wire fence and guarded by armed soldiers in watchtowers along the perimeter. The whole camp was within the forests of the Lüneburger Heide, consisting of extensive heath lands and forests.

We were put into large wooden barracks which had bunk beds, three high in pairs, down each side of the barrack. Families were separated: the men and boys of 13 years and over were together and the women and children were in different barracks. In this way we ended up with my Aunt Cissie and her son, Maurice (12 years old), and daughter, Helen (10 years old), on the top bunk, my mother and I (4 years old) in the middle bunk below them.

Our lives fell into a pattern. We were roused by the kapos (camp guards, often ex-criminals) very early in the mornings, around five or six o'clock in the dark and had to dress and get out to the washroom to share some ice-cold water with everyone else pushing and shoving before being rushed to the Appelplatz, the parade ground. There we would have to stand at attention in rows five deep, for sometimes several hours, while the SS organised the count of the prisoners to check that no one had escaped during the night. Because some were sick and some had died, the numbers standing would not be the same each day. This caused endless trouble and many times they would have to recount.

I could never understand that these omnipotent officials did not seem able to count and do additions properly. People thought they counted and recounted often to make us suffer a little longer in the bitter cold winter months of 1944, and in that way to cause more deaths. I would have to stand with my mother often in cold drizzling rain and keep quiet, not talk and stand very still. Sometimes, senior officials, wearing shiny, calf-length leather boots and black leather overcoats, supervised the counting process. They all appeared to be very tall, for on their heads they wore peaked caps with the deaths-head insignia. They carried sticks or whips, had pistols holstered on their wide leather belts and were very intimidating as they shouted their orders. I was frightened of them and always kept my head down so as not to look directly at them. I respected their power and authority and recognised their brutality which they exhibited from time to time with little or no provocation.

The adults had to keep the barracks clean and swept and I remember one occasion when, after roll-call, we had a barrack inspection. The bunk beds had wooden slats to support thin straw mattresses and were covered by a blanket (which I think we had brought all the way from home in Amsterdam). We had to stand at attention by our beds while the Officer inspected and moved along the bunks. When he reached ours he angrily pulled the blanket off and threw it on the ground. My mother and I were trembling, but he passed on. The reason for his anger: the blanket had not been tucked in smoothly and wrinkle free enough and so appeared to be hiding something. The bed had to be remade more carefully, she was warned!

At noon we had to line up and queue for the soup that was brought from the kitchen in milk churns. The soup was very watery and thin and was made from potato peelings and a little swede or turnip. To this day if I have soup using root vegetables it brings back memories of the camp, and I still dislike their taste.

Part of the daily routine was to keep oneself 'clean'. My mother would put a very fine-toothed comb through my hair to look for and remove lice and nits and she would also inspect my vest and other clothes. The nits (or eggs) laid by the lice had to be crushed between ones fingernails to avoid hatching out into more lice. I remember my mother's efforts to look after another woman (Dolly Reins) who had become too weak to care for herself, and who had become lice infested. She eventually died, but my mother also looked after and saved her daughter, Myrna, who was two years older than me and who used to tease me, my mother said, although I cannot remember that at all.

One day my mother and I were summoned to the men's barrack. When we went in I was struck by the stench and dirtiness of the place. We were taken over to where my father lay on his bunk. He had died and was lying on the middle bunk, just above my head, and I saw that he did not move, his hipbone was very prominent and his arms and legs were very thin. He had become just skin and bones. We were stunned yet did not cry; we were not able to shed a tear or show any emotion. I still have a letter that was given to my mother at the time, written by a Dutch Jewish doctor as a substitute death certificate, signed and witnessed by two other men. It is dated 31st October 1944. This occasion was the only one I could remember of seeing my father in Belsen, it seemed that we had lost contact from the time of entering the camp and being placed into separate barracks.

One day in November 1944 there was an order for all the men who had been employed in the Amsterdam diamond industry to report. About 180 men, including my uncle Isaac, were deported. We did not know where they were taken. Long after the war we learned that they were sent to Auschwitz, and that only one man survived. The following day aunt Cissie was deported together with all the other wives of these diamond industry workers. My cousins, Maurice and Helen, were collected and with the other abandoned children, about fifty in all, were sent to another section of the camp, inaccessible to us. For a while we did not see them, we thought that they had been sent away somewhere else, perhaps to join their mothers. Then, one day we saw them in an adjacent section of the camp and we went up to the fence where we were near enough to speak to them. After that we would try and meet up every day at the fence. Then one day, my mother had two sugar cubes, which she threw over to them and at that moment she was spotted by a kapo who shouted at her to get away from the fence; it was not allowed to go near the fence or to speak with prisoners in another section. She ran away and was chased by the kapo threatening and waving his long rubber truncheon at her. She managed to get into a barrack ahead of him where she was helped to hide from her pursuer. After some fruitless searching he abandoned the chase. I was left behind near the fence fearing for her life and for mine.

Life became progressively worse, harder and harsher as the winter progressed. More people were arriving in Belsen speaking in strange languages and the barracks were becoming more crowded. People used the slats in the bunks to fuel the barrack stove, but this let to sagging mattresses which meant punishment if discovered on inspection. There seemed to be more and more disease and illness and people dying everywhere. I started to see 'musselmen', people who had lost their minds and moved about like zombies, and more dead bodies were collected outside the barracks in piles, growing higher daily.

On a couple of occasions we saw aeroplanes flying over or near the camp, chasing and fighting each other. Some of their bullets hit our barracks and splintered the wood of the bunks. We did not fear the danger of stray bullets. It was very exciting and gave us a message of hope that we were not forgotten and that the allies were getting closer to rescuing us.

One day a convoy of people was chosen to go away by train. A couple of days later a second convoy was being gathered. My mother was given the choice to stay or go. By now the living conditions in the camp were so bad, with typhus and other infectious diseases, no food or water, that she decided any alternative was better than staying.

We left on a passenger train in early April 1945. It meandered along very slowly, stopping and going for about ten days through the German countryside and forests. We could make out where we were heading and it seemed that the German officers were receiving different orders each day, sometimes causing our train to reverse on the journey. They seemed to becoming more anxious and were not treating us so harshly anymore. Then one day, the train had come to a stop in a cutting in the forest and we saw the officers tearing up and burning their papers, taking off their uniforms, changing into civilian clothes. They disappeared into the forest leaving our train abandoned and its passengers 'free'. At first, we could not quite grasp what was happening. Then some people ventured out and went foraging for food in the vicinity with mixed success, but all stayed nearby the train overnight, choosing to sleep either on the train or out in the open. My mother and I slept on our seat in the train. The following morning we heard shouts of joy from those outside and then found ourselves overlooked by American soldiers. They gave us chocolates and cigarettes, for those who smoked. We felt overwhelmed with our emotions of gratitude, to be saved and free again. The date was the 13th of April 1945. As well as joy and happiness there was sadness at seeing some who being so weak and ill from disease and starvation, could not respond and died unable to take in any of the 'rich' nourishment offered.

The American soldiers took us in lorries to a small German town called Hillersleben and housed us in an apartment block which, we were told, had been army officers' quarters. They had been emptied of their families to house us, the survivors from the train. We felt very honoured. One of the first things the Americans did was to put us through showers, then dust us thoroughly with a white powder (DDT) to disinfect us and they gave us new clean clothes. In our new apartment I found my first toy. It was a wooden model airplane, but it had the German Luftwaffe symbols on its wings and I was not happy with it. I soon broke it.

At this time my mother became very ill, with a very high

temperature and fever. She had caught typhus and was taken to a nearby makeshift hospital set up and managed by the American army medicals. She stayed there for about three or four weeks before recovering to rejoin me. I was not allowed to visit her. Somehow, although I had slept next to her and been in very close proximity, I did not catch typhus and remained in the block where I was, looked after by other survivors, Hungarian and Polish women from the train. I do not remember worrying about my mother as I believed she was in safe hands and I was told that she was getting better. I was left to my own devices to play and I enjoyed the freedom of roaming around.

After my mother recovered and had regained some weight and strength, she returned to the apartment. Through the Red Cross organisation we obtained an offer of accommodation in our hometown. This came from a former neighbour and enabled us to return to Amsterdam sometime in June or July. I found it hard to understand why we could not return to our own apartment and why the people who were now living there, former NSB supporters, were not removed in order to start to rectify the wrongs that had been done to us by the Nazis and their sympathisers. I still have problems with such issues and have often got involved with fighting injustices in my adult life and taking up causes on behalf of other people.

My cousin, Maurice, who also survived, had learned a few words of English. His mother had also made him remember the name and address of his uncle in England. He could talk a little with the British soldiers who liberated Belsen on 15th April 1945. His sister, Helen, was still alive but terribly weak and emaciated. She died ten days after the liberation. The British Army then arranged for him to go to England, to join our uncle's family there.

A few months later my aunt Cissie who had barely survived her time in a labour camp and in salt mines in Germany, returned to Amsterdam, after recuperation in Sweden from tuberculosis and starvation. She was able to obtain a new apartment where my mother and I joined her. We lived there until March 1949.

Following our return to Amsterdam, we gradually obtained

information from Red Cross lists telling us that, with the exception of one cousin, Jannie, who had survived her stay in Auschwitz, all my father's family, that is mother, brothers, sisters, their spouses and children, had been murdered in the extermination camps of Sobibor and Auschwitz. Amsterdam was like a ghost city. When we walked through familiar streets my mother would mention different friends she had known before the war and point out to me the many places where they had lived. These Jewish friends and relations had all disappeared without trace, all robbed, brutalised and dehumanised, some shot, some clubbed to death, some worked and starved to death, but most just asphyxiated with poison gas, their corpses disposed via the ovens and thus all murdered without trace.

With such memories to haunt my mother, she did not want to remain in Holland. My mother's brother, Michael, had been in the British Army, captured in Singapore, jailed in the notorious Changi prison for a while, and then set to work building the railway to Burma over the river Kwai as a prisoner of war of the Japanese. He had contracted malaria from which he eventually recovered. His wartime experiences were as horrific as ours as he had lost so many of his friends during that time. He had returned to London and by 1948, had bought a house. He suggested we come to London and live with him. My mother was so pleased to take up his offer. However, she had to apply to the British Consul for permission and it took many months before they would grant her again British Nationality which she had given up on marriage. We eventually came to London in March 1949, to join my mother's family, her two brothers, one married, and a married sister with their children. She also had an elderly aunt and her children.

I was surprised on arrival in England to find that the country which had won the war, still had rationing. Rationing was something that had finished around 1947/8 in Holland; in Great Britain rationing continued until 1952. What a high price it had paid for waging a just war against such an evil regime without recompense.

My Father's Birth Certificate

The enigma I struggle with is how do I commemorate those who I have never met but cannot forget? Throughout my later life, but never during my childhood, my father talked to me of **his** murdered family. When I asked my father if he had pictures, he produced a tin box carefully buried at the bottom of a cupboard. Its contents were the photos of his mother, father, brothers and sisters together with those of my mother's parents and brothers and sister. My father always referred to them as **his** brother or sister. It took me many years to realise they were also my uncles and aunts, my family.

My mother always talked of her mother in saintly terms, of her kindness and tolerance and of her ever resourceful brother Mundek, known as Roiter, because of his red hair. Mundek had married a Polish woman Mishka and was later shot by the Nazis in the Jewish cemetery in Przemysl hiding under a gravestone. Abrumek, her younger brother, had been taken in an action and murdered in the town square. Her mother and father, Chaya Wirtenthal and Nachum Ganz, had been taken to the square where her father was shot. Her mother was transported, probably to Belzec. This was when my mother was five months pregnant with me. Her sister Lolla, who was also five months pregnant, was taken with my grandmother. My paternal grandmother Gisa had been burned alive in a synagogue near Tarnopol. My grandfather Adolf Garfinkle had died before the war, in a typhoid epidemic.

My father had fallen in love with and married my mother in

72

Przemysl in 1938. My sister Leonia was born nine months later on November 18. My father had been born in the Jewish East End of London in 1917. His Polish father had been unable to make a living and returned with his family to Poland.

When the Germans invaded Poland and divided it with the Russians, the border followed the river San which cuts Przemysl into two. My family was living on the eastern side and thus only suffered the 1939 Nazi occupation for a few weeks. However, they were incarcerated in the ghetto after the Germans invaded Russia in 1941. I was born in the ghetto on 29 October 1942. In 1943, close to the time of the liquidation of the ghetto, Himmler ordered the construction of Bergen-Belsen. This was designated an Aufenthaltlager, an exchange camp envisaged for the holding of Jews having allied or neutral nationality, to be exchanged for Germans in allied hands such as the German Templars from Jerusalem. My father registered when a notice went up in the ghetto. In the first few days of July 1943 we were transported in a normal rail carriage to Montelupic prison, the Gestapo headquarters in Cracow. On 7 July 1943, after three days of interrogation during which many of those travelling with us were shot, we were transported to Belsen on the first day it took Jewish prisoners, together with 3000 fellow Polish Jews. In the Stern Lager as it was called, we were allowed to wear normal clothes with a coloured star according to the now infamous categories. My father who spoke at least seven languages, was a Lagerfriseur (camp barber), a needed occupation with which he could earn himself a little extra bread. It also allowed him to move around the camp and communicate with most inmates. He was thus very useful to the Jewish administrators. After a few weeks most of the 3000 Polish Jews were sent to Auschwitz.

Words cannot describe Bergen-Belsen although some have tried. The now infamous film, dreadful as these images are, does not capture the stench, the fear, the total awfulness. Only those who were there, will ever truly know, and we do not need reminders or descriptions. It is imprinted in our minds and hearts forever. Despite this, there was resistance. When Irma Griese came from Auschwitz with her ferocious dogs which she let loose on us, Albella, the Greek Jewish administrator, sent my father to the French barracks to buy costume jewellery to have made up with just one real stone, to keep her 'sweet'. She never discovered the deception.

How did we all survive? That would take a whole book. Suffice it to say it was through that mixture of luck, resourcefulness and the help of other survivors, as you will hear in every camp survivor's story. I survived, in large part, because my mother was able to breast feed me throughout our incarceration. Babies need less food than adults and Belsen was not an extermination camp. We often came close to death through starvation and illness. My sister still suffers from an infection contracted in Belsen and I still have the marks of rickets. The emotional scars are less obvious but far deeper than the physical ones, and trouble us to this day.

The Nazis with their insane logic, held on to us even after Belsen was liberated. They put those from the Stern Lager on transports a week before the liberation, to wander around Germany for two weeks looking for a bridge to the east. The historians suggest it was probably to send us to the new crematoria built at Theresienstadt. We were liberated by Russian cavalry on 23 April 1945 in Trobitz, a small town near Leipzig. My father, resourceful as ever and speaking fluent Russian obtained a rifle, then 'liberated' a dog cart and a bicycle, to carry my mother, my sister and me. We were all at death's door with typhoid. Unlike the others who were liberated and quarantined, we immediately headed home to Przemysl to see if any of the family had survived. Mishka welcomed us as ever and nursed us to some degree of recovery. We discovered that of our large extended family of more than 62 members, only Dorcha Kellerman, a second cousin of my mother, and her husband Zigmund had survived. Having been threatened with murder by the Polish nationalists who did not welcome returning Jewish survivors, we left after a few weeks to try and obtain entry to Britain. My father, resourceful as ever, obtained visas to Lyon, France, from the DP camp outside Prague, after only three days.

Getting to England was more difficult than it should have been. When the British Consulate had obtained my father's birth certificate he was summoned and asked if he could prove that he was the person named. How could most survivors do such a thing? Fortunately, some of his mother's family had survived in Vichy and he was able to obtain sworn statements to verify his identity.

After nine months in France, we came to London in January 1946. We immediately went to the Jewish Board of Guardians, the predecessors of Jewish Care. The doctor and nurse had tea and cakes while we were not even offered a glass of water. When they saw my rickets which had been treated in Lyon, and Leonie's emaciation, they decided in their wisdom that what we, children, needed was country air. My parents, too fearful to challenge the authorities having only just gained citizenship, felt they had to agree to us being put in a children's home. Having never been separated from our mother and only being able to speak Polish, this was a further trauma for my sister and me to survive. We had been threatened by the cruel non-Jewish matron of Broadstairs not to say a word about our mistreatment to our parents who were allowed one monthly visit. After nine months my father defied the authorities when he saw my obvious and deteriorated physical state, and took us home.

So began our life in England in a tiny flat in Old Montague Street. My father worked at the hairdressers at the Savoy Hotel thanks to his linguistic skills. My mother suffered deep depression as the full extent of her losses hit her. We became a magnet for the East End's Polish survivor community. We were the only entire nuclear family of Polish Jewish survivors in the locality. At my mother's insistence the talk was always in Yiddish. Many evenings were spent around the dining table full of survivors with constant talk of their Shoah experiences. When I was Barmitzvah all the guests were survivors.

It was not a happy childhood. My traumatised parents could barely look after themselves, let alone care for two disturbed and traumatised children. They did their best in extraordinary circumstances and with exceptional burdens and handicaps. My sister Leonie was my protective shield, protecting me from some of the emotional turmoil of our home life which I will never forget and for which I will be eternally grateful. Looking back, it all seems almost beyond belief, but sadly it was all too real.

LEA GOODMAN

Two Autobiographical Letters to an Eleven Year Old French Niece

1995

Dear Laura,

I have made considerable headway in researching what happened to your grandmother Lola (Lydia) and myself during the war. All of what I am telling you now I know from those times, as your grandmother and I never spoke of that distant tragic past.

We came to live in Dialoszyce, your grandmother's home town, in 1941 from Krakow. On the eve of the mass deportation from that city we travelled to a labour camp which I remember by the name of Kostrze. It was run by a German friendly to Jews. I was nearly seven years old. A Polish Christian lady acted as my mother during the train journey. I thought it was quite normal to have a different parent for a while. It was very dangerous for Jews to travel, as this was forbidden. We arrived at night and slept on the floor. We woke up with black smudges on our faces and laughed as we only saw the other and did not realize that our own face was also black.

An old fort housed the camp. Part of the building was below ground. The gates had Jews on guard. There were huge concrete pipes in the foreground. I remember visiting an office in Krakow with your grandmother and I knew that some people working there were Jews.

I had stayed in Kostrze for a few weeks when the camp commandant told parents that the German authorities heard that there were children in his camp, and he was not permitted to keep them any longer. He therefore found places for them in a children's home in the ghetto.

We were about twenty children in a horse drawn cart. We were all quite happy; it seemed as if we were going on an excursion. My father Mendel (Max) followed the cart and after some kilometers, in a suburb of Krakow, my father took me off and said that I was going to say goodbye to friends, and rejoin the children in the ghetto, which of course I did not. If I had, I would probably not be alive.

I spent time during the last three years at the Archives and Library of Yad Vashem during holidays in Israel. I have been handicapped by not knowing Hebrew or Yiddish. I kept on asking where I could find records of labour camps in Poland and ultimately was referred to the "International Tracing Book of Forced Labour Camps for Jews in the General Government" published by The International Committee of the Red Cross, based in Geneva. I would like to convey to you the satisfaction of finding that name as Kostrze, District Krakau. I ask myself why it was so important for me to see a record of that camp. Was it to confirm it existed, that it was not part of my imagination?

Two cousins of your grandmother survived the war: Herman Pomocnik and his brother Henek. I have met them over the years in Germany where Herman lived, and in Israel, the home of Henek. When I was together with them we always spoke of the war years, as besides my father's sister Sala and her husband Jacob, these were the only members of our family who I knew as a child in Poland. Your grandmother's half brother Jacob also survived, but he killed himself in Israel. I shall write another time to you about him.

I remember Henek sitting on a grass verge in Kostrze and crying. He was a very young man then and this made a big impression on me as I had never before seen an adult cry. From Herman I got to know the name of the commandant which he remembered as Strauss, and confirmed that there was an office run by him in Krakow. Herman was a furrier and had made a coat for the wife of the commandant. In the Tracing Service book, under "Employer" I found "Firma Richard Strauch" and under "Kind of work" it said "Kanalisationsarbeiten und

Hoch-und Tiefbau" (Drainage works and civil engineering). The names plus the work in that camp and also its location confirm the fact that it is the camp I was looking for.

For a number of years I have made enquiries to find the group of people who helped your grandmother and myself together with a number of Jews, cross the Tatra mountains into Slovakia in 1944. We were on our way to Hungary, that magic land where I was told the cows ate water melons. I understand that our great fortune was that we did manage to get out of Poland, tragically without my father. My parents knew that there was a way to get out of Poland to Hungary where conditions were much better for Jews, but by the time we got the contact, my father had been arrested. Our cousins Herman and Henek told me that the repeated miracles which enabled us to survive that long, could not have gone on repeating and that we would have run out of luck. Our good fortune was that we left on that journey so late in the war, and never made it into Hungary. We stayed in Slovakia where we were liberated by the glorious Russian Army.

Now that I am nearly 60, our journey from Krakow to Kezmarok is etched in my memory like a slow moving film. It would be more accurate to say that part of the journey only is a path through a forest; a group of us, 6 to 8 people. I remember a girl, a few years older than myself, strapped by a belt to a person who was a relative of hers. She had partially lost the ability to walk by being hidden in a confined space. There was snow on the ground; it must have been February or March. Some people got separated. The guide told us that we should wait for him; he would join us once he found the stragglers. They caught up with us, but he had vanished. We separated again and found our way back to Krakow. We had nowhere to stay. My mother and I turned up at her old dressmaker's who kindly took us in. She and Mr. and Mrs. Soltisova (the business friends to whom my father took me) were the only Christian Poles who kept us without asking for money. The numerous other families did it only for money. We were also once blackmailed.

For our second attempt we bought a sledge. The journey on foot was 32 km; I was quite proud of having walked that distance. The sledge was of no use as the snow had melted. We had to pay again, and had a different guide this time. We halted at a farm where we had to wait for a Slovak guide to fetch us, to take us over the border. This farm we knew was often searched by Germans and therefore we had to stay under the floor boards of the stable. The farmer took away some hay to reveal a hole. It was quite a confined space; the grown ups could neither sit comfortably nor have enough space to lie down. I felt safe and quite happy there. Suddenly my mother had to get out, it was quite upsetting to see her in such a state of panic. The other refugees begged her to calm down as she was endangering all our lives. She insisted, she just wanted to get some air, and would get back immediately. When it became night time, the farmer who had a daughter and whose wife was away, took me into his house. I slept in the same bed as the girl. After a while she left to go into her father's. I was so upset to see them together; it made me miss my own father and so I preferred to spend a second night in the hole.

The Slovak guide was late fetching us, but what a relief to see him arrive. He came with two boys. We crossed the frontier at night. I could see the guards with their lanterns on an embankment. They walked towards one another and then away, two by two. The boys went ahead and signaled to us to move on when the guards were back to back, and we then crossed between them. I put a foot on each side of the path and said to myself: "Now I am in Slovakia and in Poland". I was three years younger than you are now, and I remember this tiny detail so vividly. This crossing is so memorable that it has stayed with me as a big adventure.

Once we were in Slovakia I was frightened of being arrested and put into jail for twenty four hours, if we were found by frontier guards. This I was told by my mother. When I think about it now, being found on the Polish side would have meant death. The Slovaks who at that time were still an axis power of the Germans, behaved with humanity towards illegal refugees and that could not be said most of the time of the neutral Swiss who in similar situations like ours, sent people back to occupied France.

Your grandmother used to comfort me by saying: "One day the war will be over and it will all be as before". Her saying this springs to mind when I remember the house we came to, our first in Slovakia. We came to it on foot; was it in the mountains, standing there in isolation? I do not remember, but what I do recall most vividly is the very warm, all embracing welcome we got, and the feeling that we came to a haven which was like something my mother had promised: the end of the war. I do not remember if the welcome was given to us by a couple; the people are faceless. The joy they conveyed was that we had made it, and the happiness was also theirs. Basins of warm water for foot baths were provided. For me this image is tied in my memory as a reflection of human kindness, and happiness shared. Whose house was it? We were expected just as the farmer on the Polish side of the border had awaited us.

I remember a lot of troop movement on our way to Kezmarok. Your grandmother felt that this meant that the Germans were marching into Slovakia. This analysis of the situation had a most important influence on our lives. On arrival she told our Jewish hostess that she would not go into the street as she did not want to be known in the town as a Jew. She asked the Slovak guide to help her find a job as a Polish Christian. There were no Jewish young men in that household; they had been taken to labour camps earlier in the war, but the rest of the Jewish population was free at the time of our arrival in Slovakia. This also applied to Hungary which is, as you can well imagine, the reason why we were on our way there.

An article of Robert Rozett in Yad Vashem studies which I was so exited to get, is called "From Poland to Hungary : Rescue Attempts 1943-1944". It describes the incredible help your grandmother and I got to escape the hell which was Poland at that time for Jews. The article reads: From February 1943 until March 1944 an extraordinary and, in many ways, unique rescue operation took place. Zionist youth movement members, veteran Zionist and Orthodox anti-Zionists in Slovakia and Hungary, backed by representatives of the Jewish Agency for Palestine in Turkey and aided by gentile couriers (guides), strove in lose federation to extricate Jews from Nazi-occupied Poland. Those who were smuggled out of Poland were brought to Hungary, generally by way of Slovakia, with the hope of eventually bringing them to Palestine. In the terminology of the rescuers, this operation came to be known as Tiyyul (Hebrew word for a trip or a hike) from Poland.

Our Tiyyul from Poland was one of the last ones. During my first meeting of "child survivors" I met a Jewish courier who took Jews from Hungary to Romania, and he told me that they were from Poland. He only knew one link in the chain and did not know who the organisers were. Robert Rozett gave me, amongst other names of authors on the subject of "the rescue attempts", that of Yael Peled. Before meeting me she spent a lot of time reading books on the subject which were in Hebrew, and send me information on the relevant pages which are of direct interest to me. Now I have the answer to my question of who made our escape from Poland possible.

It was an underground committee who disagreed with the policy of the formal Slovakian Jewish Judenrad (Jewish Council; Ustredna Zidov). This committee consisted of known Slovak Jewish personalities: Giza Fleishman, Oskar Neuman, Vitach Winterstein, the rabbis Armin Fiederand, Weismandel and others. This committee was known under the name of Kvutzat Avoda (working group). She writes that they are the people your grandmother and I have to thank. Most of them did not survive the war and the ones who did, are unlikely to be alive today because of age. Dr Peled gave me the name and address of her friend Gila Fatran whose book "Struggle for Surviving. The Leadership of Slovakian Jews in the Holocaust 1938-1944" had most of the information I just gave you. Subsequently, I had the pleasure to meet Gila Fatran and Yael Peled in Israel. Also Shmuel Krakowski, the senior adviser of the Yad Vashem Archives. I got from Dr Krakowski the name and address of the director of an organisation in Krakow who I hope will give me information on the labour camp Kostrze.

We came to France from Prague in 1946. Your grandmother married your very nice grandfather one year later.

When I was seventeen years old I left Nice where your mother,

Eliane, was born in 1948. I spent several weeks each year with my mother. She died in a car accident in 1981. You might have thought that there would have been many opportunities to reminiscence about our war experiences. I would love to know now so many details. How did she find most of the addresses of families to stay with, after my father was taken by the Germans? He was arrested when he left his work party to go into a shop. Jews were not permitted to do that in 1943. As you know my father was killed by the Germans.

In 1989 a conference organised by Robert and Elizabeth Maxwell, entitled "Remembering for the Future", took place in Oxford and London.

This conference which I attended for one day, was a turning point in my life. A newsletter started to appear on a regular basis. In it I read of a forthcoming gathering of children who had survived the Nazi occupation of Europe, to take place in California. I joined the gathering and have been to Child Survivors' conferences twice since then.

It was wonderful to get together with a group of Jews with a similar past to my own. I felt that we could have known each other as children and stayed friends to this day. Some women, like Gilberte, had Polish parents and survived the war in Belgium. She and I speak French together. Living in the USA for many years has kept her quite extrovert, unlike some child survivors in the U.K.

I got a British Library readers pass to research the psychology of art. The day I spend at that library replaces in a way the time I used to spend as an art therapist at a London cancer hospital. I achieve a balance to my week, with the four days at the studio making sculptures. Over the years I changed to researching the Holocaust. In retrospect it seems like a natural progression. I know that there is no answer to my question of what led human beings to commit such monstrous crimes. I get some satisfaction in hearing different voices giving a multitude of information and viewpoints on the Shoah.

So my dear niece Laura, I am pleased to be able to write to you and tell you a little of your grandmother's and my war story, also to let you know how I felt when I learned of the names of these wonderful Slovak Jews who endangered their own lives in order to help their fellow Jews from Poland. As I read their names I feel quite emotional and am full of gratitude for their deeds.

Love,
Tata Lea

Dear Laura

I want to tell you something about your grandmother's brother Jacob. If I write about him, you will also understand how his life touched mine. He was the only one of her siblings to survive the war.

Your grandmother was born in 1912, the oldest of four sisters, Mania, Esther and Bronia. Their mother died in 1922. Henoch Pomocnik, your great-grandfather, remarried a divorced lady by the name of Esther Weintraub. Their only child Jacob was born in 1926. My mother told me of her embarrassment when she went to register her brother in school. He carried his mother's name, as his parents had only married in front of a rabbi which, obviously, made Jacob in Polish law an illegitimate child. Your grandmother was the one member of her family who spoke good Polish. This I know, not because I observed it, but because my mother told me so. She read Polish newspapers regularly. You can imagine how he must have looked up to her. The big sister, thirteen years older, the modern woman. Jacob and my mother's thirteen years difference of age was the same as between her and myself. As you know, in our case we have the same mother, but not the same father.

Jacob Weintraub shot himself while on guard duty at his kibbutz in 1948. The brother and sister had found each other only a few months before. I think it was through an international tracing service. He wrote that he was not happy in Israel and wanted to join her in France. Your grandparents were working very hard at that time, establishing their restaurant. It was very important for my mother that they should be self employed. She felt that living in Israel was easier and better than where she was. In 1946, your grandmother tried to go with me to what was then Palestine, on Aliyah Beth from Prague. After a lapse of three months, having been unsuccessful to leave for Eretz Israel, we joined a train taking 500 children from Poland and Czechoslovakia to Aix-les-Bains in France. It is in that town that your grandparents met.

Your great uncle was badly injured in a road accident while riding a bicycle. It was thanks to the devoted care he got from the staff of an Israeli hospital that his life was saved. When he returned to live in the kibbutz, he wrote that his comrades made him feel that he did not contribute sufficient labour, but they had forgotten how hard he had worked in the past. He was a good looking young man. The last photograph which was taken in a garden, is dated 25.9.1948. He has a dent in his forehead, the shape of his nose is not the same, it is slightly pushed sideways. He wrote that when walking, one of his legs gave him a problem. All this happened while I was separated from my mother: I was away in Switzerland for a year and a half. During that time, your grandparents married and moved to Nice. I joined them in October of that year, around my 13th birthday. There was no room to accommodate me. They were living in a one room flat, expecting your mother. Your grandmother was working in the kitchen of their kosher restaurant. I was made to live with their partner, a Mrs Eizencweig, and in fact I never lived with her again under the same roof, that is, not until years later when I came from London to Nice on holidays. Your cousins David, Daniel and Naomi spent many happy days with me at your grandparents', by now much larger, home.

I was with my mother when she removed a large brown envelope from the letter box and opened it then and there. A batch of photographs dropped out and she suffered a foreboding of her brother's tragic death. The image of her, highly pregnant with your mother, faced with this tragic news is still with me after 47 years. For your poor grandmother, the joy of finding her brother was so short lived. The main reason for me to write about him is that I don't want him to suffer from a double death. He died at the age of twenty-two, without having a family of his own. I, his niece, am the closest relative he has. Marcel Moring writes, speaking to a child: "Don't think about death, think about the people you know who are already dead. When somebody dies, it seems as if he's gone and everything is over, but as long as there's someone who remembers what that man was like, he's not really dead. He lives on in the thoughts of other people. That's what's important". We say in the memorial service for the dead: "May his soul be bound up in the bond of life". Jacob Weintraub's photographs spanning six years of his life, have provided me with images without which my memory of him would have been nothing as intense. Now that I have told you about him, he will go on being amongst the generation of grandchildren he never had.

My mother and I were liberated by Russian troops in Kezmarok, a town in Slovakia near the border with Poland. I was left with friends on several occasions, and your grandmother went to Krakow, to the Jewish community, to see if any members of our family had survived the war. They had arranged to report their existence before we were separated. She found only one person, Jacob Freilich, a brother-in-law, who then came back and lived with us for a short time. She lit Friday evening candles and cried. She saw time passing and with that, hope fading of my father having survived, also her sisters and brother. The time between our liberation in February 1945 and our arrival in France when my mother was getting more and more depressed, was for me, a child, a grim episode. You know your grandmother was killed in a road accident in 1981. When your grandfather passed away, three years later, I took Jacob's photographs. Your mother had never seen them, even though she lived at home until she was twenty-one. Also, she tells me that she had known that Jacob was involved in a road accident, but not that he later took his life. She was told that he was killed as a soldier in the Israeli army. My mother recounted how she walked in the street and felt that her sisters were walking on either side of her. This background, I hope, will make you understand so much better how she must have felt when she heard that her brother was alive, her guilt of not bringing him to Nice, when he so badly wanted to join her. One of his photographs is of him before he was deported, it must date from 1942. He was then 16 years old. Who knows how that photograph survived the rest of the war.

I knew him at that time. We lived in Dzialoszyce, my mother's home town. His family moved back from Krakow to live there, as did my father, mother and myself in 1941. We spent the Sabbath and Jewish holidays with all our extended family. I only have vague memories of Jacob; I suppose he was not that interested in a little girl, while I remember his sister Bronia who made a big fuss of me, very well.

Several photographs are of Jacob taken soon after he was liberated. They show him still suffering from the effects of starvation. One of them is a postcard size portrait. He is wearing a cap on a shaved head, lovely large eyes staring at one. Jacob's photographs of this period are the only ones our family have which show the sufferings which were inflicted on us. The nearest I have is one of my father dating from the war. It is a passport photograph, with a face full of sadness, with eyes which, to me, look as if he was haunted.

Henek, a cousin, told me that Jacob was very musical. The same cousin was in Dzialoszyce when the Jews were deported. He said: "Our whole family was assembled on the market square, the only members missing were your mother, father and yourself". This is not quite so. The Germans ordered the Jewish population to be on the square at six in the morning, my grandfather's sister Sarah Raisel did not obey these orders and was therefore, later shot. Jacob and his sister Malka seem also not to have been on the square. However, Malka was not heard of again whilst Jacob disappeared until he reached Palestine, via Italy. The women, children and old men were told to go to one side, and the young men on the other. Henek who lives now in Israel, and his brother Herman are, with Jacob, the only ones of our family who were at that time in Dzialoszyce, to survive the war.

My aunt Mania was expecting a baby; she was married to her cousin Herman. Their wedding took place in Dzialoszyce and I remember it well. A large room with a low ceiling. The bride wore a long white dress. Music was provided by a fiddler. You can imagine this being my first wedding, what a big impression it had made on me. Even though it was war time, and some young men where in neighbouring labour camps, life as seen by me, a child, was good. The persecution of us as Jews, came later when we went back to Krakow. My grandfather was working at home; he remodeled men's hats. He and his family lived in a small house near the river. Nearby lived the extended family of my great aunt Sarah Raisel. It was a house on several floors, with a great number of young people sharing the home of their mother who was a widow.

I did not go to school; at that time school in Poland only started at the age of seven. My mother taught me to read. Bronia, my mother's youngest sister, was retarded. She must have been in her late teens when we all lived in what was a Polish shtetl, in the years 1941-1942. She was so excited by my ability to write that she snatched my note book and run home to show it to her parents. My step-grandmother made a big fuss of me. I liked flowers. She took me outside town to buy some from a nursery. She looked after Bronia with a lot of care. Bronia was a baby when her mother died. She had meningitis when she was a small child. The illness left her mentally handicapped. Number three sister was Esther who must have been in her early twenties. She was short and slim. I remember her, somehow always in motion. Grandmother Esther had no hold over her. If she punished my mother or Mania when they were children, she could not do that to her namesake who was nicknamed 'Esther sheigitz'.

As I told you in my previous letter, my mother and I did not speak about the war years when we were together; so all of what I am telling you, besides a few details, I have from Henek. What do I remember from my childhood, between the ages of five and not quite seven? I recollect events, but am uncertain which I actually witnessed or was told about. Josey Fisher writes: Memory, imperfect as it is, has its own reality. We block out certain thoughts. We cluster others. We telescope significant events to the exclusion of what seems insignificant. We incorporate details told to us by others and unknowingly they become our own.

I remember the market square, also the river, near which my grandfather and his family lived. It took me until 1993 to go and visit the town from which so many of our family were deported to the death camp, Treblinka. What miracle it was that I was not there with the rest of them, on that fateful day of 7th September 1942. A monument stands not far from that infamous square, erected by children and grandchildren of survivors of a town which had eleven thousand Jews out of a population of thirteen thousand. At the foot of it were some remnants of memorial candles, so others like myself, had come on a pilgrimage to a part of the world which has such dreadful memories for us. The river is only a small pale shadow of its former self, the square has a cluster of trees and some benches. I asked some passers by, and they confirmed the fact that the trees were planted there after the war. The river has been diverted; it used to be big enough to have powered a mill. I remember a waterfall near my grandfather's house.

I don't know at what time my grandfather moved from his home town to Krakow. I must have visited the home of Jacob and his family regularly enough to have such a clear picture of it. It was in Ulica Bozegocialo, on the first floor, a terrace overlooking a courtyard. My uncle and I lived in the same two towns at about the same time, until that fateful day in September when Dzialoszyce was made *Judenfrei* (without Jews).

Where was Jacob between the time of the deportation from Dzialoscyce and 1948, when my mother found him on Kibbutz Mizra? No letters which he wrote to his sister, survive. My mother received letters from a hospital nurse; she seemed to have become fond of her patient. Cousin Henek told me Jacob was not in Auschwitz. He must have been in camps where Russian was spoken. At the back of two post card photographs I have of him, there is a text, a loving confession to his mother. It is sad and is written with gratitude of what she did for him. It is written in Polish and Russian.

My mother thought that the shock of her brother's death was the cause of your mother being born with "club feet". I don't know how strongly she could have believed such medical nonsense. As for me, I want to conclude this letter to you, my dear niece, by telling you that this sad period of my life came to an end with the birth of your mother Eliane. She came to live with me in a maid's room I had at number 7 rue de France, Nice, when she was still a very young child.

Love,
Tata Lea

Childhood Lost

It is July 2001 and I have just returned from Israel, after the funeral of my eldest brother, Moishe. His death leaves three of us from a family of eight children. Compared to some of my friends who have nobody left in the world after the ravages of the concentration camps and atrocities, I have been lucky to have enjoyed several years in the company of my family. 'But how did your brother come to live in Israel?', I hear you ask.

The story begins in Roscova, a small village up in the mountains, in the north of Rumania. My father, Joseph, was a farmer and landowner. Some of the land was inherited from my grandfather who lived with us. In records I obtained in later years, my grandfather, David Hersch, is shown as the owner of the land in 1876. He subsequently passed it on to my father in 1914.

All the Jewish families in Roscova were orthodox – it was a way of life. My father was a man of means and he was the gabo (elder) of the shul. If a stranger was present on a Friday night, he was told to see my father who would bring him home and he would stay until the end of the shabbos.

My brother Moishe who worked on the farm where we all helped, was eventually sent to a yeshiva (religious academy for men). He hated it and ran away. My father was ready to send him back until Moishe told him about some emissaries from Palestine who had visited them and urged them to go there. My father at last agreed and from that moment on Moishe became an ardent Zionist.

By now it was 1935. My father left Roscova taking with him Moishe, my eldest sister Shosanna, my sister Rifka who was still a schoolgirl, and my younger brother Schmuel Avrum. As they rode away I remember clinging on to the carriage in great distress. They travelled with many other families, in fact, Moishe's future wife, Batya, was on the same boat having come from another town. By this time my grandfather was elderly and becoming senile. He did not want to join them in case he died at sea. In fact, he did die while my father was away.

My father stayed in Palestine for about two years. He settled the family down, found homes for them and endured harsh times. He must have missed my mother and family life. He returned with my younger brother, with the intention of winding up the business so that we could all go to join the others. This took time and as we all know, time ran out for so many people, including us.

Our part of Rumania was always changing hands and it was not long before the Hungarians, under German command, entered our village. They used mules as transport and I remember them tying up these animals on our veranda. They chewed on the veranda all night and destroyed it.

In April 1944 we were rounded up and put into the Ghetto of nearby Viseu. My father had to shave off his beard which was humiliating. We had heard the Russian guns in the distance before we left, but they did not arrive until August. After a month in the Ghetto we were sent to Auschwitz. The rest is but ugly history.

On arrival in Auschwitz, as we lined up, my father told me to stand tall. I did not realise the significance until later. That was the last time I saw my parents. I saw my sister through the wire a few days later and then she was gone. Four of us boys remained together, working in quarries and moving to other camps until we were on a death march in April 1945. My two eldest brothers became tired and decided to accept an 'offer' to ride on the trucks. They were never seen again having been shot on arrival at the head of the column of marchers. This happened only a short time before the Americans arrived to liberate us.

Eventually we arrived in England in October 1945 and then began the search for relatives. All I could remember about my brother Moishe was that he wrote to us in Roscova that he was working on a farm in Rehovot and that the farm belonged to a wealthy man called Arbeiter. I wrote a letter to him there and eventually, it reached him. At the same time the family had heard our names mentioned on the radio. My sister Baskoo had also survived. She had returned to Roscova to try and start up the farm again, however, to no avail. She married and went to Israel.

Moishe came to see us in 1948. As life was hard in Israel at that time, because of Arab uprisings etc., he said that it was better to stay in England and be educated. It was quite a few years before I met the rest of my family again.

I often wonder what life would have been like for me if we had all gone to Israel. Would I have been a farmer too? Who knows?

Moishe is now dead and is buried in a beautiful spot, under a tree. We do not know where our brothers lie, but he had specified that on his memorial stone their names, Israel and Schmuel Avrum, should be carved as a permanent reminder of their unity in death.

ZDENKA HUSSERL

Photographs of my Mother

My name is Zdenka Husserlová. I was born in Prague (Praha) on 6th
February 1939. My mother was Helena Husserlová, born on 16th
August 1910, and my father, Pavel Husserl, was born on 12th July
1904. I was their only child.

My mother was born in Zdikov, a small village in southern
Bohemia. My father was born in Vienna. On 16th October 1941 my
father was deported to Lodz, Poland, on one of the first transports, and
died. My mother took me in 1941 from Prague to Zdikov where we
lived with my grandfather.

On 26th November 1942 the Nazis came to Zdikov at night and
took us to Terezin (Theresienstadt). In 1944 my mother and
grandfather were taken to Auschwitz where they died. I was in
Terezin until I was liberated in May 1945. This part of my story I have
learned from written records. I wish I could remember my mother or
how we got to Terezin.

There are three memories I have of Terezin: sleeping in bunks,
having my hair shaved because I had lice, running around naked. I
have a small round burn scar on top of my right hand. I am not sure
where I burnt my hand, whether in Zdikov or Terezin. This burn must
have meant something, as I can never forget it.

Another part of my life that I know from being told was when I
was liberated. There were four castles near Prague: I was in Olesovice.
I was six years old but cannot remember this castle.

On 15th August 1945 I came to England with 300 other children, aged between three-and-a-half and sixteen years old, many of them from camps and from different parts of Czechoslovakia (now Czech Republic). We were brought in nine Lancaster bomber planes which I remember very well. There were no seats for us on the planes, so we sat on the laps of the grown-ups who were taking us to England. I was very attached to Edith, as she spoke Czech, and I thought she was my mother.

Edith and her husband George organised these flights to England. They had both been in Terezin, but I cannot remember them there. I remember the first part of the flight, from Prague to Holland. When we landed, there were all these soldiers who gave us hot chocolate and fruit, and put the smallest children up on their shoulders. The second part of the flight to England I cannot remember.

Alice Goldberger who was like a mother to me and to all the other children I grew up with, heard about the children who were coming from the concentration camps. She looked after us with the support of the Jewish Refugee Committee and other wonderful helpers. I remember part of Windermere, my first rehabilitation home in 1945. There I started to learn English.

In December 1945 I and the other children arrived in Weir Courtney on the first night of Hanukkah. This wonderful house in Lingfield, Surrey, was such a sight: there were so many menorahs, with the candles lit. To this day Hanukkah makes me a little sad. This house was donated by Sir Benjamin Drage.

I was nearly seven, and can remember many things we did. Beautiful countryside, a swimming pool, a wood. Alice organised so many things that I had missed in my early life. Learning to play games, dressing up for Jewish holidays, music, singing. We were all normal, happy children – except for the loss of our parents. It is hard for me to get older and know that I am alone. I have many good friends around the world.

In the spring of 1949 I moved to a house in Isleworth in Middlesex. I was ten years old, good with my hands. I enjoyed classical music, and learnt from Alice to play the harmonica. When I became a teenager, I started to move out of that lovely house. Some of us lived together in a flat, others lived in bed-sitting rooms. My first job, at the age of 16, was to train as a dressmaker at Victor Stiebel, moving to Hardy Amies, then John Cavanagh. I then did florist work for several years. My last and longest job was as a cashier at Waitrose. I retired at the age of 60.

In 1986 a friend in Israel encouraged me to search for my roots giving me different addresses to write to. I found I had two step-aunts in Vimperk, Czech Republic, who are Catholic through marriage.

In May 1987 I plucked up courage and flew to Prague with mixed feelings. My home is England, but my aunts want me to come back to them. I always tell them I will visit them. I cannot speak Czech; they cannot speak English. I picked up German in Terezin, and I also hear it spoken in England. At the age of 50 I saw the first photo of my mother – my aunts sent it to me. This was the last photo taken before we were sent to Terezin. My mother is wearing the yellow star: I am standing next to her, in a summer dress, holding my teddy-bear.

In 1995 I went to Prague for the 50th anniversary of our liberation. Hana Meryova who lives in Plzen, had read an article about me, written by Vera Hajkova who looked after me in Terezin, and recognised the picture of me with my mother. Hana lived in Zdikov, upstairs in the same house as my mother and grandfather. I used to play with her brother. For 50 years I had wished I had a brother. To my surprise, when we met, she gave me three more photographs: one of my mother alone, and two of me. All my life I had wanted a photograph of my mother. To me it is a miracle to have these photos. There are no pictures of my father. When I go back to Prague once a year, I get told that I look like my mother. Hana was the only person who responded to the article.

So this is my story. I am not married, and live in Jewish sheltered accommodation. I have a nice flat, one large bed-sitting room, kitchen and bathroom. I used to live in a small converted flat that Alice left to me, as a thank-you for all I did for her as she got older. I hope the history of what I went through in the Second World War will never be repeated.

EDYTA KLEIN-SMITH

My Last Eight Months in the Warsaw Ghetto

I am writing these words trying to recall events so unbelievable my concentration wanders … Here I sit surrounded by beauty and colour. Around me a garden of lovely flowers, majestic cypress trees, umbrella pines, delicious honeysuckle – so quiet and tranquil. Did I really live through these times I will try to describe now? Yes, I did!

For our Memorial Book I shall omit all misery of my life in the Warsaw Ghetto since November 1940 and start with 22nd July 1942 – the declaration of the Final Solution. The beginning of the end.

As we got up that morning and as always glance through the windows at the world outside, literally, since we had a wall on Swietojerska Street that divided the Ghetto from the Aryan Warsaw, the pavement on the other side with normal life activities, clean children, people going to work – life. But our side, the side of poverty, hunger, the tragic side that in the mornings contained many dead bodies barely covered with papers to be collected later in the day, our side has changed this morning of July 22nd. It was early before the curfew ended. The street was full of Polish police, rows of Germans and on the wall and exits black uniformed Ukrainians all with weapons at the ready. The Jewish police also in large numbers were near the buildings, near the gates of the buildings which just opened as if for another ghetto day, every man armed with a truncheon. Walls were plastered with proclamations in German and Polish languages, stating that only people with jobs valued by the Germans and special passes

98

could stay in the Ghetto. Others were destined for resettlement in the East. The word Treblinka did not reach us as yet. How to find a valuable job? Where to go? Where to hide? The tenants of a large apartment in which we had a room huddled in a long corridor, crying, hugging each other and whispering. All that was very strange to me since before it was always just a polite 'Good morning'. I grew up very quickly.

The deportations started immediately. The Jewish police had to deliver to the departure point, Umschlagplatz, 6000 people a day; within two days, the number was increased to 10,000 a day and more. Some poor and hungry volunteered because the Germans promised food on departure. The first victims were patients in hospitals, orphanages, and old people. My paternal grandparents came to say goodbye, and to see me for the last time. They were told that the block in which they lived would be evacuated the next morning. Hot July, blue skies – on the street complete pandemonium. People scurrying back and forth avoiding being caught, trying to get a pass from a German owned factory. Many small so-called shops opened up, employing people. Three large factories already existed – Toebbens, Schultz and Brushmakers. For the first couple of weeks we were still allowed to live in our Ghetto flat in which our small family of four lived for 20 months. We clung to the miserable normality which was slipping away. My uncle Jozef, through protection and bribery, was employed by the Schultz shop and had a pass, an Ausweiss – a Lebenskarte as we called it. One down, three to go. The 'Action' was raging. Sometimes as many as 13,000 a day were deported. The landlord of our ghetto flat became a foreman in the tailoring department of Toebbens' shop. He was a professional tailor. He tried to employ people who owned sewing machines, but he took my mother into his department and now she had the card of life!

At the beginning of August the walls were tightening up. The fortunate exempted from immediate deportation had to live near factories, or the Jewish council or Jewish police blocks. The rest of the Ghetto, called wild, was off limits. But thousands of people were hiding in special camouflaged places – attics, basements, etc.

The Action continued. Every few streets, one or two open lorries with German gendarmes, carbines and even machine guns waited to fill it up for transport. The catching, struggling, rounding up and beating of people were left to the Jewish police. The final blows were left for the Germans. All the stores and food supplies ceased to exist. The thriving black market which kept the Ghetto alive for 20 months just stopped. I don't remember eating any meals the first days of the Action. Again, through bribery and protection my stepfather Stanislaw became employed in a shoemaker's department of Toebbens. Another card of life! We had to move nearer the Toebbens factory to a miserable, rat-infested place. The workers had to be inside the gates at 6 o'clock in the morning ...My parents with their Ausweisses and the help of the Jewish police smuggled me inside the factory gate every morning in the tailoring department. My mother was finishing buttonholes of boys' clothing, all in thin blue fabric. Some days she ironed, patched and cleaned uniforms. She worked at the table approximately four feet long and three feet wide with the unfinished merchandise under the table. That was my hiding place. I was lying between the boys' clothing or uniforms at my mother's feet for twelve hours daily until the 6 pm whistle, when everyone ran to the courtyard to collect a bowl of watery soup. But that routine was too peaceful. That first big Action continued until mid-September and deported about 200,000 people. Even the cards of life were not safe. Selections started inside the factories. Mid-August my young wonderful uncle Jozef was taken from Schultz's factory. Thousands of people caught and brought to the Umschlagplatz were literally shoved into the cattle wagons. A Jewish policeman, a friend who was also a pharmacist and before the war employed by my grandfather, tried frantically to pull uncle Jozef out of the transport. He was not successful. That evening he told us what happened. It was a terrible blow. At first we were timidly uncertain that such a place as Treblinka could exist; but as the name was more and more whispered by the Ghetto inmates, our hopes of survival diminished.

At Toebbens selections started also. Whatever one reads and knows, one cannot imagine the feeling of standing in front of a tall, handsome, impeccably dressed Nazi SS officer. Looking at his black shiny boots and impeccable gloved hand which if moved to the left, indicated the inmate had to sit on the pavement or road, ready for transport. If to the right, the inmate had to remain standing and was marched back into the factory in a group. We were always facing selection in rows of five. At one selection, standing in the row with my parents I realised that we had no chance for three out of five to survive the selection. In a second I pushed my mother to the front and my stepfather to the back. Strange people automatically stepped in their place to keep the row of five. We passed the selection. Did I hasten anybody's final moment? Who knows, but I do think about it.

Blockades of whole sections, empty buildings and continuous rain of feathers – where did all the feathers come from?

Our Toebbens shop was located on Leszno Street, in what once was a gymnasium. One hot and sunny morning towards the end of August a Nazi director, Herr Bauch, called everyone to the courtyard. He said that it was common knowledge that children are hiding on the premises. 'It prevents parents from doing their best and hampers the productivity needed for the Reich.' The nice man arranged for nurses to accompany the transport to an open space for the children to play in the fresh air and a kettle of porridge to eat. All under the threat of death – down in ten minutes. Thirty or so children from different departments came down including myself. I was just about to join the group at the gate when a boy I knew stopped me. 'Come, come with me!'. He knew his way around this old school, and soon we were safely hidden in the attic. When we heard the whistle at 6 pm we came down and joined the others in the queue for soup. Everyone realised that the children were not coming back. Mothers were hitting their heads on the walls, some screamed, some stayed deadly quiet. When I walked up to my mother, she had a wild bewildered look. Without a word or looking at anyone she grabbed me and ran through the factory gates to our hovel. No soup that evening. After that tragedy it was impossible to hide in a shop. No one was allowed to stay in the living quarters. All the doors had to be left open, and the Germans continuously checked the buildings. For a couple of days I moved from place to place. My poor mother was in constant hysteria. Without telling my parents, I decided to go to Herr Bauch's office, the same Herr Bauch who a few days before sent the children to their death, and personally ask him to issue me an Ausweiss. His office was on the ground floor, guarded by the German police. With my nicest smile I told them that I wanted to see Herr Director Bauch. Unbelievably, they let me and even more unbelievably, with an even sweeter smile, I informed Bauch that my mother worked in the tailoring department, that I was very skilled in tailoring, and could I please have an Ausweiss? His secretary issued one on the spot. I had now my own card of life, and my own bowl of watery soup in the evening.

Selections continued. Miraculously, we hung on. More and more often in the evenings the Germans would have an open lorry waiting for the Jewish police to fill it up with people rushing to their hovels from work to eat their soup and have a few hours of rest. In many cases the Ausweisses did not help. One time the three of us running home realised that the street was blocked by lorries at both ends. In the Ghetto slang we called this 'in a kettle'. No way out. My stepfather had a cousin living in a building next to where we stopped. The cousin had a very ingenious hiding place. My stepfather, Stanislaw, knew it. We ran up the steps, knocked and were let in just at the last moment. In the very narrow space stood about a dozen people. The outside was perfectly camouflaged. A young woman was holding a baby, who started to cry. Without a word the young mother opened the wall and threw her baby out. No one stopped her. We all wanted to live. The Germans shot the child. The Action over, we went home.

A few days later, in an almost identical situation, caught in a kettle by myself, I did not know which way to run. A Jewish policeman on a bicycle just scooped me up and protecting me with his back drove me out of the kettle. The Germans were shooting. It all happened very fast. I knew the young man. In the winter of 1941 there was a small ice-skating rink in the Ghetto. Both of us, being good skaters, had spent some time together enjoying these moments.

Before we left the Ghetto for good, we managed to escape many kettle situations. The Ukrainians were always shooting for fun, and the Nazi monster nicknamed Frankenstein was looking for victims.

Dirty, undernourished, and lice-infested, I became very sick, with a high temperature. A strange yellow colour covered all of me, including my eyes, nails and even my gums. I had yellow jaundice, a miserable and contagious disease. My parents dressed me and carried me inside the Toebbens gates. No one was allowed to stay home. We struggled in this fashion for two days but I did not care then if I lived or died. I begged my parents to leave me. They covered me with blankets, threw some old clothing over the bed, and I stayed that way until I heard at different times each day the Germans checking the rooms, poking beds with their guns, moving to the next building. The toilet was frightening to use since the rats sitting on the pipe seemed to be waiting for me. Miraculously, my parents did not get infected, and within 10 days I was much better and back at Toebbens. No doctor or medications!

Through all the Final Solution, the worst day in my memory was September 6th. By that time, at least half the population had disappeared. The rest were told to gather together in a couple of streets which were once inhabited by the very poor. People crowded into empty buildings, sat on the pavements everywhere. We were waiting for the main selection. Only the ones with the card of life would be allowed to pass. The ones without the card of life would try to knock down a weaker person and take their precious card. In these tragic moments we were losing our sense of morality. In the meantime the Jewish police was helping the SS to keep all the thousands of people sitting. The blows were coming from all sides. One SS officer on a horse was beating people with a whip. This whip had an iron ball on the end. My mother was struck on the side of her head. This was catastrophic, since sick or wounded would never pass the selection. In a panic I somehow managed to wrap her up in a scarf. We had to hold up our Ausweisses high over our heads in our right hand. At the end of the street, more SS, more police, more open lorries. The bosses of each factory were present, but did not want everyone back. With my parents I moved towards the Toebbens group. We passed!

I estimate that after that day there were less than a hundred thousand people left. About half that number were in the factories and Jewish police; a hospital still existed, groups of people were working outside the Ghetto, doing dirty jobs, sorting rotten vegetables, working on the railways, etc. There were day and night shifts. The rest were so called wilds, hiding wherever they could. We existed in misery near our shop. In mid-January 1943 the Jewish underground killed the Jewish chief of police, had a few skirmishes and a few Germans were killed. Our shop was a separate world. We just heard about it. Early in March, yet another meeting with Walter Toebbens at the courtyard. After endless selections, kettles, diseases, we were a small group of a few thousand. He called us his faithful workers. He decided to move the factory to Poniatowa within the next couple of weeks. Lots of fresh air and good country food were promised. Amazingly, with all our Ghetto deprivations, some telephones were working. My mother got in touch with friends on the Aryan side. They said that mother and I could get help and false documents, but that they could not risk helping a man. Bribing the guards who watched the commando workers assigned to sorting out rotten potatoes outside the Ghetto walls, mother and I left. Toebbens did take his faithful workers to Poniatowa. They were made to dig their own graves on November 4th 1943, and then were all shot. One victim was Stanislaw. Mother and I watched from the outside as the Warsaw Ghetto was burning. Part of us died with the others ...

MIREILLE LIPSKI (NEE MANDELBAUM)

My Life During the War in Vichy France

When France and Britain declared war on Germany on 3rd September 1939 I was a child of six living with my parents in Paris and with an older brother and one brother a few months old.

My father joined the Free French Army and went to the South of France. My mother was left in Paris with 3 young children and complete upheaval as the war intensified and the Third Reich sent in planes bombing Northern France and the Wehrmacht marched relentlessly across France towards Paris. During this upheaval my younger brother took ill and my mother had difficulty in finding medical help for him. He died causing further distress to the family. On the 14th May 1940 the Germans entered Paris and France fell. The French army was at the end of its strength and disbanded. My father was demobilized somewhere near Toulouse.

I have no knowledge as to how my mother kept in contact with Papa but she decided that we had to try and join him in the South of France which by then had a rightwing Vichy government led by Marechal Petain. The only way she could do this was to secure a "Laisser-Passer" document which could only be obtained from the recently established Gestapo regime in one of Paris's best parts and grandest buildings. Because many people wanted to leave Paris, long queues waited outside the Gestapo Headquarters and I remember being in one such queue with my mother and older brother and waiting a very long time. I have clear memories of the room we finally entered where maman faced a German in Gestapo army uniform and being asked many questions which she must have answered to their satisfaction because we all left with this authorisation in maman's hand.

My next recollection is of a long journey during which the train stopped and an official asked all passengers to show their documents. We met Papa in Toulouse, but I have very little memory of our reunion. My father being a master tailor from Paris, must have had no difficulty in securing work, but nevertheless, he must have felt that staying in Toulouse was not safe as the Vichy government passed anti-Jewish laws long before this was demanded by the Nazis. Measures against the Jews were taken long before it was demanded by the Nazi regime.

We moved to a village called Lavaur (it is now a thriving town) and Papa secured a job with the only and very well thought of tailors shop in Lavaur. My brother, Solomon, and I went to school and life continued, though we were desperately poor, having left Paris with just a small suitcase and being known as evacuees. I made a very good friend in my class called Marguerite (whose parents proved to be very helpful to my family one way and another). The South West of France remained unoccupied and relatively safe for Jews until mid-1942 when the French police began rounding up Jews for the Nazis. Men, women and even children were rounded up and collected from their homes. They were probably given away by their neighbours. Not all French people collaborated with the Nazis. Many risked death by sheltering Jews in various places such as cellars, attics, country houses, etc. In Lavaur, during this time, I did not feel threatened for being Jewish. We knew privations and hunger but only because there was a war on. My friend's parents welcomed me into their family and Marguerite's mother always made me feel at home making sure to invite me to share the family meal whenever possible. After some time, however, my father was rounded up and sent away to a French concentration camp – perhaps Merignac or Dax–and held there by the French ready for transportation to Germany for 'work' so they told them! These concentration camps were manned by French citizens who collected new intakes of Jews considered the enemies of the New Order embraced by Vichy France. Lys also had such a camp. The staff of these camps tried to run them so that the people of these towns should not be too aware of them. Because they were never talked about or even mentioned, people almost lived under the illusion that they did not exist! They were not camps like the German or Polish ones. In the French camps there were no killings. They were camps where the French Jews were kept under strict surveillance whilst awaiting deportation. I never knew to which of these French camps Papa had been sent. We were without news of him at least for a year. How Maman managed to keep us is still a mystery to me to this day. Papa came back to us which was nothing short of a miracle. We can only explain his return by attributing it to my father's boss. I have to explain that Papa was making a complete man's suit, almost by hand, therefore producing a 'Saville Row' quality work for his boss. Consequently when these suits were no longer produced (at very low cost) they were sorely missed. No matter why he was released, the miracle of his release was appreciated all round. In Lavaur we were one of three families who were Jewish refugees and the village knew us all. I do not remember ever meeting the other two families, but we knew that the men of the other two families were rounded up at the same time as my father. We were made aware also on Papa's return that the other two men did not come back to the rest of the families and probably perished in a concentration camp, either in Germany or Poland. We were indeed very fortunate to be out of Paris and that Papa, having been interned in a camp, was released and able to come back to his family and have the ability to earn a living, even if a very modest one.

Living in France as Jews during the occupation was not to be envied. However, we had escaped into Vichy France which was considered a little more independent due to Hitler's gesture of goodwill for Marechal Petain's surrender of the French Army to the German army in 1940 during which time my father was demobilized.

Living in Lavaur where the people tolerated us without animosity, continued to be tolerable on my father's return from the French camp. There were always rumours going round and we were continually frightened that the Germans would march into Vichy France. Not all French people liked living under the German regime, but went along with it while some became Resistance workers. The South West of France remained unoccupied, but a French Resistance movement was operating. I was aware that every so often a stranger would pay us a visit and during that evening my father would be away and I never knew where he went. We would learn the next day that a bridge or a road had been blown up or something had happened somewhere which one assumed would hinder the German cause. Other times another person would pay us a visit and that evening Papa, Maman, my brother Solomon and I would take a few belongings with us and walk into the countryside to hide in a pigeon loft for the night. Maman would leave in the morning to reconnoitre and come back to tell us that it was safe for us to go home. The reason given for this hiding would be that a rumour said that the men were going to be rounded up again, or some such story. There were always lots of rumours and life always felt precarious. I enjoyed going to school and mixing with all the children. Having a special friend in Marguerite was a bonus, especially as her family always made me so welcome. Marguerite used to take me to her Catholic church which was next door to the flat we used to live in and show me round. She involved me in many of her religious activities though she knew I was Jewish, this never bothered her in the least. We were best of friends. I remember also making friends with Spanish children who lived in Lavaur with their parents because they were refugees from Franco Spain. These children spoke mainly in Spanish and I learned quite a lot of Spanish from them. We had the fact that we were refugees in common, but they had no worry of being interned in any sort of camp.

My brother being four years older than me, did not adjust to school life very well. He did not make friends as I did and rebelled against life in a small village. I believe he caused my parents additional worry. We had no radio so Solomon decided to build one so that we could hear the news. He managed to build what turned out to be a crystal set. Where he found the components to build this set I have no idea. However, I remember listening to the BBC World Service and distinctly hearing Churchill which gave us all a thrill. We could not understand what was being said but nevertheless it gave us hope. Papa explained to me who Churchill was. My understanding of politics was nil but I knew he was on our side. The fact that it was forbidden for us to listen to the BBC did not escape us but we only listened at night. I don't know how long we had this crystal set but I do know that I enjoyed the thrill of trying to listen to it.

During my stay in Lavaur one of my strong memories is listening to gunfire coming from a great distance. (I think I was told that the incredible sound came from the direction of Toulouse, but I cannot be sure of this). Apart from this I have some pleasant memories going with my brother Solomon to the river which ran along Lavaur to bathe or walking in the countryside. We lived then in the main street of the village. We were always hungry and eating a slice of bread and very runny jam represented a feast. Nevertheless I was with my family and I was content.

A lady came to our flat, brought us a tin of Ovaltine and talked to my parents. I later found out that this person was from the organization O.S.E. (Oeuvre de secours aux Enfants), an organization to save Jewish children from deportation to Germany. I cannot remember leaving my family and my next memory is of walking along a long avenue of tall rhododendron trees and arriving at a beautiful 'chateau' which I was told was called Montintin. Montintin turned out to be a former hunting lodge many kilometres from anywhere and surrounded by open ground and in point of fact quite a lovely place to be. I found myself with many children, some of approximately my own age which was about eight years old, some older ones up to maybe fourteen or fifteen years old, but I could not say for sure. Boys and girls, but the only adults were young men and women who were our leaders or carers. I do not remember how many adults were involved in looking after us. What I do remember is their caring and kindness. There must have been approximately a hundred children. Most of these children did not know where their parents were – some knew that their parents had been deported, but did not now where to. The atmosphere was a happy one. The home was run on very strict rules. We woke up at six in the morning, went down from our dormitories which were in the towers of the chateau, to the wash rooms on the ground floor. We always washed in cold water as there was no heating or hot water on the premises. After ablutions, we all went out in shorts in what to me was an enormous park and did some form of exercise, i.e. running and P.E. This we did until breakfast time when we went into the main hall which was enormous and had a large fireplace in which a whole beast could be roasted on a spit, but in which I never saw any fire. Before eating any meal we had to say our prayers. We also had to say our prayers after any meal. These were always sung and I certainly remember enjoying them as much as eating. I cannot remember any schooling as such. We had activities and these seemed to me always agreeable and pleasant. There was also lots of music played on some gramophone. The leaders must have worked very hard and I always thought them fantastic. We went on nature walks, we learned and performed plays and somehow our days were very busy. There was always so much we had to do that I was never homesick or miserable during the day. However, night time was a different story. I suffered bad ear ache and can remember being perpetually cold. I felt very homesick every night and very often cried myself to sleep. My ear ache was always worse at night. We were allowed to write to our parents but, though I wrote home every week, I never received any news from home and certainly no reply to any of my letters. For some reason I have some recollection of what I think was my ninth birthday and I believe Maman came to visit me which must have been a horrendous journey and very much walking for her. I was also totally devastated when she left without taking me with her. My other recollection of Montintin was when I was taken with a few other children to Limoge to pay a visit to the dentist where I had to have a tooth extraction. This entailed a journey by bus and train and lots of walking. In fact walking was always the order of the day and because I was a very small child I found having to walk anywhere very tiring. The O.S.E. did a fantastic job in looking after the children they saved from being deported although things were not quite as safe as I believed. The Germans knew about the safe houses, of the O.S.E., and often tried to remove the boys. For this reason, every so often, a group of children was sent off with a leader to reach the Swiss border but sometimes the group might not be successful, with disastrous consequences. For me life in Montintin was totally different. We were very involved with observance of the Jewish religion and prayers before and after every meal. There were no formal lessons as such, but we learned about things and enjoyed music though I have no recollection of learning anything as one did in school. I remember enjoying playing in the 'garden' and climbing trees. We stayed in Montintin for quite some time, but exactly how long I cannot say.

My next recollection is of a house which I think was in Montmerency but again I cannot be too sure. I don't actually remember moving away from Montintin – all I can remember is being in a completely different environment, a much smaller house, with other children. During the length of time I was away from my parents I cannot remember making any close friends so moving away from Montintin could not have been so distressing. The new home was very comfortable and I did not feel the cold so much there. I recollect looking forward to Wednesday afternoons because that was when a ballet teacher came to the home with a violin player and we were given a ballet class. I thought that was one of the most wonderful things for me to do. I must have been there for Rosh Hashana and Yom Kippur because I was made aware that when you became an adult you had to fast on Yom Kippur.

I cannot say how long I stayed in this second O.S.E. home but it seemed that soon after this move I was reunited with my family, though I cannot recollect how this reunion came about. How my parents and my brother Solomon coped while I was away from them I never knew. We were reunited in our old home in Paris although my parents did tell me that the flat had been completely ransacked and my parents had to start again from nothing – but at least we all survived. It must have been the end of the war because I remembered lining the street with many other people and cheering the American soldiers marching in and giving away sweets and chocolates to the children. I somehow was given a soldier's sewing kit which I still have and still use to this day.

I went back to school and had a lot of catching up to do. My mother and father's family all perished in Poland, but one sister of my mother's survived by fleeing to Siberia and my father had one sister who had moved to England long before the war and therefore we thankfully arrived in Britain. My father never spoke about his internment in the French concentration camp and to my utter regret I never enquired about his stay there.

We came to settle in England after the war in 1948 and that is another and much happier story

HENRI OBSTFELD

A Bridge Too Far

During the Summer of 1944 Allied Troops had advanced from France through Belgium into the Southern part of the Netherlands. I was four years old and had been looked after by a middle-aged couple, 'Aunt Hennie' and 'Uncle Jaap', for about two years. However, before I continue, let me first tell something about my background.

My mother was born in Amsterdam in 1906. Her ancestors had lived in Holland since before 1800, many in small provincial towns in the Southern part of the country, others in small towns North of Amsterdam. She went to a neighbourhood primary school, and later to a secondary school with an economics related syllabus. Afterwards she worked in several offices including that of the Hoover electric carpet-sweeper company.

My father was born in 1896 in Krakau (now Krakow, Poland), when it was still part of the Austro-Hungarian empire. He was sent to Vienna for his education, and lived there from about 1910 until 1925, when he moved to Amsterdam. He became a shoe designer, and worked as such in Vienna for many years. During the years 1917-28 his whole immediate family gradually moved to Amsterdam.

My parents met at dancing classes in the early 1930s. They married in November 1933, and moved into a very small flat 'under the rafters' of a relatively new block of flats in the Lekstraat, in Amsterdam–New South. My father and his brother Simon owned a small slipper factory which had been started by their father Selig. Over the years they managed to increase the turnover, and eventually had to move to larger premises. In December 1935 the factory was relocated to the 1e Oosterparkstraat 126A, and both brothers found flats in the same street: Simon and his wife lived above the factory, and my parents a couple of doors away. My grandfather Selig was a bit of an inventor. According to another brother, Dolek, grandpa had invented a helicopter during the First World War and had offered the design to the Austrian military authorities. He was told to come back when he got the "vehicle" in flying order … Dolek added to the story that he had destroyed the parts, then stored in Amsterdam, before the German invasion (10 May 1940) so that the Germans would not be able to benefit from them.

I was born in Amsterdam in April 1940, exactly one month before the Germans invaded the Low Countries and France. There is not much to tell about my early life. Gradually, the Nazis, with the help of their Dutch collaborators, made life more difficult for the Jewish population. Jews were not permitted to sit on park benches, were not permitted to ride on the trams or go to the cinema, had to wear a yellow star with the word 'JOOD' embroidered on it, on their clothes. In February 1941, the situation was such that the Amsterdam dockworkers started a strike in support of the Jewish population. That day, the trams stayed in the tram sheds, and many factories and offices remained closed. However, the Germans soon saw to it that life returned to 'normal'. Simultaneously, the 'resistance' started to get itself slowly organised. From time to time, there were also skirmishes between Jews and Nazi collaborators. Young Jewish boys were picked up during razzias. Amongst them was a cousin, Marco, who was deported to Mauthausen were he died soon after arrival, in September 1941.

During the summer of 1942 the 'Jewish Council' had been ordered by the Germans to arrange for Jews to be selected for 'work in the East'. My parents received call-up papers for me … I have learned from an older survivor that children of two upwards, were sent such papers. Having done some research at the Netherlands Institute for War Documentation NIOD in Amsterdam, I learned that there are no records of who was called up.

My parents were alarmed when they read that I, all of two years old, had to present myself, with a rucksack, clothing and food for a few days, to be sent to work in the East. They took me immediately to uncle Dolek, who lived with his wife and son in another part of the city, and left me there. Fortunately, the call-up date came and went, and nobody came to see why I had not turned up!

My parents decided that it was not safe for me to stay with them. They started looking around for somebody who would be prepared to look after me – whatever that might mean. A friend of my mother's from her secondary-school days was prepared to take me in. However, he was unmarried and lived in a small village near Arnhem called Huissen, where everybody knew everybody's business. That was probably the reason why it was decided not to send me to him. With hindsight, perhaps just as well, because Huissen lay in the front line of the Battle for Arnhem, in 1944. There were not many houses left standing after the war.

How my parents found my foster-parents, I do not know: neither does their daughter (who passed away in January 2003, aged 87). It was safer not to know ... However, both of us assume that the fact that Uncle Jaap was a free-mason, had some bearing on the matter.

My 'aunt' and 'uncle' lived in a large house in the centre of the city of Arnhem, on the corner of Bovenbergstraat and Oosterbeekseweg, near the railway station. Their surname was Klerk, and when I came to live with them, some time during the late summer of 1942, my name became Hendrik Klerk. They called me Hans, just as my parents used to do. The story of my sudden appearance in Arnhem was that I, a nephew of the Klerks, had lost my parents during the bombardment of Rotterdam by the Luftwaffe (German air force) in May 1940. It was only a few years ago that I learned that my story was far from unique: quite a few hidden Jewish children were supposed to have lost their parents on that occasion.

During the two years in Bovenbergstraat I did not play with other children, nor did I go to school: all that was too dangerous.

In the course of 1944 it became clear to the authorities that the centre of Arnhem could become a battle zone, because the bridge across the river Rhine at Arnhem was one of the few suitable for military vehicles. Hence civilians were made to leave the centre of town. The three of us moved to one of the suburbs, where we stayed with the Klerks' daughter, 'Aunt Els', and son-in-law, 'Uncle Jan', and their baby daughter, Emmy. They lived in a block of flats on top of a hill, from where one had a very nice view along a dual carriageway called Bakenbergseweg, which had tram rails in its central reservation. Watching the electric trams come and go, was always entertaining, that is, while there was still electricity! The threat of an all-out battle for the city (as recorded for posterity in the movie *A bridge too far*), was in the air for some time.

On Sunday, September 17th, around lunchtime, the first gliders bringing British and Polish Airborne troops started to appear. We all watched these silent planes from the windows of the flat. I had seen lots of noisy planes in my days, but this was something different. Next, we saw pastel-coloured dolls emerge from the planes. Almost immediately, a pastel-coloured umbrella unfolded above each doll. We had never seen parachutes before! They drifted slowly down and out of sight, behind the woods at the end of the dual carriageway. A short while later a few of the dolls appeared at the end of that road, and then moved out of sight again. I was at least as excited as the adults, but probably for different reasons!

Meanwhile shooting had started, but that did not stop us from finishing Sunday lunch. Our block of flats was situated around the corner from the large Diaconessen hospital. Both the Germans and the Allies wanted to have possession of the hospital, for obvious reasons. Ambulances, often no more than horse-drawn carts flying a Red-Cross flag, came and went while the battle raged, mainly in the centre of town, near the bridge, and a good distance away from us.

We stayed another two days in the flat. By now it had become clear to the adults that we had to leave, because of the fighting going on all around us. A doctor who had a motorcar which ran on a 'gasbag', came to fetch us at dusk on the 19th. We put as many of our belongings as we could in the car. I sat on the floor, between the front and back seats, with parcels above me and the breadbin on my lap. Aunt Hennie kept asking 'Hans, are you still alive?' This was a not an idle question, since there was shooting going on all around us.

We passed a restaurant called 'De leeren doedel' (the leather bagpipe), which was burning spectacularly in the night. Somehow, arrangements had been made for all of us to stay with the headmaster of the village school of Harskamp, some 20 kilometres away from Arnhem. However, our hosts whose names were Jan and Nel Eshuis, had not been told about me. When I appeared from behind the skirts of Aunt Hennie, they were asked whether they minded having one more little evacuee staying with them. They did not.

We stayed in Harskamp for the next nine months. Harskamp was a small village that had served the Dutch Army camp where, before the war, soldiers had undergone their primary training. The camp had since been taken over by the Wehrmacht (German army), and was full of German soldiers and their equipment.

I recall very clearly the very harsh winter of 1944-45. Because of food shortages, Aunt and Uncle would take me on long walks, visiting farms and begging for food for their little boy. For some time a central kitchen, situated in a model farm near the village, had provided hot soup at lunchtime. I remember going along with an adult at midday, to collect a kettle full of the liquid which we called 'blue-bean soup'. Nobody had ever seen blue beans before. The liquid was tasteless, but it was warm!

A few hundred people, also evacuated as a result of the fighting, occupied the school building. Hygiene did not improve as time went by. I was not allowed to play with the children who lived with their parents in the classrooms, for fear of infection with lice, etc.

Another problem was drinking water. There was no piped water in the village: each house or farmhouse, had a well or pump. The headmaster's house had its own modern pump which could not be run because there was no electricity anymore. Everybody had to make do with the one pump in the school playground. One of

Uncle's daily chores was to pump water. Fortunately, the pump did not freeze up during that severe winter. Another of his tasks was sawing wood for the stoves. Since there were woods surrounding Harskamp, there was no lack of that commodity.

Because there were so many people living under one roof, tempers would sometimes flare, particularly over the use of the stove in the kitchen. First, Aunt and Uncle's daughter and her family moved out, having found accommodation in one of the village bakers' baking houses. Later, we moved in with a farmer's family whose farmhouse was situated near the centre of the village.

One day, 'Dolle Dinsdag' (Mad Tuesday), the rumour went round that the Germans had lost the war. Soon German soldiers on stolen bicycles started passing the farmhouse in an easterly direction. All the village inhabitants were standing along the roads yelling abuse at them. Unfortunately, we had been shouting much too soon: the rumour proved unfounded. The Germans returned and stayed several more months.

Almost every Sunday afternoon we would go for an hour's walk to the nearby village of Wekerom where friends of Aunt and Uncle had found accommodation. Sunday, April 17th 1945 was no exception. However, by now the Allies were so close to Harskamp that we had to cross the lines between German and Allied troops in order to make our weekly visit. When I think back about it, crossing the lines – just by walking along the main road – appears to have been sheer madness! However, when we arrived that day in Wekerom, we found a Canadian troop carrier parked in the drive of our friends' house. We were FREE, after five long years of occupation!

That is not the end of the story. Around five o'clock, Aunt and Uncle decided that it was time to go home. They discussed with the locals whether it was safe to walk along the main road back to Harskamp, the way we had come. It was decided that it would be better to walk along farm tracks, through the fields. And so we set off. Somewhere we passed a farm where a Canadian tank was just leaving the yard, and in doing so, toppled a brick gate support. We passed the model farm, and joined the road into Harskamp. Soon after we arrived back, shooting started. It did not last long: the German soldiers just fled, and we welcomed the Canadians, thus having been liberated twice that day!

The liberation festivities went on for several days, with the village brass band giving concerts some evenings in a bandstand which had not been used for several years.

What about my parents? After they had left me with my foster-parents and returned to Amsterdam, they found a hiding place in the City of Haarlem, only a quarter of an hour's train ride west of Amsterdam. They, together with my father's brother Simon and his wife, and one other Jew, a Mr. Elkeles, lived from the autumn of 1942 till May 1945 above a kindergarten-school on the Stoofsteeg, in the centre of Haarlem. The head of the school was a lady, a Rosicrucian, who used the money paid by her 'lodgers', to feed seven dogs and innumerable cats. The latter were not allowed to catch mice.

Members of the resistance who brought food, knew the whereabouts of these lodgers. I should mention here two names: Mr Piet Zegwaard, who, after the war, lived with his family in the nearby village of Heemstede, and with whom we were in contact for many years, and Dr H.A.L. Trampusch, whose wife was Jewish. The latter couple were Austrian nationals and lived on the Falkstraat in Amsterdam. After retirement from his post at Amsterdam University, they moved to Blaricum, a village east of Amsterdam. Dr Trampusch was a well-known resistance figure. Originating from Vienna, he would put on a German army uniform, speak German with his own Viennese accent, 'retrieve' Jewish children, give them shelter in his house and then take them to safe houses. A radio programme about his war-time exploits, was broadcast after his death. He was recognised by Yad Vashem in 1979 as a Righteous Gentile. His wife was also deeply involved in resistance work.

During their stay above the school my father and his brother sometimes drew pictures on the blackboard in the classroom for the children. This could only be done overnight, because the lodgers could not move during school hours, in case the children might become suspicious of the noises upstairs.

After our move to Harskamp my foster-parents had sent a postcard to my parents at their last-know address in Haarlem. It told them that we had been evacuated from Arnhem to Edeseweg 174 in Harskamp. That postcard was delivered notwithstanding the war conditions.

A few days after the end of the war my parents moved back to Amsterdam. In their absence, their flat had been occupied by other people. However, the factory had remained untouched since they left it to go into hiding. Thus they recovered official papers such as birth certificates, photographs and the like, left in the boiler of the central heating system. They lived in the factory for some days before they decided to try and locate me.

Travelling through the war-torn country was not easy. Trains had not run since the railway employees had gone on strike in 1944. Many tram carriages had been removed to Germany. In short, transport was at a standstill. The only way to get from A to be B was to hitch a lift on the few vehicles that were on the roads, or walk. Having started out early one morning in May, they hitched lifts on a milk transporter, a fire engine, and so on. They also had to cross the border between 'Fortress Holland' and the rest of the country – a border that had been put in place to trap fleeing Germans and collaborators. However, these two Jews were allowed to cross. Towards late afternoon they reached Wekerom, where they were told that Harskamp was an hour's walk away. It would be easy to find, because you could see the church spire from a distance. So they set out on the last leg of their journey. What the villagers in Wekerom did not know was that the spire of the Harskamp church had been shot away by the Canadians, because it could have been used by the Germans as a lookout post ... and so they found themselves suddenly in the village. The locals could point them to the headmaster's house, and they were welcomed by Uncle Jan and Aunt Nel. Yes, their little son was safe and well, but no longer staying at this address. Someone was sent to the farm where we were now staying. It was only a few minutes' walk away. According to the recollections of those present (Aunts Hennie and Nel, Uncles Jaap and Jan, my parents, and possibly a few other people), I recognised my mother and said to her 'You stayed away a very long time'. Having sat on her lap for a while, someone asked whether I would not like to sit on my father's lap, too. I slid down and went to him, but soon went back to my mother.

My parents stayed for about a week in Harskamp with the Eshuis family. Then, the day came to return to Amsterdam. So, one morning we set out on the journey. What I remember about it were the trams of Utrecht city. It was the first day after the war that they had returned into service. What struck me was their dark brown colour, so strikingly different from the trams I had known in Arnhem, which had been sand-coloured.

We reached 'home', the factory, that evening and lived there for a while.

From that point in time, my parents began the slow process of rebuilding our lives.

★ ★ ★

During the period that we lived in the factory, I remember that my parents took me several times to a building where they looked at notice boards. I had no idea why and what for, but they talked about people, and with other people who had come for the same reason. It was only many years later that I realised that they were looking for relatives and acquaintances whose names, whether as survivors, as missing or as murdered, might appear on these lists. I wonder whether that building was, what I later knew as the building of the Amsterdam Jewish Religious Community, at Plantage Parklaan 9.

Eventually, my parents were given a house in Heemstede. The previous occupier, a Mr Slot, had been a collaborator who was now under investigation. I clearly remember that one day men, to do with the police, came to our house, had a look in a large metal cupboard which had handles like a safe, and put on a seal. It probably contained Mr Slot's documents.

My mother told me many years later, that I told her every evening my recollections of the war period. That went on for about a year; after our reunion, every evening the same stories. As she said many years later. she felt very depressed during the period we lived in Heemstede. I think that this had to do with her trying to come to terms with the loss of her parents, her oldest sister and family, and so many others.

One of the things I insisted on doing, was going for a walk on my own every evening. Much later she told me that she had once followed me, to find out what I was up to. It turned out that I only went for a walk, along the river Spaarne, and then home again. Was I imitating my foster father perhaps who would have taken our dog called "Beer" (bear) , a chow-chow, for a walk?

My father travelled daily to Amsterdam, to the factory. From Heemstede it was a problematic journey. Public transport was hardly operational. He first had to get to Haarlem railway station, by tram which didn't run all day, because of the limited supply of electricity. The trains were sometimes no more than goods wagons: much of the rolling stock had 'disappeared'. Once in Amsterdam, he had to catch a tram. Eventually, his brother Sem who lived in London, sent him a bicycle! Now the journey from Heemstede to Haarlem became much easier.

My mother knew no Hebrew at all. Her background was secular. Why she took private lessons in Hebrew, I do not know. However, her teacher, a Mr Wolf, lived in Haarlem. She had to use my father's bicycle to get there, and back. For a lady to ride on a man's bicycle was a problem (in those days!) and I recall the problems she had getting on and off. Hopefully, she would not have to get off on the way...... Eventually, my mother also received a bicycle from Uncle Sem.

I also remember the first night that the street lighting – gas lamps! – was switched on again. For us, children, it was a great event and we were allowed to stay up beyond our usual bedtime!

For my sixth birthday, my father had bought me a second hand scooter – without inner tires though. He tried to improvise by stuffing the outer tyres with pieces of garden hose. That didn't work at all. I don't recall the end of that story.

My first school was a Froebel-type school. It was about five minutes' walk from our house, at the home of two spinsters. The class room occupied the whole downstairs area, and they lived upstairs. The most memorable incident was when I was sent out of the classroom because I could not remember the word for the number nine. Having been given a small wooden tablet with the shape of that number on it made out of sandpaper, I had to sit on my knees at the bottom of the stairs going with my right index finger over the shape and repeating the name of that number.....which I promptly forgot again! Fortunately, the school mistress's friend came down the stairs and asked me what I was doing there. I explained and even dared to ask her to tell me the name of that number!

The primary school was closed on Wednesday afternoons. During the summer, my mother would wait for me outside the Kraaiennesterschool, and we would cycle to Zandvoort, the nearby seaside resort. I would sit on the 'luggage carrier', behind her. The dunes were littered with bunkers, part of the Atlantic Wall which had been built as defence against a British or Allied Forces invasion. One of the bunkers at the end of the Zeestraat leading from the tram terminal in the village to the beach, had been turned into a police station. On one occasion, my parents had arranged for my father to join us after work travelling by train to Zandvoort. My mother would meet him at the station. She had left me at a certain spot near the police station with the instructions to play and stay put. After a while I decided that she had stayed away too long and so I took myself off to the police station where I explained the situation. The policemen were, of course, well accustomed to 'lost children'...so they let me stay and wait. You can imagine that my parents were very upset when I was not to be found at the appointed spot, and very relieved when they found me in the end.

I have no recollection when and how my parents reintroduced me to my surviving aunts, uncles and cousins. I do remember that my father's sister who lived in Antwerp with her husband and little son, came to stay with us in Heemstede. I wonder how that was arranged, communications and transport still being so tenuous at that time. Other surviving members of the family also came to visit us there, as did my foster parents.

My first memory of being taken to a synagogue must have been for Rosh Hashanah. The synagogue building was at Kenau Park, near the Haarlem railway station. I recall that the services were held in an upstairs hall, and that you entered through very heavy red, velvet curtains.

I have often wondered about my transition from a Christian to a Jewish, although not orthodox, household. When I went to stay with my foster parents, I would have to eat what I was served, as before. Although Tante Hennie was reluctant to give me pork to eat, Oom Jaap said that all that was nonsense, that I had always eaten it and so I was made to eat pork. I recall clearly that I tried to stuff that meat in my cheeks until there was an opportunity to get rid of it…!

A happy ending? Most certainly. And so I sit here, having typed my story, and I cry again. The late consequences of my experiences.

Postscript: My 'aunts' and 'uncles' Hendrika (Hennie) Klerk-Igesz and Wilhelmina (Els) Willemsen-Klerk, Jacob Klerk and Jan Evert Willemsen, were honoured (posthumously) with the Yad Vashem 'Righteous Amongst the Nations' award during a ceremony at the synagogue of Arnhem on 10th April 2000. I also made an application for the recognition of Jan Eshuis and Nel Eshuis-Rodenburg, but the circumstances did not fulfil Yad Vashem's strict requirements.

EVE OPPENHEIMER

Two Lucky Events

My life by the end of the Second World War included two events which made a great difference to the lives of my brothers and myself. The first one was that I was born in London, in fact, in Golders Green. I will first say something about my family.

My parents, as their parents before them, were Jewish and born in Germany. My father was born in Nuremberg, my mother in Heidelberg. They met at the university of that city, where they both received their doctorates. They got married in 1927. They then moved to Berlin, where my father was offered a career as a commercial councillor, at a family-owned bank called Mendelsohn.

My brother Paul, known in the family as Bikki, was born in 1928, and my other brother, Rudolf, known as Ruzzi, arrived in 1931. By all accounts it seems to have been a very happy family, with visits to grandparents, and being visited by father's younger brother, Rudi, who was to move to London, and his sister who was to immigrate to Palestine.

My mother and brothers came to London in 1936. By this time the Nuremberg Laws had already been introduced, and life for Jews who led a Jewish way of life was getting progressively more difficult. My family was very assimilated, but this had no bearing in the eyes of the Nazis.

It was during this trip to London, and while my parents were staying with my Uncle Rudi and his wife, Lotte, that I was born. Rudi and Lotte had got married in 1934. The piece of paper saying that I was a British citizen was to play such an important part in the lives of my brothers and myself.

At this time my father had recently moved to Heemstede in Holland, where he had been offered a job with the Dutch branch of the Mendelsohn bank. It was three months after my birth that I was introduced to my father. My father managed to get his parents and his wife's parents out of Germany, as well as his much-loved Steinway piano.

Many years later, when we were grown-up, while my Uncle Rudi was clearing up his attic, he came across a battered suitcase with our names on a label. Inside was a chumash, dated 1592, which belonged to my mother. It has an extensive family tree in it. When I find someone who is fluent in both Hebrew and German, and has some free time, perhaps this can be sorted out. In the case was also a kiddush cup with my father's name on it. I was very interested in these two items. The third item was a set of silver fish knives and forks which I let my brothers have. I was not really interested in these, especially since I am a vegetarian. This case and some other items, were hidden by our Dutch friends.

I cannot really say what my parents were like as people, what made them tick. My father was rather stocky, with thick dark hair, and wore glasses. Going by photographs I have seen, he looked rather serious. He had a great love of music, stamp-collecting and train-spotting. My mother, by contrast, was tall, slim, with light brown hair, and a lovely gentle face. She was a fantastic knitter, and most of our clothes were made by her. She also made muesli long before it was heard of here, with oats and fresh fruits. I especially remember the strawberries.

My early years were extremely happy, with visits to Zandvoort, the local seaside town, during the summer. In the spring we walked through the tulip fields. In the winter I learned to skate on the canals, pushing a chair in front of me for support.

This happy life changed dramatically in May 1940, when the Germans invaded Holland. After the port of Rotterdam had been heavily bombarded, Holland surrendered. Soon we had to move from Heemstede to Naarden, where we stayed for eighteen months. In May 1942 we were forced to move to the south side of Amsterdam. We lived there in some tenement flats on the second floor. Below us lived a lady whom I used to call tante (auntie) Fie. I used to go and visit her very often. She took great care of all the family. She also wanted to hide us, but my father would not hear of it, as it would have endangered her life. What I remember most of Amsterdam is the window-boxes with bright red geraniums in them.

As said, I had a British birth certificate, although not a passport. My father registered me with the Swiss embassy, as there was no longer a British one. He received correspondence from them saying that we could be exchanged for Germans interned in Britain. It was for this reason that I sometimes did the shopping: I did not have to wear a yellow star. I often forgot, according to my brothers, what I was meant to purchase, and had to run out of the shop to find them and ask for repeat instructions. I, of course, was unaware of the goings-on outside our home.

It was on the 20th June 1943, just before my seventh birthday, that the German police came, shouting and barging into our flat. I was very scared, but remember how much I admired the shiny buttons on their uniforms. There was no panic, although we were very nervous. For some time we had had our rucksacks and suitcases packed, with clothing, eating utensils, blankets, soap, and some food. And most important of all, we had little bags, which we hung round our necks. They had been made by my mother. Inside the bags were various documents, like the address of my uncle in London – he was to move around several times during this period – and also my birth certificate. We went to the local railway station, and met up with many of our fellow Jewish prisoners. It was a very warm day, and we all wore extra clothing and were all wondering what was to happen next. It did not take long to find out.

We were herded into cattle wagons. Around lunchtime they started to move slowly. Later that day we arrived at Westerbork which was a transit camp in northern Holland. The scenery looked very barren, with no colour whatsoever. My mother, Ruzzi and I went to one hut, and my father and Paul went to another, in the barracks. In these huts were three tiered bunks, and we stored our luggage underneath them. There were about 800 people in each barrack.

As soon as we arrived in Westerbork we looked for our grandparents. There was joy at finding my father's parents, and great sadness at not finding my mother's. They had been shipped to the east, to Sobibor. None of us knew what this meant. Later we were told that this was the Nazi way of telling us that they would be killed. My father's parents were shortly to make the same journey.

Life at Westerbork was degrading. There was a bath house: each of us had a card to tell us when it was our turn to have a bath. Paul still has his card. Every Friday afternoon at three o'clock was his turn to report for his bath. There was also a wash-house. Everyone hung the wet clothes on a nail which was by or near their bunk. And there was a double row of toilets, ten in each row, with no partition between them. What I remember of Westerbork was the boredom. We got up at six o'clock, had roll call, and the rest of the day was our own. There were lots of other children, so I most probably played with them. However, there was nothing organised. We, I mean the family, still had our meals together. My parents worked through the day, as did Paul. Ruzzi was learning a new skill which was to help later on, namely, how to forage for food by the kitchen.

Every Monday evening names of people were called out and they had to be ready for the next day, to board the waiting cattle train. Everyone was scared – and everyone felt for the people inside the train, wondering where they would be going and what their fate would be. Monday evening was the time that everybody dreaded. If your name was not called out, you had at least another week to live. On 1st February 1944 it was our turn to board the waiting train. The doors were locked, there was hardly any water, no food, and a bucket to use as a toilet. The next day we arrived in a very dreary countryside, with no station sign, let alone a station – just a ramp. We were told that we had arrived at Bergen-Belsen. We could see straight away that life here was going to be much more difficult then it had been at Westerbork. The family was put into the Star Camp, my mother and I went to one hut and my father and brothers to another.

The Star Camp was for people who had connections in Britain, Palestine or South America. They could be used to exchange for prisoners of war. Again the day started with a roll call which seemed to last for ages. Today I get fed up waiting for a bus for five minutes; I marvel at myself at how long I stood there, often in the cold, waiting to be counted. Boredom was the main occupation again. No books, no pencils or paper, and certainly no toys. However, there were some unofficial lessons. My father's work was sorting out shoes, looking for leather that could be used again. My mother worked in the kitchen, and Ruzzi ladled out the so-called soup. Sometimes it had a bit of potato or turnip in it. He used to ladle a bit of vegetable to his family or friends. Naturally he was found out, and was put into solitary confinement for a couple of days by the Jewish Council which did the everyday running of the camp. However, this did not deter him; as soon as he was released, he would do the same thing again. For some reason Paul did hardly any work at all.

In January 1945 my mother died, mainly from starvation. I used to go and visit her every day in the so-called hospital, after visiting my father. I still remember saying to him that I must now go and visit mother, and he replied that she was no longer alive. I think I screamed the hut down, as I did not believe that bit of news. I had seen people die before. One minute people were standing or sitting, the next they had fallen to the ground. Death was nothing new to me. However, somehow I could not believe that it would happen to someone so close to me. She was the practical one, the one who kept up our spirits when we were feeling low; a very lovely, intelligent lady. How could this have happened to us? Two months later, my father died in the same hospital, from starvation, disease and exhaustion. A lovely but serious family man, who would never ever break the law for his own needs.

In Belsen the sun never seemed to shine. We were there for 14 months, and throughout it was always so grey. In 1995 I made a return visit to Belsen, and the atmosphere seemed very eerie.

In the beginning of April 1945 the Star Camp was suddenly evacuated. My brothers and a family called Birnbaum who seemed to take care of all the orphans including me, were put on a train. There were three such trains. It seems that nobody knew what had happened to the first train; the second was meant to go to Theresienstadt, but it never arrived there; and then there was our train. Survivors call this the train the phantom or lost train: it criss-crossed Germany for fourteen days. There was no food or water, and the Allied air force bombed it. Small fires were started and a few people got killed. By this time the guards were not interested in us any more, but looked after their own skins. The train used to move at night and stay still during the day. Many passengers would then alight and dig up potatoes that had been planted at the side of the railway track, collect some firewood and cook them. I was unaware of all these events as I was ill with typhus as a result of all the lice and dirt around us. Eventually we arrived at a place called Tröbitz and were liberated by the Russians. By now I had become separated from my brothers, although we were on the same train. It was here that the second event which I mentioned in the beginning took place. My brothers only spoke Dutch. They were afraid that if they spoke German, they might be returned to Germany. Eventually, the guards let them go. They were put on an open truck, bound for the station. When they reached the exit gates they had to stop and let an incoming open truck pass. I was on that truck. My brother Ruzzi spotted me immediately, shouted at the truck driver to stop, and after formalities I joined my brothers on the trip back to Holland.

On arrival there, because my brothers were German, the Dutch authorities put them in a camp with SS officers – what a welcome! By now my aunt and uncle in England had written to their Dutch friends, to see whether they had heard from us. They had traced my brothers at the camp, and had them released. In the meantime I had gone back to tante Fie who had welcomed me with open arms. My uncle had been in the Intelligence Corps during the war. He had been given special leave to travel to Holland and visit us and, in my case, to take me to London. I was far from eager to go. I wanted to stay with tante Fie, I didn't want to go on another journey without my brothers, and I wasn't happy to meet new people, none of whom spoke Dutch.

However, I landed at Northolt Airport on the afternoon of the 18th September, in an RAF Dakota. On the plane travelled some British soldiers. Sitting around the fuselage, they tried to cheer me up by teaching me my first English song which was 'My Bonnie lies over the Ocean'. I don't think that I was too impressed, because as soon as we landed, I was violently sick. I was nine when I came to this country.

My aunt and uncle lived in a flat in north London and they had two small children: Peter who was seven, and Ruth who was nearly one. And then I arrived, causing a lot of disruption. I was certainly resentful, and didn't trust anyone. My brothers were still in Holland. They didn't come till November. I first went to a local junior school where I learned English. This was the first time that I underwent any formal teaching. I then went to a Jewish boarding school in Hove. I soon hated it there. I had visited the school earlier with my aunt, and had thought that it would be exciting, like the Chalet School Stories or Enid Blyton which I had begun to read. How wrong I was. My aunt and uncle saw that I was unhappy there, and by a stroke of luck heard from the paediatrician whom they were using for Peter and Ruth about the perfect answer: Lingfield House.

The West London Synagogue had been bombed during the war. Luckily, no-one was hurt, and the only damage was to the ornate ceiling. After the war the government of the day gave a grant to all places of worship which had been damaged. However, that grant was not large enough to repair the roof: so a fund raising appeal took place. Just before the contract was signed, a member present at the meeting – no-one seems to know who it was – suggested that, instead of spending all that money on the ceiling, it would be better to rescue some children from Europe. That idea was immediately accepted, and people who had given donations also agreed. And so Lingfield House was born.

The first children arrived in Windermere on the birthday of the person who was to play such an important part in their lives. Alice Goldberger was herself a refugee from Nazi Germany. One of the members of the synagogue had a very large country house called Weir Courtney, outside Lingfield, overlooking the racecourse. He was prepared to let the children stay there keeping a few rooms to himself. The house with its beautiful gardens could not have been a more perfect place for these twenty-four children. They arrived there on the first night of Hanukkah in 1945. The house is still remembered fondly by the children. The move to Isleworth, to Lingfield House, in 1950 was mainly so that the children could go to services and attend the Religion School of the West London Synagogue, and could also go to larger schools..

It was to Lingfield House that my aunt and uncle sent me. Right from the beginning I felt safe and at home. To be with children who had similar backgrounds, with a loving and caring staff, made a lot of difference to my life. It was to Alice that we turned when we had anything that worried us; it was Alice who used to come to our bedside every night, to say goodnight, and it was Alice who made sure that we had the best of everything. She encouraged us with our interests, whether they were music, dancing, drama or painting. She made sure that we took care of animals; we all had one. There were: a dog, three cats, chickens, rabbits, guinea pigs and a tortoise. Alice also made sure that we looked to the future, when we would be standing on our own feet.

Today some of us are still in touch with each other. Some live in Israel, Australia, the United States, Europe and this country. We were brought ever closer last October, when one of the youngest children,

Denny, died suddenly of a heart attack. It was Denny who had the wonderful idea of having a reunion on the occasion of Alice's 100th birthday.

Today, I am retired from work, and lead a fairly full and happy life.

CLARE PARKER

Klara's Story

My name now is Clare Parker but when I was a child in Hungary, I was Klara Hochhauser. Even now nearly seventy years after the Holocaust, I find it difficult to speak of the terrible things which happened to me and my family. The tears still flow when I think back but I am determined to leave my testimony in the hope that it may be a deterrent to further genocides

We lived in the suburbs of Budapest, Hungary. I was an only child, and went to an ordinary state elementary school. My father had a metal-plating workshop in the courtyard of where we lived in a ground floor flat. He owned a nice big car for his business, so in the summer we were able to drive to some picturesque old inns on the banks of the Danube. We would enjoy the view of the river as boats floated by. Until my problems started at school, I led a happy, carefree life.

Sometime in 1942, a priest came to give religious education and as I was the only non-Catholic child in the school, I had to remain outside in the cold while this took place. From that day on, because of my glasses, the other children taunted me with shouts of "dirty four-eyes Jew". When the time came for me to move up one class at school, forms had to be filled with many details, including nationality and religion. The teacher brought back the form I had handed in and told me that since I am Jewish, I cannot be Hungarian. She has crossed out 'Hungarian' and replaced it with 'Israelite'.

By 1943, with the war raging in the rest of Europe, I would hear whispers within the family about plans to escape from Hungary. The children at school had become so horrible to me that I was afraid to go to school. But I told no-one at home.

Then the situation worsened rapidly. Suddenly all Jewish men between the ages of sixteen and sixty were sent into forced labour camps under the guise of work for the war effort. My father was sent to a place called Katzko in the Carpathian mountains. At first he was able to come home for a few days now and again, but my mother could not run the workshop and it had to be shut down. In any case, soon all Jewish businesses were to be closed anyway.

For the majority of non-Jews life went on as usual in spite of the war. One day on the way home from school, my classmates, no longer content with shouting insults, pelted me with stones. So my family decided I should stop going. I was eleven-and-a-half years old. In family discussions, I would hear comments in my family to the effect that Hungarians were not as anti-Semitic as Germans, Austrians and Poles and that Hungary would never maltreat its Jews as the others did. As the situation worsened, I heard more whispers. On one of his visits, my father told my mother that he had been offered to convert to Catholicism: "In return I would no longer have to do forced labour". He refused saying: "I cannot do this. What would happen to everyone else in the family? If the others have to die, I would rather die, too."

My twelfth birthday was in January 1944. Now the sanctions and atrocities against the Jews escalated rapidly. Every minute of what should have been everyday life, became terrifying for us. I remember the day the German army poured in: long columns of soldiers, some on high tanks, and some on motorcycles with side-cars, arms stretched out in front of them in the Nazi salute.

The head of the Hungarian government was Admiral Horthy and the head of the Catholic Church in Hungary was Cardinal Mindszenty. These two men created a new uniformed gendarmerie (*Csendör*), for the purpose of collecting anything valuable from Jews and to gather us for deportation. Admiral Horthy gave the order that all Jews living in Budapest's inner city were to move into houses especially marked with a yellow star: this was the ghetto.

We lived in the suburbs and, at first, did not have to move, but one day the *Csendörs* came and looted everything of value, even my father's car. We had to wear the yellow star during the short periods that we were allowed on the streets. But it was difficult to buy food as printed signs had been put up saying: 'No Jews and dogs admitted'. Shortly afterwards we were made to go into a ghetto. We had a very small room where my grandmother joined us and the three of us slept in one bed. We had to carry water from a standpipe and the toilet was a wooden shed on the ground level.

Two weeks later we were awakened at night by the gendarmes who ordered us to go silently into the street, five by five, and to start walking fast all the way to a disused brick factory. There we joined a large number of people sitting on the ground beside a railway line. We sat there for two days and then were herded into cattle wagons by Hungarian soldiers commanded by an SS-man. They shouted at us. We sat, closely packed together, on the wagon floor. The train started and much time passed. We were very hungry and did not know where we were being taken.

The train arrived – we were at Auschwitz extermination camp, C Lager. A selection took place between two tall electrified fences amid constant shouts of: 'Schnell!' I was twelve years old but, when asked how old I was, I said 'thirteen'. I am sure that was why I was allowed into the camp. I learned many years later thirteen was the lowest age limit. Anyone younger was steered to the right which meant death. The person who decided whether you went to the right or the left was Dr Josef Mengele. Because I lied about my age, I am the youngest survivor of this side of the Auschwitz concentration camp.

We were made to go into a large room full of overhead pipes with shower-heads at every junction; but no water came. Afterwards we were stripped naked and had our heads and bodies shaved. Some – not all – of us had a number tattooed on one arm. They gave us ragged 'dresses' to wear but no underwear and we became unrecognisable.

In total, there were thirty-two barracks set out in two rows facing each other across a long alley like street with two toilet blocks at the end. I was ordered to go to one of the barracks but did not go in and started searching for my mother. I was sure that she too had been sent to the left but could not pick her out among the many women. I shouted her name at each barrack door, but it was no use. Then I went to the toilet block where a large number of women were waiting to be told which barrack to go to. Here, at last, I found her – we hardly recognised each other.

Over the next period of time, somehow I managed to survive, escaping the selection 'to the right' time after time. We were in Auschwitz until 3rd November when the camp was partly emptied. Of the 32,000 women who had arrived with us in C lager, only a few hundred were left. All the Hungarian women were sent to Mauthausen labour camp in Austria. Here we were each allotted a pair of lace-up boots with wooden soles and a uniform which was like a pair of striped pyjamas and still no underwear. We had to walk a long way to work each day in wooden clogs. We were in groups, each sent to do different work. My mother's group had to clear autumn leaves from the railway lines and, later, snow but were not given any warmer clothing.

I was in a group working in a large factory using machinery to make large bales filled with cotton wool. I worked long hours, whether on day shift or night shift, and then had a fast forty-five minute walk back to camp. We could never sit down. We had no knowledge of time, date or day – only cold and snow, four months of winter. We had only our canvas striped uniforms to keep us warm. We never talked about our work, or conditions. My mother told me that her group of women was working outside, clearing snow, without any extra clothing.

We were getting fewer and fewer in numbers. We naively believed that the missing people had been taken to other camps, perhaps better one, because one of the women who spoke German said that she had heard the guards discussing this between themselves. It was just as well that we did not know how they died.

On 11 January 1945 five women did not come back from work; one of them was my mother. It was just two days before my 13th birthday. I was too unwell to go to work and the other women told me that one day we would go home and meet the rest of our families and find out where they had been.

On 5th May 1945 there were only a few of us left in the camp; the Germans and their Alsatian dogs had gone. We saw American soldiers coming in at the gate which had been left open. Just inside the gates they stopped. Some of them even stepped back. Their faces register deep shock. One explained that they would organise transport to take us somewhere. We could see some of the soldiers wiping their eyes. They left. They did not come near us, only stood there just inside the gates. They seemed almost afraid of us, petrified by the sight we present, creatures hardly recognisable as women.

I was sent back to Hungary where I was immediately taken into hospital. One day I had a visitor. Margit, my grandmother's former housekeeper had traced me to the hospital. We both burst into tears. When the troubles had started, my grandmother had advised her to find a safer household. Margit had refused explaining that having no family of her own, she considered us her family and she wanted to stay and help us. Since she was a Catholic, she could do the shopping for us in safety. She had stayed with us until we had been forced into the ghetto. Now, with the war over, she had spent the last six months looking at lists of survivors. Of my family, she had been unable to find anyone else besides me and my father who was in another hospital having survived Bergen-Belsen. She had managed to save some family photos which she gave to me together with a bar of soap which was in short supply.

The news of my tremendous loss was so hard to accept that I was crying all the time. I adored my mother and would not accept the fact that she would not come back. I wanted to believe that she was alive, somewhere... I had to be given some tranquillisers. For two whole months I could not stop crying until I took this medication.

When the day came for us to leave the hospital, doctors and nurses gave us what was thought at the time to be the best possible advice which I tried to follow until quite recently: "Your new life begins today. Never look back. Look forward and plan your life step by step."

We know better now. We know that you need to face up to your past and work it out of your system before you can build a mentally healthy future. So it was nearly fifty years before I looked back and began to research my past and to tell my story.

I only discovered in 1998, when my son went to Mauthausen Museum library to help me to write my story, what had become of my dear mother. She, with the other four women, was clearing snow at a railway junction in the early morning darkness when a high-speed train passed; the barrier had not been lowered.

Many of the dates and details of my experiences I only discovered through research done in 1998 for my book, Klara's Story.

ABRAHAM POLLACK

Who Else Had Survived?

I was born to strictly Orthodox Jewish parents who observed shabbat and all festivals. We lived in Nagyvarad, a large market town in Transylvania. This area, which came under Hungarian rule, held a large Jewish population. There were all denominations among us, from Liberal to Orthodox. Our family was part of the Wiznitze Kehilla. My brother was a student in the Yeshiva, and I might have followed him, had Nazism not changed our lifestyle in the 1930s.

Because of severe economic hardship affecting our family, two of my sisters went to Budapest to seek work. Their meagre income helped towards the maintenance of the children at home. I was the youngest of five children, three girls and two boys. My two sisters who lived in Budapest, were either deported to Auschwitz or murdered in Hungary in 1944. In those chaotic years, no communication was possible and no record or information became available after the war. Their dedication to the family's welfare, and their vigilance over me, will always shine as a beacon in my life.

We lived close to the synagogue which eventually became surrounded and part of the ghetto. It would serve as a springboard for further deportation, but not before gross cruelty emaciated the poor victims. My own father's beard was torn off by one of the sadistic fascists. We suffered starvation while in the ghetto, and the future looked hopeless. We were waiting to be included in the 'resettlement programme' which was, in reality, extermination in Auschwitz where both my dear parents were gassed.

I desperately wanted to join the Jewish labour battalion to escape the misery of ghetto existence. Many were refused because of age, but I was fortunate in having my name called out one morning. There were thousands of Jewish men in the labour camps when I arrived.

The setting up of the labour camps was the initiative of General Revitzki who, fully aware of what awaited the Hungarian Jews, conceived the idea that volunteer labour could be used to repair roads and farms; but its main purpose was to save lives from Nazi brutality. Everyone was anxious to join. Youngsters, including myself, gave ourselves an older age to be eligible. We worked on farms, and repaired bombed railroads. However, eventually the SS took charge and life became hazardous in the extreme.

There was routine shooting at us. Those who survived were shipped to Mauthausen. A few lucky ones, including myself, survived the bestial treatment by the SS in Mauthausen and Gunzkirchen.

On liberation by the American Army, the few survivors needed medical care. I was hospitalised in Linz, and when I felt stronger, I began my search for my family. I managed to join up with Russian troops. We believed that they would help us to get back to Hungary. However, lack of clear communication deluded us, and we soon discovered that we were destined for Siberia. We quickly escaped during the night, and boarded trains when we could. We had neither money nor passports. We discovered that Nagyvarad had reverted to being Romanian territory.

My one surviving sister and brother were at 'home', waiting to see who else had survived. We soon realised that nobody else would return. 'Home' in Nagyvarad became meaningless. Soon after came the realisation that, if we were to have a future, we had to begin anew, and so we all left.

I was 17 years old at the end of 1945, and burdened with the most traumatic life experiences. I parted from my sister and brother – both had married in the meantime. They, too, soon left. Where to and what possibilities might there be for us? We had little idea. With some luck and determination, I managed to get across borders to Belgium. I learned a skill there and worked until an assisted passage to Canada was offered. There I met my wife-to-be, and we raised a family of three lovely daughters. My own family provided me with a sense of purpose and brought happiness in my life.

I am often asked whether I have been able to come to terms with the cruelty suffered in my early childhood, and whether forgiveness is possible. Avenging the atrocities committed against my family and community, could not reinstate the innocent lives of the many children lost in my family alone. However, perpetuated hate has no place in my life which holds dear to welfare and love, not only for my own family, but for the society I live in. Surely, forgiveness for the Holocaust cannot be one of the pillars of civilised society. Justice, acceptance and tolerance are the chief aims I value.

She Had Not Recognised Him ...

The responsibility of recalling those terrible years of the late 1930's until 1944 weighs heavily on me. After all, I am now the only survivor of a family of some 50 members – uncles, aunts and their many children, whose names are now erased, but whose faces are permanently etched in my mind. My own parents: my dear mother Gisella was gassed on arrival in Auschwitz, my dear father was deported earlier from Felsögöd where we lived, and murdered in either Hungary, Poland or Germany. There are no graves, no death certificates, only another number included in the six million. My, now deceased, brother Laszlo was used in the Sonderkommando unit carrying the bodies from the gas chamber to the ovens. These memories haunted him all his life, and he did not need the number tattooed on his arm to remind him what had been forced upon him at the age of 15.

I, Zsuzsanna (Susan) was born in Felsögöd, Hungary, not far from Budapest, on the ninth of September 1930. We were observant Jews, who enjoyed the festivals. As a young child I was entrusted with taking our Passover food, the pure white matzos we ate, to the police station. Was this evidence required after the late 19th century blood libel case that shook the entire Jewish population, to convince the authorities of the purity of this crisp, white bread? Or was there an implicit meaning, in this annual pilgrimage, of what the future held for us? Anti-semitism did not begin in Hungary with the rise of Hitler in 1933. There were many home bred Hungarian fascists instigating racist laws and brutal attacks. My own brother was attacked and brutally beaten up with impunity. The Numerus Clausus law which prohibited Jews, beyond a small proportion, from entering colleges of further education, excluded him as well.

The tragedy that befell my family was, I suppose, reflected in the majority of the rural Hungarian Jewish communities. Most have perished; there are very few witnesses.

My late father Erno Blau often told us, his son and daughter, of his capture by the Russians during the First World War, and how he managed to escape via Omsk, Tomsk, Irkutsk and Vladivostok, back to Hungary. He was decorated for bravery, and he was very proud of this honour. The exhaustion and disease he suffered did not embitter his sense of loyalty to Hungary, as he proudly announced that he kissed the Hungarian soil on his return. I often wonder whether the memories of the blood-libel case in Tisza-Eszler in 1882 had not necessitated that deep commitment to the country of his birth, but then again, when the Nazi crisis shook the foundation of our existence, there were no other countries that offered asylum. We were certainly patriotic. In my local primary school I sang of the strong yearning to recapture the territories lost in the First World War.

We were well integrated into local community affairs. My parents were involved in many volunteer duties. How disillusioned my father must have felt when Admiral Miklos Horthy waged the 'white terror' against the Jews, in particular, after the short lived Kuhn regime. Time and again, the Jews were accused of surreptitiously installing a communist government, to subvert the economy. Anti-semitism grew stronger, and open racism found fertile ground in Hungary, some imported from Germany by the politicians.

In this environment I grew up with a sense of unease and open hostility when shouts of 'Jews go back to Palestine' were aimed at us. However, we were still a family together. We had a small coal and wood business which provided us with our livelihood. In 1942 all Jewish-owned shops had to close. Very few Gentiles would employ Jews, and the only available work for my father was carrying heavy loads on his back. By then, my father was a mature man for those times, but the family was still intact. However, when a summons was received by all Jewish households, for all men to attend a meeting concerning the welfare of the families, we feared the rumoured 'East resettlement plan' might be put into action. I clearly remember the doubts and hesitation expressed by my father and the other heads of families. They decided that, to safeguard the families, they must appear the following day. A short time later, we were all asked to come and say goodbye. There, on the lorries, they were brutally beaten up, taken to an internment camp in Hungary, or eventually transported to one of the camps scattered over Germany and Poland.

Closer to the time of our own deportation, wearing a yellow star did not allow us to use public transport. However, we managed to send a local Hungarian woman to the camp where the men were kept. She was able to hand to my father the little basket of food she took with her. She had not recognised him at first. 'Just as well you did not see your husband,' the woman told my mother, 'he was not the same person'.

We knew then that we were doomed. There was no escape, nowhere to hide, no passports, no visas, no support. We were the very last group of Jews in Europe to be sent to Auschwitz where, on arrival, my mother was gassed. As I said, my brother, 15 years old at the time, was used to clear out the gas chambers in Auschwitz and Treblinka. A year's suffering in various camps, destroyed most of us, Hungarian Jews.

I was then thirteen years old and reasonably well developed, still of some use for slave labour. Hence, I was selected in Auschwitz and consigned to swell the numbers made to walk on one of the many 'death marches' to Bergen-Belsen, as part of the Nazi genocide. I was liberated in Bergen-Belsen. The physical and emotional recovery took many years.

I have been fortunate in that I was able to have my own children who instilled a sense of purpose and joy in my life, and my husband, also a survivor, whose love and understanding helped create a stable home environment.

WLODKA BLIT ROBERTSON

Surviving In Warsaw –
My Wartime Experiences

My twin sister Nelly and I were born in Warsaw in 1931. In August 1939 we were with my parents on holiday in the Polish mountains near Zakopane. Rumours of a German invasion meant that we had to cut short our holiday and hurry home to Warsaw where we lived in a small apartment. Within days war broke out, and Warsaw was subjected to incendiary bomb raids.

My parents decided that they had to leave Warsaw because of their known political activities. My father was a leading member of the Jewish socialist Bund organisation and my mother was headmistress of a Yiddish primary school and active in Poale Zion. They thought that taking young children on foot to the Russian frontier, along with thousands of other fleeing people, would be too dangerous. We were therefore left with our grandparents, aunts and uncles, and cousins Jerzy and Pavel aged fifteen and four. When my parents were leaving, my uncle Jakub cried; I knew then that awful things were happening.

Then, following the Russo-German pact, Soviet troops invaded Poland from the east, and my parents found themselves in Russian-occupied Poland. My mother managed to smuggle herself back to Warsaw to be with us. My father, Lucjan Blit, also tried to get back to Warsaw to help with the underground organisation of the Bund. But he was caught by the Russians and imprisoned in a labour camp until 1942 when he was released and joined the Polish army (and eventually

147

came to England in 1943). After my mother's return to Warsaw we moved in with my paternal grandparents. They had a large apartment, but we all lived in one room because the winter of 1940 was very cold and fuel was in short supply.

As soon as the Germans occupied Warsaw they began issuing anti-Jewish laws. I remember being chased by gangs of Polish hooligans organised by the Germans. A high brick wall topped with barbed wire was constructed around a quarter of Warsaw which became the Ghetto. We had to move there. My mother's family, my grandparents, aunts and uncles and two cousins, already lived in that part of Warsaw, and we moved in with them. My father's parents found a room in another part of the Ghetto.

Conditions in the Ghetto were appalling – random shootings, beatings, hostage-taking, typhus, overcrowding, homelessness, people dead from hunger in the streets. Hungry children used to snatch parcels from passers-by and immediately stuff the contents in their mouths, hoping that it was food. But there were also secret self-help committees, secret schools, secret libraries, synagogues and clandestine political organisations. My mother was in charge of one of the few soup kitchens for starving children. There I saw many of my school-friends swollen from hunger. My sister and I and our cousins spent most days playing with other children in our courtyard.

Then posters appeared in the Ghetto announcing the evacuation of everyone to 'work camps' somewhere in the east, with only those who were working for the Germans being exempted. We soon knew that these were in reality extermination camps. People were obviously terrified. My family built a bunker in the cellar with a hidden entry, and we used to run there and hide when the raids began. We could hear the Germans and Ukrainians shouting for everyone to assemble in the courtyard or be shot. My mother at first had exemption papers from the Jewish Council because of her work. But as we watched our neighbours being taken away, some quietly, some struggling, we understood that these bits of paper would not save us for long.

My grandfather gave away his small metal factory to the German industrialist Toebens, hoping to get in return some protection from the raids and some food for the family grown-ups who worked there. The factory repaired arms and mended helmets brought back from the Russian front.

More and more people were caught and taken in cattle trucks to the concentration and extermination camps, mainly to Treblinka which was near Warsaw. Occasionally someone would escape and tell terrible stories of gassings. We were told not to bother to take belongings with us if caught. We knew we would be killed.

My mother's family was still together. As the Ghetto was emptied, we moved to other abandoned apartments and our uncles and grandfather built other bunkers. My father's parents and sister had already been taken away to be murdered. Because of my parents' connection with the Jewish underground organisation ZOB through Poale Zion and the Bund, Michal Klepfisz, who was a Bundist courier on the Aryan side (outside the Ghetto) found a Polish Catholic family who for payment agreed to shelter my sister and myself in their home at great risk to themselves.

At night we were smuggled out of the Ghetto, climbing a ladder over the Ghetto wall. The policemen and Ukrainian soldiers were bribed. Other people were smuggling food and arms at the same time. We were dressed in double clothes and told that we now had new documents and new names and were never to mention to anyone who we really were. The decision that we should leave the Ghetto was taken so quickly that I cannot remember saying goodbye properly to my family.

The Polish family Dubiel were kind to us and very devoted to Michael Klepfish whom they knew from before the war. From the window of their apartment we could see over the Ghetto wall and often our mother would come in the evenings and walk discreetly on the other side of the wall. For a short time Michal Klepfisz shared the same apartment and talked to us about his smuggling of arms into the Ghetto and making incendiary bottles for the Jewish underground.

Five weeks after we escaped, during the Passover and Easter

holidays of 1943, German and Ukrainian troops surrounded the Ghetto and entered supported by tanks. They started systematically setting fire to buildings with petrol and flares. I saw people shot whilst trying to escape with their clothes burning. Everyone outside the Ghetto knew of the armed Jewish resistance which was maintained for four weeks. Michael Klepfisz fought in the Ghetto and died there. The Dubiels became afraid to keep two Jewish-looking children, and I was taken by Wladka Mead – another Bundist courier – to a railwayman's family outside Warsaw. When that did not work out, because of the hostility of their daughter, I went back to Warsaw to a caretaker's family called Serafin. Here the young husband became drunk and violent almost every day on home-distilled vodka, and often beat his wife. I was frightened of him but he never harmed me or their small daughter.

In the street I was often recognised as a Jew, usually by taunting teenagers, and had to run away. Wladka Mead normally came to pay for me once a month, and I waited impatiently for her visits as I had no contact with anyone else I knew, except for occasionally meeting my sister secretly in the street.

I was excited when the Polish Warsaw uprising began in September 1944 but knew that it was still very dangerous to be recognised as a Jew. The Germans were obviously on the run now, and we could hear the Russian artillery getting nearer. However, the uprising was put down after heavy bombing, and the Germans evacuated Warsaw of all its remaining inhabitants. The Serafins and I were put on a train, but managed to jump off when it slowed down, and went to a village where the Serafins had distant relatives. There we were sheltered by very poor and hungry peasants who lived without electricity or running water. They guessed that I was Jewish, and often made anti-semitic remarks, but treated me not that much worse than their own children. They were never paid by anyone.

By chance Wladka who had also escaped from Warsaw, met the Serafins in the small market town near my village. She could not offer money because the contact with the underground was now broken. I hoped that she would come and collect me when the war ended.

When the Russian soldiers finally arrived, I thought I was the only Jew left in Poland apart from Wladka. For some weeks no one came, and I felt completely helpless. The Serafin family and I eventually set out that winter to walk back to the ruins of Warsaw. My only footwear was a pair of torn sandals. We found a habitable room but, without proper shoes, I could not go out. At the same time, my sister Nelly came back to Warsaw from another village. She was still with Mrs Dubiel and together they found a Jewish committee set up to help survivors. There she recognised Wladka, and soon another underground Jewish courier, Ala Margolis (wife of Marek Edelman, one of the surviving leaders of the Ghetto uprising), came to look for me.

So I was reunited with my sister, and later – miraculously –with my two young cousins. I did not know that they had escaped from the Ghetto through the sewers just a few days before the liquidation of the Ghetto. In 1946, aged 14, my sister and I came to London to join our father. It felt strange to meet him again after those terrible six years. Strangely, we hardly talked about what happened.

The rest of my family whom we left behind in the Ghetto, were all murdered. They were my grandparents Mordechai and Lea Herclich, Fela and Wolf Blit, my aunt Pola Blit, my young aunt Bella and her fiancé Jozef, my aunt and uncle Gucia and Jakub Felenbok who looked after the children of the family so selflessly, uncle Leon and aunt Niusia Herclich who had the means to escape but would not abandon their parents, and my mother Fela Herclich Blit, who tried to help the starving children in the Ghetto, and is praised for it by Professor E.Ringenblum in his diaries *The Chronicles of the Warsaw Ghetto*.

A Family Apart

My passport identifies me as Joan Frances Salter, British citizen. I have had this persona for so long that in my everyday life I never think twice about it. Indeed there is nothing to distinguish me from my fellow Londoners. Nothing except for a slight inflection in my voice which no-one can quite place. Because of my fair skin, deep-blue eyes and once very dark hair, some assume I am Irish while others place my accent as West Country. In fact it is the now faint remnant of an American accent. Only that is not my country of origin, but that of a child named Joan Farell.

Hidden away in the jumble of my filing cabinet is a file marked Certificates: Birth, Death, Marriage, Insurance etc. Inside is a green certificate written in French bearing the title and seal *Ville de Bruxelles*. It states that a daughter, Fanny, was born to Jakob Zimetbaum (born in Zabno, Poland) and to Sprynca nee Perleman (born in Warsaw, Russia) in Brussels on February 15, 1940. This is my birth certificate. Although Warsaw was in Russia when my mother was born there at the beginning of the last century, by the time I was born it was in Poland. Today Poland is part of the European Community, its citizens free to travel and live all over Western Europe, but times were very different then. Indeed had I been issued with a Polish passport at the time of my birth, it would have identified me not as Polish, but as a child of Jewish or Hebrew nationality. With this, the only journey I would have been entitled to make, would have taken me direct to a concentration camp.

When the Germans invaded Belgium on May 10, 1940, one of their first acts was to round up all male aliens over the age of 15. I was barely three months old when Jakob, my father, was deported. At the time, Germany was busy moving troops down into France and the logistics of supplying an invading army meant that diverting resources to the deportation of the Jews was given low priority. So, instead of being sent straight to the 'East' as the camps were euphemistically described, Jakob was taken over the border into France and interned first in an ordinary French prison in *Angouleme* and subsequently in another prison, in Bordeaux. The previous occupants of these prisons were, no doubt, freed to commit more of the crimes for which they had been convicted, in order to facilitate the incarceration of those deemed to have committed the worst crime of all: being born Jews.

Jakob languished in prison for approximately six months before being put on a train with a group of fellow Polish Jews, bound for a camp in the East. It was an ordinary train, and although they were in a separate carriage from 'normal' travellers, they were guarded by only a handful of young German soldiers, who soon settled into a game of cards. Jakob tried to persuade some of his friends that their best bet was to slip out unseen and jump off the train as it slowed down approaching Paris. But they thought he was just making trouble. 'Why endanger yourself? A labour camp is better than being on the streets without papers!' So Jakob slipped away quietly by himself and jumped. He lay on the tracks watching the train move painfully slowly away, expecting it to squeal to a halt when the others alerted the guards. The lives of his companions would be safer if they informed on him. But surprisingly the train continued on its way. Whether their destination was a labour camp or not, it is unlikely, ultimately, that any of his fellow deportees survived.

Before moving to Belgium Jakob had lived in Paris for many years. His journey from the family home in Tarnow, South East Poland, to Western Europe started in 1920. His father, my grandfather, was a very tolerant man, but he had run out of patience with his second son who preferred playing cards to working in the family-run garment factory. So aged seventeen, he was sent to Antwerp to be apprenticed to a distant cousin as a trainee gemstone cutter. This apprenticeship didn't suit him at all. For one thing the cousin was ultra-Orthodox and the day was punctuated by frequent prayers and by punctilious adherence to the minutiae of religious observance. Although Jakob's ideology diverged sharply from that of his younger siblings, both active in the Communist Party, he shared their non-religious outlook. So to him prohibitions like not smoking on the Sabbath were clearly meant to be broken. His other problem was with the long hours he was expected to work. After about six months he decided he knew all he needed to know about precious stones and moved on, causing yet another rift with his parents.

After leaving the diamond cutting business in Antwerp, Jakob settled in Paris, first as a gemstone salesman. He found the nightclubs and casinos a good source of income. He always had something in his pocket to offer a man on a winning streak for the attractive lady on his arm. And his prices always were wholesale! A gregarious, flamboyant personality, Jakob's entrepreneurial skills enabled him to diversify, and he took to attending fashion shows put on by the Paris couture houses to make surreptitious copies of their designs. By then he had again made peace with his parents, and would make regular trips back to the family business in Tarnow, returning to Paris with a consignment of 'ready to wear' clothing. At a time when only the wealthy had access to haute couture, the sale of these stylish copies made it a very profitable business.

By the 1930's Jakob had become a very rich man with a wide circle of friends. Their lives were a continual round of social events. In 1937, still a bachelor, he met my mother who was known by her Polish name, Bronia. Though only in her mid-thirties, she had already known much sorrow. In 1932 she was 28 and still living in her parents' home in Warsaw, when a marriage had been arranged for her, after which she moved to Paris with her new husband. The seventh of eight children, most of whom had also moved to Paris, Bronia adapted happily to her new life. But her first child, born in 1933, died only a few months old, and, while she was pregnant with her second, my half-sister Liliane, her husband died of tuberculosis. Two of her older sisters, themselves already grandmothers, took her under their wing, and she stayed on in Paris with her baby daughter. Aged thirty-three she met Jakob. She was a very attractive woman and romance blossomed, though her sisters opposed the match. Both sisters were married to professional men, and considered themselves quite genteel; Jakob and his entrepreneurial ways seemed very déclassé to them.

In February 1938, my parents travelled to Tarnow to be married. The celebrations were nearly spoilt when my grandmother and an extremely religious aunt accompanied my mother to the *mikvah*. This ritual was essential for the majority of Jewish brides at that time and meant purification by total immersion. So assimilated was my mother that she had never heard of it, and thinking they were trying to drown her she fought against the dunking. After this slight hiccup, the marriage went ahead, festivities lasting seven days as tradition demanded. The newly-weds had planned to travel to Vienna, but delayed their departure to stay with Jakob's family for the festival of *Purim*. This was the first of many strokes of luck with which they were blessed: on March 11th, the first detachment of German troops crossed the Austrian border. Had they been in Vienna as they had planned, they would probably have been among the first deportees to the concentration camps.

Instead they were able to return to Paris and resume their society life. Photographs of them taken at this time show a very attractive, cosmopolitan couple. But in spite of their virtual assimilation, the shadow of Nazism increasingly blighted their lives. Non-Jewish friends, with whom they had previously shared their social life, became ever more reluctant to be seen with them in public, simply out of fear. Nazis were everywhere and there was a growing expectation that Germany would soon invade France. Being seen with Jewish friends was tantamount to having your card marked.

Jakob thought the Germans would not bother with Belgium, but would march straight on into France. So at the end of 1939, the family moved to Brussels where I was born a few months later.

Before leaving Paris, Jakob converted all his wealth into easily negotiable currency, mainly gold coins, jewellery and precious stones. He squirreled away small caches of them in a number of places: in an unsuspecting friend's cistern, under floorboards, even under a churchyard headstone. The rest he carried to Belgium. When he jumped from the train in 1941, he headed for the churchyard and retrieved his nest-egg.

As an escaped Jew without papers, he was in grave danger on the streets of Paris. But he had other resources which helped him to survive these dangers. One of his greatest strengths was his ability to merge into any environment, and he had always had an eclectic group of friends. As long as he could play a fair hand of cards, he was happy to spend time drinking with anyone. During the 1920's and 1930's, Jakob's sister Salle had attended many Socialist and Communist rallies in France and Belgium, and though their divergent political philosophies always embroiled them in heated arguments, they were close. Through Salle, he was introduced to young people who became stalwarts of the French and Belgian resistance movements. So with the combined benefit of his hidden jewels and his sister's contacts, he was able to get himself smuggled back into Belgium. But these were dangerous times. Brussels was a small city compared to Paris, and even if he stayed hidden in our apartment a chance remark by my seven-year old sister Liliane could endanger all our lives. My father decided it was safer for us to move to Paris.

My mother went to the authorities and explained she was unable to support herself and her two children since her husband had been deported, so she was seeking permission to travel to Paris to stay with her sisters. We were given the necessary travel permits. My mother hid her jewellery in my feeding bottles and we left Brussels by train to move into her elder sister's home.

Jakob had to travel clandestinely and it was several weeks before he arrived in Paris. My aunts considered him a danger to their families because he was effectively an escaped criminal, and they refused to have him in their homes. He stayed hidden with a cousin of his who had an apartment in Boulevard Voltaire in the *11e Arrondisement*. My aunts were so terrified that my mother would be putting the whole family at risk that she had to visit him in secret. Eventually she fell out with her sisters and moved into a small hotel in the *Place des Foires* run by a Madame Roux, a contact of my aunt Salle. By this time Salle had risen in the ranks of the Communist party. Somehow she had escaped the ruthless purges of the Polish Communist party and had gone to Russia as a party official.

During the night of June 22nd, 1941, my father woke up to a surprising silence. The window of his bedroom faced a busy road and although it was lighter than in the daytime, there was always some traffic throughout the night. During his months in hiding, he had whiled away his time, playing cards and sharing a drink or two with the concierge. So now he woke him up and asked him to find out if anything was going on. The man came back with bad news. The road was blocked and army trucks were moving from house to house rounding up the Jews. Jakob's cousin, a French national, was certain the only danger he personally faced was to be discovered harbouring Jakob. Therefore, he ordered him to leave immediately. My father, always a fast thinker, pointed out that if he was caught without papers, he would be tortured into telling who had hidden him and the truth would be out. Accepting the reality of this risk, his cousin reluctantly agreed to Jakob's plan. Passing over a few brightly coloured gemstones, Jakob asked the concierge to board up the door, the custom when families left the city for their summer vacations. 'When the soldiers come, tell them that M. Ada had left earlier that night to join his family in the country.'

The two men hid under the bed waiting for the lorry pulling up outside their block. They listened as the soldiers knocked on the door of the apartment below and heard someone being escorted away. Their knees knocking and their teeth chattering, they heard the soldiers return and head for their apartment. They had no confidence that the porter would put his own life at risk for them, but to their surprise they heard him turning the soldiers away. When, later that afternoon, my mother made her usual visit, the concierge intercepted her and told her what had happened. Through her landlady, Madam Roux, arrangements were made for all of us to be smuggled out the next morning. It has become such a cliché, the laundry van smuggling out potential victims under the noses of the Gestapo, but that's exactly how it happened.

We joined Jakob and his cousin at a 'safe' farm on the outskirts of Paris. The cousin was still certain he was in no personal danger, so he joined his family at their summer home. Jakob felt that it was much too risky for us all to travel together to the unoccupied part of France, and at that time it was still unthinkable that women and children would be deported. He acquired false papers and travelled by train towards unoccupied Vichy France while we returned to Paris. Fifteen miles before the boundary between occupied and unoccupied France he got off the train and walked over fields and hills unnoticed. In July 1941 he arrived safely in Lyon.

Each week my mother took us to the local police station for the required registration of aliens. This took place in a small room manned always by the same two policemen: one a kindly young man, the other known for his hostility and rudeness towards foreigners. One week in the summer of 1942, there was as usual a long queue for the 'nice' policeman, and as my mother was in a hurry she took her place in the shorter queue. My sister's demands to be picked up and for me to be put down resulted in the pair of us screaming at once, causing absolute fury from the man behind the desk. Terrified, my mother took us both outside and waited for hours until everyone else had registered. Then taking her place in front of the gentler of the two men, she announced our name: Zimetbaum. The policeman perused his list but insisted, in spite of my mother pointing to our names, that 'no, you are not on my list.' He turned to his senior officer and asked him to search in another room for another list. When he left the room, the friendly officer turned to my mother and warned her, 'Madam, tomorrow they are starting rounding up the women and children. Your name is on that list. If you have anywhere to hide, go.'

Frantic my mother returned to the boarding house. Again Madame Roux arranged for us to be collected by the Resistance. The van turned up at 5 am, an hour before expected. It is a measure of my mother's innocence, that in spite of everything, she insisted on taking the time to wake us gently and to give us breakfast before the journey. She was told in no uncertain terms that either she bundled us into the back of the laundry van immediately, or they would go without us. Miraculously, we were safely smuggled over the occupation border into Vichy France. Madame Roux wrote later to say that the Gestapo had turned up for us at 5:50 am; little more than half-an-hour stood between our life and death.

The first round up of women and children in Paris is well documented. They were initially kept in a sports' stadium for several days in blistering heat with inadequate sanitation, no shade and virtually no food or water. By the time transport had been arranged to the internment camp at Gurs, many were dead, dying or seriously ill. The conditions at Gurs were little better and those who survived were soon deported to camps in the East. There is little doubt that at barely two-years-old, I would not have survived.

We joined my father, Jakob, in a little village near Lyon. But despite the Vichy Government's stated 'independence', Nazi influence was increasing and internments had started. Jakob was rounded up and taken to a camp near Annecy. Here he spent each day working with other Jews building a railway track intended to transport them to the concentration camps as soon as the Nazis occupied the whole of France. In his usual way, my father played cards with his guards who were Corsicans and sympathised with their complaints of being treated as second-hand citizens by the French. We were allowed to visit at the perimeter fence and bring food to the prisoners. At my father's instructions, my mother smuggled in a few of their remaining jewels. Uncertain as to how much trust he could put in them, Jakob passed these on to his Corsican 'friends'. They helped him to escape and he was taken by motorbike to Perpignan, at the foot of the Pyrenees.

Dressed roughly, like any other French worker, Jakob sat in a cafe, drinking coffee and smoking cigarettes, studying the activities of what were clearly groups of refugees bartering with locals to take them to safety over the mountains into Spain. He stayed in the shadows and witnessed the 'guides' returning and bragging to their friends how they had stripped the Jews of their possessions before turning them in. This was clearly not a place to trust anyone, so Jakob headed off to a small town further along the base of the Pyrenees – I believe it was St-Girons - where he found someone prepared to take him over the mountains and across the border into Spain. In fact the guide took him down as far as Barcelona where the Quakers, acting as agents for the Joint Distribution Committee, were supplying food and shelter for the refugees. My father handed over virtually the last of his wealth to the guide as an advance payment for smuggling Bronia and the two children into Spain.

The Quakers advised him that he was still in danger, as all adult male Jews were being interned in a camp at the town of Miranda de Ebro, in anticipation of a German occupation of Spain. The only help they could give was to suggest that if he managed to get to Lisbon, as a Polish national he might be able to join the Polish Free Forces, by then part of the British Armed Forces. It seemed there was nothing for it but to head towards Portugal.

For several weeks Jakob hopped on and off trains, hiding in bushes and stealing what food he could. At Vigo he talked a friendly fisherman into smuggling him down the coast into Porto. From there he made his way down to Lisbon and the British Embassy. Diplomats advised him they could do nothing for him without proper documentation, including an exit visa, from his own Embassy. Jakob, by now a discouraged and broken man, turned up at the Polish Embassy. As Vichy had fallen and we had not turned up in Spain, he assumed that we had been deported to the camps. Three years of running and hiding like a sewer rat had taken its toll on his health and his wealth, but far more importantly, on his spirit. He was a penniless Jew in a hostile world.

Jakob had no illusions about the attitudes of his fellow countrymen towards a Jew. Frankly, he no longer cared what happened to him. He was ushered into an interview room followed by an official who sat at the opposite side of the table. Jakob did not raise his eyes from the ground. 'Name?' the official asked. 'Isaac Jakob Zimetbaum,' he replied. Home address '20 *Urszulifska, Tarnow.*' There was a silence. The man spoke again. 'You're Jerry Zimetbaum's brother, aren't you?' The voice was friendly. Amazed, my father looked up. Sitting opposite him was the son of Tarnow's Chief of Police. He and my uncle, Jakob's oldest brother, had been close childhood friends. Many a time the three of them had played truant together, to enjoy a clandestine game of cards. So my father received the necessary documents to enable him to return to the British Embassy.

On January 1st 1943, my father arrived in Gibraltar. From there a troopship carried him to Scotland. In London he informed the relevant officials that he had no wish to join the Polish Free Forces because he believed them to be as anti-Semitic as the Nazis. Instead he was drafted into the Pioneer Corps and spent the rest of the war in England.

And what became of us? True to his word, the guide had returned for us and after Vichy fell, sometime in the winter of 1942/1943, we made the hazardous journey across the mountains. We were captured at the border – but luckily it was by the Spanish police. My sister was put into a convent and I was allowed to stay with my mother in prison in Figueres. Although history puts Spain politically in the Fascist camp, everyone I know who was a refugee there – my mother included – spoke highly of the Spanish people and their kindness. The guards allowed the children to wander freely, and local people brought my mother food and cigarettes. This was a very kind and generous gesture, given that their own people were suffering appalling food shortages. Moreover, it was expected that the Spanish would be suffering German occupation themselves within weeks, with all the consequences that having helped Jews could bring down on them.

In June 1943, I was put on a boat from Lisbon to the United

States of America. When the deportations started in France, Polish parents whose children had been born in France were offered the choice of either taking their children with them or of leaving them behind. Approximately 5000 children were being kept in children's villages in unoccupied France, and pressure was applied to the Americans to give visas for these 'orphans'. The Vichy government promised safe passage for the children and that they would be allowed to exit France under the care of the Red Cross. A relief team left the USA in November 1942 headed for the neutral port of Lisbon with visas for 500 children. When their ship arrived in Lisbon, Vichy France had fallen and the majority of the children remained trapped by the German occupation.

The Americans bringing the visas were informed that approximately 100 child refugees had managed to reach Spain and Portugal. As it was expected that Spain would shortly be occupied, it was agreed to allow these children to travel on the visas and those in Spain were transferred into the care of the Portuguese Red Cross. Although a handful of children – like me – were not orphans, no such concessions were given for our parents. Indeed the U.S. authorities made it clear that the children's entry to the USA was only a temporary measure. Parents were given the opportunity of sending their children to safety in anticipation of Spain's occupation and their likely deportation and that the children were not to be seen as 'anchors' to enable their surviving relatives to gain entry to the USA at a later date. I can only guess at what my mother must have felt as she agreed to let us go while she remained in Europe.

Our sea voyage was not without danger. Though she was flying the flag of a neutral country, our ship, the Serpa Pinto, was stopped by a German submarine which surfaced silently beside her: a vast grey shape with an enormous logo on its fin. Our ship was boarded and one of the older children remembers hearing a splash. As we stood, silent and terrified on deck, the submariners returned to their ship which rapidly submerged and vanished. The Serpa Pinto continued safely across the Atlantic; one person on board, the cook, had disappeared.

On arrival in the USA we had health checks and were sent to an orphanage. My sister, Liliane was thought to have tuberculosis, later correctly diagnosed as pneumonia. She was sent immediately to hospital where she stayed for a long time. A report at the time notes that I was the youngest child the local Committee had received into their care. 'Fanny is a very winsome little girl, lovable and responsive and is well developed physically and mentally who speaks flawless French'.

Dr and Mrs Farell, a local physician and his wife, became my foster parents. Another report concerning me from the U.S. Committee for the Care of European Children to its Field Staff states: 'This little girl walked into the arms of her foster parents and has a very secure place in their affections. The foster parents are middle class people living in a suburban community and have fine standards of living. Fanny fits into such a home, whereas Liliane has to strive very hard to meet their standards.' A report of an interview with my mother in Barcelona includes the comment: 'Mrs Z. makes an excellent impression. Although obviously very much moved by news of her children, she was restrained and intelligent in speaking of them.' Hysteria, tears and emotion were given short shrift in those days. The as-yet-unrecognised Post-Traumatic Stress Disorder would also have been dismissed. Gratitude, acceptance, and a smile was what was expected of us.

I was young enough to adapt to my new life, but my sister, like many of the older children, was too traumatised to be able to cope with the expectations placed on her. She was first returned to the orphanage as being 'unmanageable' and subsequently passed onto a series of foster homes. My name was changed to Joan, my language from French to American. Over the next few years, little Polish Fanny Zimetbaum morphed into all American Joan Farell.

But then the war ended. It took the refugee agencies time to locate splintered families and to untangle the bureaucratic demands necessary to unite them. It was not until 1947 that I was reunited with my parents in London. This might seem like the 'fairytale ending' but it was anything but. I remember being taken onto the plane by the man I regarded as my father. He settled me into my seat, told me to be a good girl and kissed me goodbye. He then returned to the tarmac and stood waving until the plane took off. I looked down at the document he had put into my hand. It had my picture on it and identified me as Fanny Zimetbaum, Stateless Person. What on earth was that about? People had tried to explain this to me, but how much meaning could this concept have for a seven-year-old? As far as I was concerned, I was Joan Farell and this was the person I wanted to be. The last thing on earth I wanted was to be a refugee.

When I met my parents things were no better. Both of them were severely traumatised – I think beyond any possibility of recovery – by what they had lived through in the preceding seven years. To me, looking through the eyes of a child, their behaviour seemed irrational, incomprehensible. My mother was the sole survivor of her family. Her parents, her seven siblings, their spouses, their children had all perished. Even my aunts' grandchildren whose toys I had shared, were dead. The only trace of their lives survives as a handful of sepia photographs which my mother carried with her on all her journeying. Of my father's family only one sister survived, as she was in Russia, a member of the Communist Party. His parents, two brothers and their families all died in the camps.

My parents were broken in health, spirit and mind. They were working all hours of the day and night to try and pick up the pieces of their lives, and were ill-equipped to deal with the return of their angry and alienated children. I spent the next ten years shuttling between my two families, becoming more and more confused as to who I really was. Nobody's adolescence is easy; mine was a nightmare. I would stand for hours by the window watching passers-by. All I wanted to be 'normal' like them.

In 1956, I was offered the opportunity of studying at a college for Youth Workers in Israel. I jumped at the chance to get away from the never-ending tug-of-war between my two families, my two personae. Israel itself meant very little to me; it could have been China for all I cared. I had very little affection for my Jewishness. Everything terrible which had ever happened to me was because of it and I certainly was no Zionist. In America, at the Reform Synagogue we attended, I was taught that I was an American of Jewish faith. In England, at the ultra-Orthodox school my parents sent me to, more out of an intense fear of the outside world than any religious inclinations, we were taught that it was only when we were redeemed by the Messiah would we be returned to the land of Israel. Until such time it was not for us to take matters into our hands. The Anglo-Jewish Community were grappling with the hostility the British Mandate in Palestine had brought down on them and, in the main, were leaning over backwards to identify as being British and to play down their Jewishness. In fact, I was the first candidate from the AJY – at that time a strongly non-Zionist Youth Organisation – to go on the course.

We sailed from Marseilles in January 1957 on a rickety old ship. The passengers were an oddly assorted bunch, many of them refugees. These were the dregs of European Jewry who, more than a decade after the liberation of the concentration camps, still remained in Displaced Persons' camps waiting to be offered a permanent home. There was an amazing hotchpotch of languages and cultures. I became friends with a group of young and very secular Israelis. We steadfastly stayed sitting down as the blessing was said over the Friday night candles, arms folded across our chests and ignoring hostile demands to show respect for the Sabbath.

On the morning of our final day an excited wave of emotion rippled through the ship. Not understanding a word, I followed the others up onto the deck. There, just coming into view over the horizon, were the green hills of Haifa, the golden dome of the Baha'i Temple reflecting the sun. Suddenly these brash young Israelis and the motley bunch of refugees all broke into spontaneous song: *Ha' Tikvah*. There were many tears; the refugees' knuckles white as they clung to the rail as if letting go would make the mirage vanish. It was a heart stopping sight, but I still could not identify with them. Then the Israelis joined hands, singing *Hinei Mah Tov* –how good it is for brothers to join together – pulling all the refugees into their circle as they danced round the deck in a spontaneous show of unity. To me it all seemed very strange and terribly un-British.

The year in Israel was important for me. The country, like me, was young and enthusiastic. It radiated idealism and great optimism for a future where all Jews would live in harmony, not only with fellow Jews but with their Arab neighbours.

I returned to England and married. My husband and I had two daughters and this became my family. At this stage of my life the past was truly another country I hardly remembered, let alone visited. Only when my daughters had grown up and my foster-father died, was I able to take the first tentative steps back into my origins. My birth parents were still living, and though my mother found the past too painful to revisit voluntarily, my father and I were at last able to find some peace in our relationship, in our travels back through his memories.

It was not only what he told me which recreated the past for me. I visited many countries and trawled through realms of archive material to find the documentation which verified the truth of his reminiscences. I researched the archives of the Friends' Service Committee (The Quakers) in Philadelphia, and the Joint Distribution Committee in New York. Among the papers I unearthed were the social workers' reports on my sister and me; a telegram reporting that the US Ambassador to Barcelona had refused me a visa because I did not have a passport; many original documents concerning the plight of children in France including a letter to the JOINT dated June 25th 1941 from Albert Einstein in his role as Honorary President of the OSE – the organisation in France which had responsibility for the care of the children – urging them to '...keep the problem of the evacuation of the refugee children in the forefront of your attention...' I was lucky enough to interview Irene Arnold who as a young lawyer had overseen the visas for these children and who had travelled with the first relief ship in November 1942. There also was, as my father had spoken, the evidence of the internment camp at Miranda de Ebro in Spain, of which very little had been reported. I found the ship's manifest of the Serpa Pinto which arrived in Philadelphia on June 22nd 1943. On this the name *Fanny Zimetbaum* is stamped: REFUGEE. The most poignant reminder of all from the past is a photograph I found at the Portuguese Red Cross archive. It is of a group of fourteen children; the trauma they have lived through etched on their faces. At the front is a skinny little girl of three-and-a-half. This is Fanny Zimetbaum – the child I once was.

I found no records of what happened to my parents' families. When, post war, my aunt returned to Poland from Russia, no-one from the family was at their home. Despite registering with all the agencies, no contact has ever been made. I can only assume that my father's parents and his brothers, along with all the other Tarnow Jews either died in the massacres in the town or nearby forest or were exterminated in Belzec in the spring of 1942.

I returned to Warsaw several years ago to try to find out about my maternal grandparents. The only documentation I could find was a pre-war telephone directory. There was the name and address of my mother's youngest brother, a paediatrician as she had told me. None of my mother's seven siblings, their children or grandchildren are known to have survived the Shoah. It is most likely that those of her family who remained in Warsaw, were murdered in Treblinka; those who lived in Paris, deported and perished in other camps. Her closest surviving relatives were an aunt and a handful of cousins who survived hidden in Paris.

Only now, sixty years on, am I able to open the door behind which I left Fanny, locked firmly away, for so many years. It would be comforting to think that no other mother would have to make the choices my mother did; no child would have to take the journeys that Fanny took. But you only have to turn on the news to know that the lessons of history are never learnt.

★ ★ ★

In 2005 I 'returned' to Tarnow. I use the term loosely. Born in Belgium in 1940, I had only visited before in my father's bitter-sweet memories. The town he had grown up in a lively family where he had lived in friendship with his Christian school friends. The safe place he had left as a young man to seek his fortune in first Belgium and then France. The secure place he had returned to frequently over the years, just barely escaping the Nazi invasion; the place where my grandparents, aunts, uncles and cousins had lived until their lives were extinguished. Post war he had been unable to return; now I felt it my duty as his proxy to return to pay homage to my ancestors; to bear witness that they had existed, to say Kaddish.

I had no idea what to expect. My first shock was on the hour journey by train from Krakow. Cattle trucks sat rusting in sidings. My first instinct was that they couldn't possibly be the same ones. Then logic said 'why not'. What does a railway do with redundant stock, no matter how horrendous its past.

At the hotel, I was warmly welcomed and handed a booklet: In The Footsteps of The Jews of Tarnow written by Adam Bartosz, the director of the Regional Museum in Tarnow. It was this which guided me through the streets as I, literally, walked in my father's footsteps. In the Plaza of 'The Auschwitz Prisoners' is a relief mural depicting the citizens of Tarnow (some but not all were Jews; all were considered political dissidents) being sent to Auschwitz in June 1940. These Tarnovian inmates, as they became known, were tattooed with the numbers 31 to 758, signifying there were amongst the first at this camp.

I look across to a magnificent Moresque style building where on June 13th 1940 these men were locked up before being forcibly transported. This building was erected in 1904 as the Jewish ritual bathhouse (mikvah). Another image of the history of this building comes into my head. On the eve of their wedding in February 1938, my mother had been brought here by my father's mother and aunt. My mother, originally from Warsaw, but having lived most of her adult life virtually assimilated in Paris, was completely unfamiliar with this ritual. As she was being totally immersed, thinking her new mother-in-law was trying to drown her, she had grasped at the two women by their hair, thereby removing their sheitles (wigs). Today the building is used as a retail outlet. How does one make sense of all these contradictory images?

Adam Bartosz could not have been more helpful. He hands me the key to the local cemetery. As I unlock the gate I notice I am not alone. In the distance someone is taking photographs. Much of the cemetery is overgrown with brambles and there is a work party clearing these. Later, I learn from Adam that these are local prisoners 'released' to do useful community work. I walk amongst the 4,000 tombstones looking in vain for a family name. But time and the wind have made this a thankless task. I stop in silent contemplation at the site marking the mass grave of the 3000 Jews shot in the cemetery in June 1942. The monument is a broken column excavated from the ruins of Tarnow's largest synagogue. At the top the inscription "And the sun was shining and it wasn't ashamed" At the base it commemorates: 25 Thousand Jews murdered by German Thugs between 11 June 1942 and 5 September 1942, are resting in this grave. There are no records of names, so I don't know if this, or the local woods or Belzec is the final 'resting' place of my family.

The next day I travel to Belzec. Started in November 1941, this camp was purely and simply a factory of death, the first to use stationary gas chambers. Here over a period of a few weeks in June 1942 the remaining 10,000 Jews of Tarnow were transported and taken straight from the trains to the 'showers'. In June 1943 the Nazis attempted to obliterate all traces of this camp even grinding the bones into dust. There remains no significant physical evidence or records of the people murdered here. The site is now marked by a huge mound of volcanic rock, surrounded by steps which each marks the date of a specific transport from individual towns and villages.

At the stone commemorating the transport from Tarnow, I light a candle and say Kaddish. In Jewish tradition only the men are permitted to say Kaddish. However from what I know of my paternal roots, it is a family of strong women, so if there were any ghosts with me on that day, I believe they would have approved and recognised me as one of their own. Before I leave I walk to the back of the site where some of the original trees still stand. I scoop up some of the leaf mould and place it in a plastic bottle.

Afterwards I travelled to Warsaw and onwards to Treblinka. There, alone, I walk through the monuments commemorating the murdered Jews. Again, there are no records of the individuals, only the places they came from. So I light a candle at the Warsaw stone and say Kaddish for my mother's family. Again I collect a handful of soil.

Back in England I visit the graves of my mother and father and tell them I have honoured our past and my heritage. I scatter the earth gathered from Poland over their graves. The souls of my ancestors are now left to rest in peace.

In June every year, The Regional Museum in Tarnow in co-operation with the Committee for the Protection of Monuments of Jewish Culture organises a week-long series of events to commemorate the fate of its Jews. I returned to Tarnow the following year to join in. The main event is held in the nearby Buczyna woods where about 6000 Tarnow Jews, including 800 children, were massacred in June 1942. A middle aged woman wearing a large Star of David joined us. Sadly she spoke only Polish, but by the universal language of hand gestures, we learnt that she is from Tarnow.

Surrounded by an Honour Guard of Cadets and children from local schools, Adam Bartosz leads a most moving ceremony which includes speeches by The local Bishop and The Israeli Ambassador, both emphasising that Jewish and Polish history with all its painful twists and turns are irrevocably entwined. A rabbi recites Kaddish. Later in the week, we join a Kletzmer concert held at the site of the oldest Tarnow synagogue. The original wooden building dating back to 1581 was replaced in the 17th C and it is the fire scarred bimah of this building which is the sole remainder of all the prayer houses and synagogues of this town. There must have been an audience of over 1000 local residents, with others hanging out of windows and balconies from the buildings in surrounding streets listening to these traditional haunting melodies, but only one - the same lady I met earlier in the week – wears a Star of David. Possibly there were others there of

Jewish descent, probably without any knowledge of the Jewish blood flowing through their veins. We tell the band how much their music had moved us. They humbly thank us, explaining that while the music was Jewish, they are not; an apt simile for the whole of post-Holocaust Poland.

A booklet and accompanying leaflet about the Jewish Cemetery has now been published. Amongst the photos of tombstones, there is one showing a woman standing before the monument placed at the site of the mass murder of ghetto Jews. In my distinctive black leather coat, with white collar and cuffs, it is irrefutably me.

Escape to Kazakhstan

In fond memory of my unforgettable father and all relatives who perished in that awful war with German Fascism and the ferocious Stalinist terror.

"I want you to be good." – I remember your words, Father, when I asked you to do my mathematics homework. I do not know if I have become 'good': I never lie, do not betray friends, live within my means and I work hard; I worked as a teacher for thirty-two years and never gave a single mark for a bribe. In Russia many colleagues boasted about this endemic bribery, but my pupils still write to me fondly today. We have raised a daughter, Valentina, who is now also a teacher in London, she is kind and good and I am now asking her to help me!

I am writing these recollections for her and her future children.

Your granny, my Mother Betia Naumovna Verkhovskaya (1911–2000) told me that she lived with her parents in the village Dobrolubovka in the Ukraine, in the pale of settlement. It was during the Civil War when White Russian bandits made pogroms and Red ones attacked the house and the small leather workshop where my grandparents worked. They had three children: your granny and her two brothers, David and Boris who perished during the War. Your granny Betia did not speak Russian until she was nine. She spoke Yiddish and Ukrainian. To give the children a decent education, the parents moved to Krivoy Rog, a small town, but their hopes were dashed by financial reforms in the country which rendered worthless the money that they had been paid for their home. This trickery left them without any money which caused grandfather's death soon after. My mother went to work at a stocking factory at 15 years of age. They lived in a cellar apartment. She met my father Isaac Alexandrovitch Okunev at an industrial construction site – they lived together in peace and understanding for twenty-two years. My father was born and grew up in the Ukrainian city of Dnepropetrovsk. His parents had passed away early and the children – Isaac and his three sisters, Anna, Vera and Masha – grew up in an orphanage. Later, Masha perished during the bombing of a hospital, Vera in Riga, and Anna was called up to build Konsomolsk-on-Amur, now a large city, when the Komsomol [1] issued an appeal for workers.

Isaac went into the army and remained a military man until the end of his life. For him, the war had begun earlier than for many others when he was posted to the Polish border. War clouds thickened and he sent Mother to Krivoy Rog for safety and, as it became clear later, on the last train. Those who did not believe that it was too dangerous to stay, fell victim to fate because the planes of the Fascists [2] had already started bombing, even before the 22nd June 1941, when the all-consuming war began for us.

I was born on 16th July 1941 and we needed to flee east immediately because the Germans were moving very quickly. Mother prepared Granny and seven-year-old Shurik (my brother) and with me – a babe in her arms – was not able to take anything, except documents. We left exactly as we were, with only clothes on our backs.

Where to run? And where to hide? At first they fled south to the Caucasus but Fascists were eager to take the oil reserves in Baku. Mamma decided to go north, only to discover that this too was impossible because of the evacuation of the administration and industrial plants. She said that we were lucky with the train which was only a freight train for carrying goods. The train was mercilessly bombed, often stopped with the sound of sirens and people had to run and hide in the gulleys. In these cramped and stinking conditions children began to fall ill and I contracted whooping cough. When I couldn't breathe, my brother Shurik cried and screamed for help. Men lifted me high in their outstretched arms above their heads – it was the only way to get some fresh air. Against all odds, I was saved by a miracle.

Where was the train heading? In those circumstances no one knew, but we eventually arrived in the capital of Kazakhstan, Alma Ata. The evacuation point gave the refugees a place in a former public canteen with thirty beds, one bed between two people. Mamma was with me and Granny with Shurik and I remember Mamma saying: "What happiness it is – to lie down on a clean bed at long last!". Later a small allotment was given to the refugees for a vegetable patch. The crop depended on water, but how could we get water? A Khazakh neighbour accepted tobacco from my Mother in exchange for building an "Arik", a small water channel.

The potatoes that grew reminded my Mother and my Brother of the time in Kazakhstan for the rest of their lives.

Extraordinarily, in that hell sometimes we got post. How was it possible? My Father learned of the birth of his daughter, me, while he was at the front. Though the uniforms, epaulettes and loyalties changed, there remained an unchangeable belief in the ultimate victory. My photographs always carried patriotic messages: "Dear Father, I wait for victory and for the moment when I will meet you. Do not forget my childhood. Defend my happiness!" Mother wrote on my behalf and Father replied on the front of the card, "Wait for me patiently and I shall return" (in the words of K. Symonov, a famous war correspondent and Russian poet).

The Ukraine was liberated in 1944, after three years of war. We returned, but everything was lost. We had to go to Dnepropetrovsk and stay with Dyadya (Uncle) Isaak whose surname was Brodsky. My Father returned from the war in the autumn of 1945. A noisy officer's voice but especially the metallic clatter of the boots when walking, put me under the bed out of sheer terror. I was so frightened that even the trophy of a hard-to-come-by chocolate bar could not draw me out! I am always touched by Mamma's small blood donor card. She gave blood for the wounded. What a gaunt face I see on her donor card photo, she was only

34 years old! I have faint memories of a nursery school where I went in Riga, a city that I fell in love with. Ominously, soldiers were being killed every day and I can still hear the screams of widows.

We moved south to Armavir, Krasnodar Region, the Caucasus, in 1953 – "Stalin's year". Even for me, a ten-year-old girl at the time, it was clear that this move was a sort of exile, a punishment. We ended up living in an unheated barrack with water outside, in the neighbour's garden. What had happened? A radio report brought us news of the Doctors' Plot in Moscow; who had been arrested, accused of treason and plans to poison Joseph Stalin. All were Jews; they were tortured to death and the Stalinist terror was launched. Jewish people lost their jobs and awaited the decision about their fate. We were among them. Father was dismissed from the army and he could not take this so he wrote letters to defend his rights, stressing that he had been awarded medals and citations, "The Order of the Red Star", "The Order of the Great Patriotic War, Second Category", "For Exceptional War Service:", "For Liberating Königsberg", "For the Victory over Germany in the Great Patriotic War.". He had been at the front line from the start of the war and had served for a total of about twenty-five years in the army. Only after Stalin's death, he was informed that he had permission to work an extra three months to be granted the war pension. Those who had been in the war counted two years for each one in service and they were supposed to get a war pension based on that. He needed to work an extra three months in order to receive the money. He was sent to Novocherkassk, near Rostov-on-Don. There, he had a heart attack and died in the army hospital on 11th July 1954. He was only 43 years old.

We did not know then that the threat of future anti-Semitism, and fear of openly fascist demonstrations would cause me to undertake radical measures to reach safety in England.

(1) Komsomol – the youth division of the Communist Party of the Soviet Union.
(2) Fascists – Soviet terminology for Nazism.

JACQUELINE SHELDON NÉE ANISFELD

Why had We been Brought Here?

My story as recounted by my older brother Marcel Anisfeld

I was born on 2nd May,1937 in a small town in Poland called Nowy Sacz in the area of Galicia near Krakow and very close to the Carpathian Mountains dividing the old Poland and the old Czechoslovakia.

My parents, whose names were Regina (née Laub) and Osjasz Anisfeld, had a son called Marcel (born on 17th September 1934). My parents were well off and lived in the centre of the town in a luxury flat. My father was a director of a local bank across the road from where we lived. He also had a wholesale and retail food business which he took over and ran from the age of 13 with his brother Motek, aged 14. Their parents both died at a very young age. The Anisfelds and the Laubs were large families and all lived in the area. Life was very good for us and although there was quite a lot of anti-semitism from the Polish people, we did not suffer from this as my father was very kind and very generous to the locals.

In September 1939 the Germans started marching into Poland and were getting very close to our town, so my parents decided to move east and travelled to Przemysl. The Germans arrived soon after us. We were not badly treated by them and I even remember a German officer offering some sweets to my mother for my brother and me. When the officer left my mother would not give us the sweets because she said they may be poisoned. There were very bad stories going around that the Germans were taking all adult men and sending them to labour camps.

We moved once again, further east, to a town called Lvov (the Germans called it Lemberg), which was under Russian occupation. We found things very difficult during this period. Food was very scarce and we had to queue for everything including bread. Some of our family, including my maternal grandmother who remained in their home town, wrote to us and told us that there were no shortages under the Germans and life went on normally. My father, as did many other people, put our names on a list to obtain a permit to travel back home to Nowy Sacz. This list was getting longer and longer, but no one was allowed to leave Lvov.

Some weeks later, in the middle of the night, we heard banging on the door of our flat. My father opened the door and there standing in front of him were two Russian soldiers with fixed bayonets. They screamed out orders "you have ten minutes to get down to the street". Other people on the same landing as us asked politely "where are we going?" and the answer was "you put your name on a list to go back to the Germans and now you are all going". By the time we got down to the freezing cold and dark street there were hundreds of people already there. We were marched to the railway station with very few belongings as we could not pack much in the ten minutes they gave us and we were afraid of being shot. At the station we were pushed into cattle trucks without any windows or seats. Again people kept asking where we were being taken, but this time there was no answer just screaming soldiers pushing and shoving the people into the carriages. The train with about twenty carriages soon left for an unknown destination. It stopped once a day and the doors were opened with a bucket of soup being placed inside for everyone to feed.

Days went by and we realised that we were not travelling back to Poland, but eastwards where the temperatures were lower and lower and the snow was deeper and deeper. Eventually after about six weeks we were told that we had arrived at our destination, a village in Siberia called Asino, in the district of Omsk. "Why had we been brought here?" we asked, and the answer was that we were considered to be German spies. We had supposedly learned all the Russian secrets while we were living in Lvov and wanted to pass these secrets and information onto the Germans. How ridiculous! – families with young children and babies and elderly parents all spying? At that time we hated the Russian regime, but we did not realise that, in fact, the Russians saved our lives by taking us away from the Germans and imprisoning us in the wilds of Siberia.

On arrival, we were marched from the station to the centre of the village where we were told to make ourselves as comfortable as possible in a large wooden communal hall. Hundreds of us all lay down on the hard floor without any seats or bedding. Within a few days of arriving we were told to cut down trees in order to build houses for the newly arrived prisoners – us. It was the middle of winter and it was Siberia, so one can imagine the situation. The snow was very often higher than the doors to the building and tunnels had to be dug for the men to leave for woodcutting. We were quite lucky with our food supply as my father was put in charge of the food distribution to all the people in our large group.

A few weeks later a number of wooden houses were finished; no heating, no lighting and no indoor toilet facilities, but one room, split by a hanging blanket for two families was our home for the next few months. I remember the other family who shared our room. They were a kind middle-aged couple by the name of Zalcwasser (translation – Saltwater). Mr Zalcwasser was a very knowledgeable engineer who fixed up various gadgets in our home to make our lives more bearable. He also taught my father who was then thirty-seven years old, how motor engines worked and how to drive them – not that we had any chance of owning a car.

A few months later we heard the news that Hitler had declared war on the Russians and that we were not considered enemies of the state any longer. We were allowed to leave Asino and to travel and settle in any part of Russia, but we could not leave the country. Most of us decided to travel to Uzbekhistan which borders Iran and Afghanistan. We chose to settle in an ancient city called Bukhara which is famous for its hand-made rugs. There was also a large Jewish Uzbekh population. One of these families gave us a room on the top of their large house. We had to climb about a hundred stairs from a large square courtyard onto a terrace with a room at the side. The Uzbekh family made us feel quite welcome although they did not want us as permanent guests. Who knew how long we would stay there and who knew how long the war would last? – no one.

Two of my mother's brothers and my grandfather Abraham settled in another town in Uzbekhistan called Samarkand. We were not allowed to travel to see one another. This part of Russia was mainly desert and the heat was unbearable. My father's brother, Motek, who had been taken away from his wife, Bronia, in Lvov to a labour camp in the Ural Mountains, found us and came to live with us. There was no news of his wife or her brother who we thought was taking care of her. She had lost her son, Monek, just before war had started, with meningitis for which, in those days, there was no cure.

My father, having been a businessman since early childhood with his brother, found a source of food. There were many hungry, growing children. My father's activities of buying and selling made him a 'spekuliant' (a speculator) which was in communist Russia one of the most serious crimes. Had he been caught he would have been thrown into jail for at least ten to fifteen years. My brother, Marcel, at the ripe old age of eight or nine, used to help my father carry some of the products to the buyer as it was safer than my father carrying things. My mother, whose father in Brzesko, in Poland, was one of the largest egg wholesalers and exporters, got a job in an egg-sorting government factory. Between them they could not earn sufficiently to support us all, so Marcel tried one or two things , as there was no school for us to attend. A couple of things that come to mind: Marcel woke up extremely early to buy one or two newspapers (which were in very short supply) and then went back home and sat outside our house on a street called Bibliotechnaya (Library Street), cut up the papers into small pieces and sold them to people for cigarette rolling as people used to make their own cigarettes with the local tobacco. The other money making scheme was to go with a heavy metal bucket to the nearest well, fill up the bucket with as much as he could carry and start making his way back home, often spilling half of the water on route. With what was remaining, he stood outside with a metal mug and sold mugfulls of water to very hot and exhausted passers by.

For fun, we used to ask our local milk salesman if we could ride his mule which he usually tied to the big wooden gate of our building. We used to play with the local children, but not too often, as they used to insult us about being Jewish. They used to punch us until my parents came along to rescue us.

In the summer of 1943 there was an epidemic of typhus all over Uzbekhistan, mainly due to the lack of sanitation. There were no proper toilets, just holes in the ground, and no baths in most of the houses. People who could afford it would go to the local public baths, but it was very expensive. The other causes of the disease were malnutrition and lack of medication. My brother, Marcel, was the only one in our immediate family of four who did not contract this horrible disease, but both my parents and I were laid up with it and only survived due to selling or bartering any valuables that we had for medical help. Marcel was the nurse and the breadwinner at the age of only nine. Thousands of people did not survive this epidemic, including my grandfather.

At this time we received a letter to report to an office to be transported to Iran (or Persia, as it was then called), to join the families of the Polish army of General Anders. From Iran we were to be taken to Palestine where we could spend the rest of the war, but unfortunately my parents nor I were in a state to leave our beds and that opportunity passed.

We started receiving some parcels through the UNHRA organization which contained some second hand clothing, some tins of tuna and Carnation condensed milk. It was not much, but better than nothing. We were very excited every time a package arrived for us and it was nice to know that we were remembered, by whom I am not sure.

We were receiving postcards from one or two members of the family from our home town. The news was always bad. My mother's brother, who would not leave home mainly because of his mother and the family egg business, was questioned by the Germans as to where the family fortune was. When he would not tell them, he, his wife and children, and his mother (my grandmother) were taken out into Brzesko's town square and he was shot in the back of his head in front of his whole family and many of the town's people. This was confirmed to me when I was in Poland in 1987, by a man who witnessed this murder. We did not hear any more about the rest of the family so I feel they were probably sent to Auschwitz where they ended their lives. My father's remaining brother, Dr Josef Anisfeld, and sister, Dr Helena Sternlicht, also did not survive. She fought until her death in the Warsaw Ghetto.

We saw very elegantly dressed foreign delegations come to Bukhara which made us very jealous because we hardly ever had a change of clothes and my brother and I walked barefoot during the five years in Bukhara. There was no schooling for the immigrant children so my parents tried to do what they could with our education.

Eventually, in 1945, the war ended and we enquired from the authorities about any surviving relatives. All we had was a telegram (in English) which we could not understand at that time, that everyone was dead. It was another year, in 1946, that we were allowed to leave Russia back to Poland although not to our home town, but to a town called Wroclaw (in German Breslau), from where German families were escaping into eastern Germany, away from the Russian and Polish armies.

In our home town of Nowy Sacz, there was nothing left for us. Our beautiful apartment which was taken over by the Germans during the war as the Gestapo headquarters was now being used as the local police station. My father's business premises had been taken over by some local people. The Jewish population which was about 40 – 50 percent of the total of 30,000 people, were all wiped out apart from the people like ourselves who escaped eastwards. We were taken by the Russians as prisoners, but I must say this saved our lives.

My brother and I were brought to England on a kinder-transport by a kind and loving man called Rabbi Solomon Schonfeld, in November 1946. My parents could not get a permit to enter England until 1948, when we all re-united to start a new life. Unfortunately my parents, Regina and Ozjasz Anisfeld, died in 1959 and 1961 respectively aged 56 and 51. I married at the age of 21 a kind and loving person called Jack Sheldon and we have four sons and seven grandchildren.

Marcel is married to Irene Forman and they also have four children and nine grandchildren.

DORRITH M SIM

I Can Still Picture that Farewell

I was born in Kassel, Germany, on 8th December 1931. Vati and Mutti, my parents Hans and Trude Oppenheim, were very sporty people who enjoyed all outdoor activities. They tried hard to give me as normal a life as possible. With haversacks on our backs and carrying our walking sticks, we climbed the hills at the weekends. Occasionally we would reach as far as the Herkules statue which overlooks the town. Then we would pass the Schloss Wilhelmshöhe, a museum and art gallery.

In the wintertime we went skiing. I hated climbing up the hills, but loved coming down. We went skating also and I have a photograph of myself skating between two Hitler Youths. I can still recall how terrified and helpless my poor Mutti felt. In the better weather we paddled down the River Fulda in Vati's collapsible canoe and sometimes camped alongside the banks of the river. I recall a festival with everyone dressed up in fancy clothes, the boats all decorated and the river aglow with water lilies.

Other memories are not so happy. We were walking by the Fulda one day when we were approached by a Brownshirt with his wife and daughter. He insisted that I should share his daughter's lilo, (inflatable air bed). I was very frightened. The little girl kept bouncing up and down until the lilo capsized and we both finished up in the deep murky water. Our fathers had to dive in and rescue us.

One day I arrived at school to find a large crowd outside and the school being vandalised. Desks, chairs, books, slates and much more were being thrown out of the windows while a large crowd stood by jeering. It was very frightening. "You'd better go home," a man said to me. "It'll be a long time until you're back here again." I began running towards my Oppenheim grandparents' apartments, some streets away. Grandmother ('Oma') was horrified by my story and insisted I wait with her until she managed to contact my parents.

"There will be more trouble" Vati prophesised. "The children at the Weisenhaus, (the Jewish orphanage) will need our help." My parents brought some of the children home with us, but that night, Kristallnacht, the Gestapo also ransacked our flat and did much damage. They took my father away and dropped him many miles out of town. The Weisenhaus children had been in grave danger too, but they missed the Molotov cocktails that were thrown through the windows of the orphanage.

We had to move house shortly afterwards, but not before my parents had set the wheels in motion for my removal to the UK. This necessitated repeated visits to the Rathaus (Town Hall) to obtain my passport. Two enormous stone lions guarded the entrance and I was more afraid of them than of any Nazi. They gave me bad nightmares and Mutti had to drag me past them up the stairs into the Rathaus for our regular confrontation with Herr Schmidt.

It was around 24ᵗʰ July, 1939 before I was ready to depart with a Kindertransport*. Mutti and Vati travelled with me to Hamburg where I was to catch the train to Holland. I was wearing a red shoulder bag and carrying Droll, my toy dog. Parents were not allowed on the platform at the Hamburg station. There were so many other children. Many were crying. In all the commotion I dropped Droll and he fell beneath the train. I was terribly upset until a kind helper climbed down to rescue him. Then the helper took me over to where my parents stood behind a barrier so I could kiss them goodbye. I can still picture that farewell today.

In Holland we were taken to a large green field where some

---

* **Kindertransport** refers to the rescue mission during the nine months prior to the outbreak of the Second World War. It brought nearly 10,000 predominantly Jewish, unaccompanied children from Germany, Austria, Czechoslovakia, Poland and the Free City of Danzig to Britain.

Dutch people, including Queen Wilhelmina herself, gave us a picnic before taking us to our boat. I shared a cabin with other children. We left it during the night to look for toilets and wandered miserably around the corridors getting more lost all the time.

The next morning, the 26th July 1939, our boat docked at Harwich where a train was waiting to take us to London. My new foster parents, Fred and Sophie Gallimore, were waiting for me at Liverpool Street Station. They could not speak German. Luckily for me Fred's brother Jack had come too. He could speak German. All I could say in English was "I have a handkerchief in my pocket." Whenever I learned a new word I would put it into that sentence. "I have a dog in my pocket." "I have a teacher in my pocket."

The Gallimores lived in Edinburgh with their dog Rogie. We drove to Scotland in their Austin Seven motor car. Life was very different there. I was able to play with the children in the street and soon I was going to school. The Gallimores tried hard to bring Mutti and Vati out of Germany also, but without success. Just after the war began, Vati's sister Auntie Alice turned up unexpectedly. Although they had little room, they let her share my bedroom until she left for New York in 1940. Shortly afterwards I was evacuated to Innerleithen in the Scottish Borders, for a year. In 1942 my foster parents had their first baby daughter followed by a second girl, in 1947.

I stayed with my foster parents until 1952, emigrating with them to Brazil for eighteen months before returning to the UK to be married to Andrew, a Scottish lawyer. We met when I took up secretarial work with Mylne & Campbell, the Company where Andrew was apprenticed. I still live in Scotland, but sadly was widowed in 1992. I have four daughters, a son, ten grandchildren, six great grandchildren and one step great granddaughter. My children's picture book "In my pocket" tells the story of my journey from Germany in more detail.

I never saw Mutti and Vati again. They were deported to Theresienstadt in June, 1943 and from there to Auschwitz in October, 1944.

From Budapest through Hell and Back

My family name is Schwet. I was born in 1932 in Budapest, the capital of Hungary. The whole family was Jewish; Austrian and Czechoslovak on my father's side, and Hungarian (Svab) on my mother's side.

My father was a civil servant, and had the job of personnel manager of the Hungarian Provincial Food Manufacturing Factory (Kozsegi Elelmiezer Uzem). He held this position for 19 years. My grandfather was the editor of the German-language newspaper *Pester Lloyd* for some eight years, and had been deputy mayor of Budapest for four years and a member of the city council. He died from natural causes in 1942.

By 1939 anti-semitism was so great in Budapest that my parents and myself were forced to take out Roman Catholic papers. In this way, my father was able to keep his position for some four more years.

I attended elementary school for four years and grammar school for the years 1942-3, and part of 1943-4. Although my papers certified that I had been a Roman Catholic since 1939, I was the only Jew, and was almost every week beaten up by boys from my own class, as well as by boys from higher forms. Unfortunately, the teaching staff in charge did not protect me, but encouraged the boys in these incidents.

The Arrow-Cross party became very powerful. My grandparents lived practically next door to its headquarters, in Andrassy-ut 60. Hence I have some personal knowledge of how this party operated, and aimed at breaking the spirit of the Jews.

On the 19th March 1944 Budapest was occupied by the Germans. From that date onwards the position of the Jews in Budapest deteriorated very speedily. We had heard already that Jews were being deported from all the Provinces to Germany, and that the fate of the Budapest Jews was going to be the same. The occupation passed quickly, since only a division of SS soldiers and tanks came to Budapest. They kept on going round a block for many hours, giving the impression that there were quite a few divisions. From this date onwards, so many things happened that, unfortunately, I cannot remember all the dates. However, I shall be as accurate as possible.

My father was dismissed from his job, and for a short while had a job in a coal mine. He kept this job until he was called up for the labour-army (Munkaszelgalat). Because he was not used to this sort of labour, and worried about his family, he became very nervous. Moreover, his colleagues, some of whom owed their career to him, turned against him because he was a Jew. At this time, our movements were not yet restricted, and he came home every night to sleep. Later, he could come home only once a month or so, and finally, only when the superior officer gave him permission 'against regulations'. Each time he got permission like this, we had to give something to the officer's wife. In all, we gave her a large amount of cash, food, clothing and furniture. Some time around the end of October 1944 we received a postcard from my father to say that he was on his way to Germany, and that he would pass through a certain railway depot where he would be for a few hours. I immediately forged a document, working against time, showing that his immediate release was required by his employers. By this time the factory he used to work in, had become one of the no. 1 secret factories, and one of the most important in the city. I took off my yellow star and met him for a few minutes, taking him food and cigarettes. There were about 19 carriages, all originally used for the transport of animals. They were now filled with Jews – men – aged between about 18 and 50, and guarded by soldiers wearing an armband signifying that they were loyal members of the Arrow-Cross party. I immediately realised that there was no chance of helping my father to escape, and did not make an attempt. At this time I was only 12 years old, and although I was not in the least frightened, I felt that it was not worth attempting it, since there were too many guards. If there had been an attempt to escape, they would undoubtedly have shot my father and me. I spoke with my father who was in a state of complete nervous exhaustion, partly because of the heavy work he had been doing, and partly because of the lack of food, water and cigarettes. He had, of course, heard the rumours that Jewish women would shortly be deported, and he worried about my mother anyway. It was the last time that I saw my father alive. In fact, after that meeting no-one ever heard any news of him, although someone came back to Budapest after the war and said that he had seen my father die, shortly after the liberation, in hospital. There is nothing to prove this, and no records which might have given us some concrete information about him, were ever found.

My mother was born in 1909. She did not go out to work, but always kept house for my father and me. Until July 1944 we lived in a four-roomed flat in Vorosmarthy utca, a street near the centre of Budapest, in District no. VI. Our home was most comfortable, and we lived a very happy family life. In about July a regulation came into force directing all Jews to wear a yellow star on the left side of the chest, and their movements in the street were controlled. Soon houses were set aside for Jews to live in. Our house had not been chosen for this purpose, and so we moved with whatever furniture we could take, to my grandparents' house which was in the same street, but was an 'appointed' house. This was shown by a very large yellow star of David displayed above the main entrance. For this move we had been given only 48-hours' notice. This made the removal conditions extremely difficult, and the removal people exploited the Jews by charging fabulous amounts of money.

My mother and I were deported on 10 November 1944, and I was with her until we were separated in Ravensbrück concentration camp on about 26 November 1944. She was taken away and I never saw her again. Some records show that she was later transferred to Dachau, but there is no other information available about her.

Soon after the occupation I had to stop going to school, because Jews were only allowed out for two hours daily, and then only in a certain quarter. I was 12 years of age then. Having moved to the Jewish house, I volunteered to clear bomb-damaged houses, and was appointed as runner for the police district commander. In this capacity I had free movement at all hours and, with an armband, I was recognised by all officials. I would go to a bombed house and would assist with first aid of the injured and the digging out of the dead. My first task was usually to try to identify all dead persons by means of the papers in their clothes, and then to collect all valuables from them and make out a list which I would then deposit with the police officials. My most memorable job was in connection with a house which had been bombed in July 1944, where 97 persons died from suffocation in the air-raid shelter. I worked all night getting the dead out, most of them Jewish. During one of these duties I was slightly injured by a machine-gun bullet from a Russian plane making an attack on the city.

Later on I worked for the SS, since, having a free pass and being paid a small wage and given food, I was assisting my family a little. During another bomb-clearance duty I had to look after the individual rooms and the dining room of the SS officers residing there. I was injured by a sheet of glass which cut my leg through to the bone. It was a serious injury and I required immediate medical attention, but this was refused by the Germans who said that as a Jew, I would have to die sooner or later. I panicked and cried and with a trail of blood, I tried to make my way to the street, but was ordered by an SS sergeant to carry a heavy mattress from one building to another. This I did, but as I could hardly walk, he hit me and then lifted up the heavy mattress which he dropped on my back. From the shock and the wound in my leg, I collapsed.

I was taken home by a fellow-worker who carried me on his back. Once at home, a nurse who lived in the same house gave me first aid and stitched my leg with 13 stitches. After this incident I was at home for some five weeks until my leg healed. I went out to another place where I obtained work, again clearing bomb-damaged houses, until 15 October 1944. On that day Horthy resigned and Szalasi, the leader of the Arrow-Cross party, took office.

From that moment Jews were not allowed to move at all. Food was obtained by Christians. One Christian was in charge of each Jewish house, but I cannot remember whether we had sufficient food at that time. From time to time I took off my yellow star and ventured out of the house, to obtain food and other necessities from our Christian friends. The penalty for this was death. Two persons were shot outside our house for this offence.

On another occasion I was looking out of the window which was forbidden to Jews, when two young SS soldiers (Hitler Jugend) appeared. When they saw me, they came to the house immediately. As I opened the door, they grabbed me and took me with them. I was terrified and as my family was not aware of what had happened, they could not do a thing. Screaming and shouting, they took me with them. Luckily, the Christian in charge of our house who knew me well, heard the noise and came out. He rescued me from the two soldiers who would not let me go at first. Later, they told me to run, and sent me back to the house with a kick in my back which required medical attention.

On 10th November, members of the Arrow-Cross party came to the house and gave us ten minutes to get ready for a 'long journey'. They wanted men and women between the ages of 16 and 45, and those young children whom the parents wanted to take with them. Mother got into a terrible panic, and was crying and terrified, because we knew that this meant going to Germany. We had all heard by this time of the wide-scale deportations, and the use of gas chambers in Germany for the extermination of Jews. Mother did not want to take me with her, but as I was crying and begging her, she agreed. By this time the ten minutes were up, so we did not even have time to put warm coats on or get some food. Each flat in the house had an

Arrow-Cross man supervising. The one in our flat said that, unless we got out instantly, he would shoot us. My mother's father tried to reason with him, but he was hit in the face with the butt of the soldier's gun. He fell down with a bleeding mouth and, seeing this, mother fainted. I helped to carry her out to the yard where all eligible Jews were collected, and she was revived there, but was in a state which I cannot describe.

While in this yard, a Jewish neighbour, Mr Goldberg, would not leave his pregnant wife who was, therefore, not forced to come along at that time. He was thrown down from the first-floor landing by a soldier and, having fallen onto the concrete, could not get up. He was whipped by a young gangster and when he shouted something at this soldier, the latter just took out his revolver and shot him. His wife, having seen all this, in an attempt to save her husband, jumped from the first floor on top of the young man who had shot her husband. However, this was looked upon as an attack by a Jewish woman on the Arrow-Cross man, and so another soldier shot her with his machine gun. The effect of this incident was terrible, particularly as all the adults were crying and were in a terrible panic. We were told that the same fate awaited us, too.

We were then taken to Hunyasi Place where already 1000 men and women had been collected. They were guarded by German SS and by Hungarian Arrow-Cross men. It being November, a very cold month, the snow was deep and the temperature was well below freezing. I was terribly cold already. We stood there for some seven hours. One had to stand because the place was small and there were so many people that to sit, or even more, to lie, was impossible. During this time a heavy air-raid took place and we were not allowed to move, probably in the hope that some bombs might hit us. Some bombs, in fact, dropped very near us, but luckily we were not hit directly. As a result of this heavy air attack, some Germans and Arrow-Cross men shouted out from the top of one building overlooking the place where we were waiting that the attacking Russians were Jews, and that we had asked them to bomb the city. With that, they promptly fired into the huge crowd 10 to 15 shots. One of these bullets hit a woman in front of me. She was standing there with her little girl. The woman was hit in the stomach, and as there was absolutely no medical attention available, she died very soon after. Even then, the body was left there and not moved. The little girl was crying terribly for her mother. As a result, she was taken by a guard, and that was the last we saw of her. She may have been killed although I have no evidence of that.

After seven hours waiting we were moved to the brick factory on the other side of Budapest and about five miles from the previous collecting place. On the way, no food or water was given and no facilities for using toilets were provided. It began to snow heavily and those with no coats on, or with only light coats, were soon soaking wet. As I could not stop to urinate or go to a place to do so, I had to do it in my trousers during the long walk. Certain people tried to escape on one part of the journey, but were caught and to the horror of all the others, they stopped everybody walking. We had to watch while some six men were hanged on the lampposts lining the street. Ordinary rope and leather trouser belts were used to tie their hands and legs. The same things were used to hang them so that they were in terrible agony. It was just as terrible for us, the onlookers, and it must have taken at least 20 minutes before they stopped breathing visibly. We were then moved on, and the six were left hanging on the lampposts. As a result of this incident, lots of people fainted. They were collected and again, their fate is not known to me, but they never rejoined the march. All this was seen and witnessed by the Hungarians who happened to live in the houses along the streets through which we walked. Lots of SS soldiers about the town joked about our looks, etc.

By the time we arrived at the factory it was about 10 pm and dark. The place was floodlit and the snow also helped to make the night look lighter. We were told that we could use the small toilets on the outside. One can imagine the chaos when the guards gave permission to the whole crowd to go ahead. Thousands tried to rush at once to the few places, with the ultimate result that women and children were knocked to the ground. After that we stood around for another few hours before we were let into the big barracks where usually bricks were stored. We were told that we would await transport here. We had no food or drinking water for the next 30 or so hours. Then we were given some dirty watery soup, and some dry bread and water was available in limited quantity. The whole crowd was greatly upset by all this, and there were lots of men and women crying.

The train, with about a dozen carriages, came late the next day. We were packed into the carriages, 60 to 65 in each. After the steel doors of the wagon had been closed, we could not move for some time. It was dark, very stuffy and dirty. From the smell we could tell that horses were usually carried in it, and manure was everywhere: it was indeed a sickening place. Eventually, we managed to sit down and tried to relax, but in vain, and we were by now slowly giving up hope. Many hours after we got into the wagon, the train began to move slowly. From what I remember, we were shut in there for three whole nights and days, without any food, without any drink or even a chance to go to a toilet. It was terrible, particularly after the second night, during which some gangsters machine-gunned the carriages as they passed by. In our wagon, some six persons were hit. They were screaming and shouting for help, but nothing happened. Eventually it seemed that one man had gone mad and started to attack us. So one person had to hit him so that he would not cause any additional suffering to others. From this, the man died. At Hegyeshalom, after three days, the wagons were opened, one by one, and the dead and injured were taken out. We saw some people being taken into a large yard, from where shots could be heard almost immediately. No-one ever saw anyone come out from there alive. The wagons were full of blood, urine and stools – it was almost unbearable to remain there. Nevertheless, after about ten minutes, while a little dirty water in a can and some bread and sausage had been thrown in, the wagons were sealed again.

This time we only remained shut in for about ten hours. At

Wiener Neustadt the wagons were opened once again and this time there were SS guards, and the Hungarian Arrow Cross men disappeared. The Germans seemed more humane and gave us some food and some more water, and left the wagons open for the day. However, by the evening the guards who were to escort the train to the camp had taken over. Later we found out that the camp was to be Ravensbrück. These guards were horrible and assured us that we would not live for very long. They promptly shut the doors of the wagons. We were not given any food or water for two days. Since the air was so terribly bad inside, we all felt that we would suffocate, since there was very little air getting in from the outside.

Our next stop was outside the Ravensbrück camp. We arrived one morning early, but the date is unknown to me. We were told to leave everything behind in the wagons and just come out as we were, without carrying anything at all. We were lined up in three lines: men, women and children separately. We were then selected, given a number and told to get into another line, and wait. It was here that I was separated from my mother, and I never saw her again. One cannot imagine the scenes that occurred when children were separated from parents and wives from husbands, and would not go. SS guards would beat them up, and pick up the children and carry them away upon which the mother, or father, would run after him. Of course, as soon as the parents left the line in which they were supposed to stand, they were shot. These brutes just shot people in the legs and backs, and did not kill them instantly. It was unbearable to watch these people in their terrible pains and without any hope of any aid. They bled to death or died of shock in due course. I was crying bitterly for my mother, but with me there must have been some 200 other children. We were almost all crying as they marched us into the camp where we had to undress completely. Our clothes were exchanged for very thin short trousers, shorts and wooden shoes – very cold at the end of November in Germany. Eventually some dirty watery stuff was given to us to eat, but only very few could eat it, as it was so bad, and we were so terribly upset by the separation. The latrines were very bad:

planks led to a very big hole without seats. Many times I saw people fall into it, including children. We were very afraid of falling in, as there was no hope of getting out, since people were too weak and the hole was very deep. Those who were found to have wetted their bed and clothing during the day or night were punished by being refused food for two days, and sometimes they would get a good hiding from the SS guards. There were men and women guards, whose names I cannot remember; they were brutal at times and not too bad at other times. I myself was not beaten while in the camp, but I was told that my mother would probably die and that I would follow her soon. That upset me, and I was very afraid of dying.

Some of the children in our huts became very ill. But they were left there and not removed, so that after a time, each morning when we woke up there were some dead all around us. We would pull their clothing off and use it ourselves. It was so very cold that the SS guards allowed us to do that. All through that time, the food was very bad and I soon had stomach trouble. This became so serious that I could hardly move. There was no medical aid, or anything, and we had to stand sometimes for three or four hours at 'roll call', in very cold weather. Once, a Red Cross man came, but he went over the hut so quickly, and there were so many SS men around him that he could not possibly see anything; and we had been told that if anyone cried or fell ill that day, he would be killed. I saw thousands and thousands of inmates arrive, but I could never speak to them. There were public executions when someone did something wrong or tried to escape. I could see through the barbed wire that these men and women would be lined up and shot, or else, hanged. Once I saw a woman SS guard bite a woman who was screaming very loudly. Some of her inmate-friends came and pushed this woman guard away. She whistled, and within a few minutes I saw the men appear with their machine guns and they shot anyone they could. There were many similar incidents which I cannot exactly recall

At the end of November 1944 we were transferred to Dachau. We had to walk a long way, and were then put into wagons. It was very cold and we did not get anything to eat. In Dachau I was placed with the men and had some soup to eat. During roll-call we had to stand in the snow for many hours, and I was feeling ill.

Suddenly they took about 100 men and children out of our hut and marched us off towards the gas chambers. By then we knew where they were. On the way a German officer and two soldiers passed us. I don't know why, but I called out 'Gute Morgen!' The officer stopped and asked if I spoke German and took me out of the group. Later I found out that all others had been killed in the gas chambers. They took me to the officers' quarters, just outside the main camp, and told me that from now on I had to clean the lavatories, deal with all rubbish, sweep the area and clean boots. So I was saved from extermination.

In the evenings soldiers returned me to the barracks and took me very early in the morning back to the officers' quarters where I worked all day without stop. They gave me left-overs from the German soldiers' food, mainly rubbish collected from the plates. I also managed to steal some cigarette-ends which I took back to the barracks and exchanged for food, mainly bread.

About the end of March 1945 there were lots of air-raids and shooting and we heard of lots of people being gassed, as the Germans were close to defeat, and the Russian army was very near. I saw very many corpses being moved on lorries and open trucks. One night the German nightguard asked the children if they would save him when he got into 'trouble', and as he was not too bad a man, we said we would, and he said that he would soon leave us, and we would be able to go home. I gathered that the guards were trying to run away from the Americans. By that time there were four or five children a day dying all around me, and I was feeling very bad. I believe I had some disease: I had spots all over and had to keep scratching myself, and it was very painful. I could hardly get up, and urinated in my clothes, since I never had a hope of going out to the latrines. The clothes dried and got wet and dried again, but the smell was very bad; however, as we were all in the same state, we got used to it.

One morning there were only a few guards left, and some of the women prisoners were marched away and were told to get ready to move. However, some hours later, in the midst of heavy artillery and machinegun fire, some soldiers came in tanks straight through the wire fence, and were shooting everywhere. Soon men and women inmates who had children here, rushed over madly looking for them. My mother did not come, and lots of other children's mothers did not come. We were told that we could go home soon, because the Americans were here, but we were too tired and ill even to move to get something to eat from the food stores. These had been broken open by the inmates, and they were eating anything they could lay their hands on.

The Americans would not come near us, for fear of infection, and we were made to understand that we should go back to our huts and lie down. This lasted for two or three days when some Red Cross and American doctors and other people came to inspect the camp. Eventually we were fumigated, and given some medicine to strengthen us, and some food and drink.

The ill ones, including myself, were soon removed to Berlin and then flown over to Stockholm where I was in a hospital for some six months, recuperating, and very ill indeed. I eventually realised where I was and had some excellent treatment. Thanks to the Red Cross to a great extent, my life was saved during those few months. When I was reasonably well, I was repatriated to Hungary where I eventually found my grandparents.

It is very interesting to reflect here that all the old people of Budapest were safe. They were too old to be deported and were put into a ghetto, and some into houses under the protection of the various neutral countries. My grandparents and all my older relations were safe, and we occupied the flat that we had had before.

I hoped that my parents would come back, but they did not. However, friends who witnessed the death of both my parents, did come back.

PIETER STEINHARDT

From Varsseveld to London Town

My mother must have drummed in to me, probably for some weeks, that I had to be vary brave. Right from the German invasion of Holland, my parents knew what would happen.

My first experience of anti-semitism occurred in winter. Of course we had to wear the Yellow Star of David. I was only 4 or 5 and was playing with my sledge on the Scheldeplein in Amsterdam. Some big boys took it away and called me a Jew Boy.

My father was arrested by the Gestapo very early on. I remember the night he did not return. I was in my cot, and my mother was wandering around, chain smoking. So my mother decided to have Ruth, my cousin, and myself put into hiding. On the night I left home, Tante Roosje (Auntie Rose) came to pick me up. Above all other feelings, a sense of guilt engulfed me about leaving my mother and maternal grandparents. Grandmother ('Oma') could not understand why I had to go away. I knew, I knew. I was only 5 or 6 years old. I knew I would never see any of them again. And there was Oma, with her hearing trumpet, asking Opa 'why must Pietje go away?'. I felt embarrassed, because Oma could not understand. I must have been a monster. This and all of it came back to me, just now, like a flash. I entered hell. For the first time since 1942, I grieved for my Grandmother.

Auntie Rose took me to a safe house, for the night. In the morning we started the journey. I remember being in the train leaving

Amsterdam. Our destination was Arnhem. There were Germans in uniform at every station. Papers were checked frequently so my forged papers must have been good. In due course, we arrived in Arnhem where I was handed over to a man with whom I boarded a local steam train. Eventually, we arrived in Varsseveld where we were met by another man who put me on the back of his bicycle. I was delivered to the 'Huisstede' (Homestead), and Uncle Johan and Auntie Dina (Mr & Mrs te Lindert).

These people were very strict Dutch Reformed Church members. They lived by their principles in a remarkable way. I owe them both, my life. They must have been just married and they had a daughter called Johanna who was only one or two years old. Apart from hiding me, they also hid a married couple and two teenage boys. I cannot remember their names other than that one of them was Bennie Mestriz. Nowadays, he lives in Jerusalem and has a large family.

Life soon formed a pattern at the 'Huisstede' which was a mixed farm. Like all such farms in the Province of Gelderland, the animals' quarters were built onto the house, and for the first time in my life I became aware of farm animals.

The Te Linderts were extremely religious people. Prayers were said before each meal and, immediately before grace after meals, a portion was read from the bible. As I was at a very impressionable age, I probably took to it like a duck to water. The goodness of these people and their sincere belief is something I shall never forget.

There were various hiding places, in case of raids. Under the floorboards in the bedrooms, and one above the cow stalls. We slept in the beds and within minutes could be hidden away.

Life was very pleasant at the 'Huisstede' although even I, as a child, knew there was still danger. Someone had turned Quizling for the reward. One night there was banging on all the doors of the farm: the Germans had arrived. Normally, I would have been hidden under the floorboards, but as one of the teenagers was ill, I had been put to sleep in the box above the cow stalls. Entry was effected from below and the trap door could be wedged locked shut. Bennie

Mestriz joined me in the box and locked it. The Germans came into the farm and demanded to know where the Jews were hidden. At first it was denied that we were there, and this denial persisted. There was also a non-Jewish boy staying at the farm. He also denied knowledge. However, the Germans had been well-briefed, and started chopping up the floorboards. It was pitch black in our box; I was terrified. We were so frightened, I tried to breathe quietly, but the more I tried, the louder it seemed to us. The search seemed to go on for ages. All of a sudden there was a shout of triumph. There was much hooraying and a sudden crash. A German swore and our horse neighed. They had found my small suitcase with all my town clothes in it, and this resulted in laughter. The chopping sounds continued from the living quarters. Time passed, in our little hole. Then suddenly, there was another shout of triumph from the Germans. This time they had struck gold: the couple and the teenage boy had been found hidden under the floorboards. We could hear them underneath us being manhandled out of the farm.

Uncle Johan was once more asked to tell them where we were hidden. He was promised his freedom if he would talk, and he would be left on his farm with his wife and baby daughter. He, however, refused to talk. I remember he asked them why he could not protect his own countrymen. The Germans started beating him again.

All this was going on below our hiding place in the ceiling. In the end, as he refused to talk, they took him away too, and told his wife that when they came again, she had better hand us over, otherwise she and her baby daughter would be taken to a concentration camp too.

I owe the Te Linderts my life. When they opened the door and were asked by the Germans to hand us over, they could have easily done so. Instead, they risked imprisonment and possible death in a concentration camp, for themselves and their baby daughter. No one in the world would have blamed them. Even when three of us had been found, despite the offer by the Germans to let the Te Linderts stay on their farm, they both refused to talk. What these two people did, showed courage beyond what any other two persons would have done. Their sense of what was right and their religious conviction is a memory which I will bear with me forever.

Time passed in our little dark box. I had lost all senses of time. We had no food or drink. More time passed in the pitch-blackness. Eventually, we heard some movement near us. People were removing the roof tiles. The box was tilted, and we saw moonlight. Uncle Johan's brother, from the next farm, was letting us out. It was then that we discovered how near we had come to being discovered by the Germans. They had been tunnelling under the eaves, and had pulled back sheaves of straw. Had they removed two more, they would have found the box in which we were hidden. Why they stopped I will never know. Perhaps, when they found my suitcase they thought Bennie and I had been moved elsewhere. Whatever the reason, it was a very lucky escape.

It became very clear that both Bennie and myself would need to be moved as soon as possible. There was always the danger that the Germans would come back, after having questioned the people they had captured. It was also unfair to put Auntie Dina and Johanna in further danger.

We had been brought down from the loft, climbing down a ladder outside the building. After Bennie and the other adults had discussed these things, we returned to our box again. More time passed in total darkness, until once more we were let out. Someone had come with a bicycle. After saying goodbye to Auntie Dina, I was put on the back of the bike and we pedalled away. To say that I was frightened, is probably an understatement. It was dark, and once again, a stranger was in charge of me. After some time we arrived at another farm, the home of the Schuurman family, an elderly couple who had three grown up sons, and there were also two girls. One of the girls was my cousin Ruth, and the other was called Inge Pollack. My memory of my previous life was already beginning to cloud: I did not recognise Ruth. I should have done because my baby book contains picture of Ruth playing with me.

So there were now the three of us hiding at the Schuurman's

farm. The girls were in their late teens and I was about seven at the time I arrived there. What had happened, apparently, was that Ruth had heard of my predicament, and had arranged for me to join her.

The hiding arrangements at the Schuurman's farm were much more sophisticated. Although their farm was smaller, the basic design was the same. Where the farmers' living quarters joined onto the animal stalls, a false wall had been built. The cavity was just wide enough for one person to lie down, and just a little bit longer. How did three people get into this space? Easy: one above the other, in bunk beds. Access was from the top via the loft, with a ladder fixed to the end wall going down to the bottom of the pit. In the evening we were put into our hiding hole, and the access panel was put into place. This was then covered with straw, etc., by old man Schuurman. Nobody could find us unless they knew the precise details of how to get to us. By the same token, I don't think the girls could have got us out in case of an emergency. However, that thought never entered my head at the time.

What I do remember about the hiding hole was that the girls didn't know the best place to put me: in the middle, the top or the bottom. Part of the problem was that most of the time we had no light. We did have a potty. It being pitch black, you can imagine what happened when I used it: bang down it would fall. Perhaps it is surprising, but I don't have a potty problem! The girls used to chatter in the evening, and many times they got told off because they could be heard outside the farm.

It is at this time that my education started. Mr Schuurman senior and Ruth, between them, started me on the 3 R's. Right from the start I was taught the script I now use. I had some exercise books from Holland right to the time that Auntie Lilli's house was sold. My writing was like a monk's from the Middle Ages. I wrote very slowly in those days, all the letters were regular and identical. When I started going to Grammar School in the UK, my writing via scrawl turned into the compromise you see now.

I was very good at arithmetic at one stage. Mr Schuurman used to correct my work. One day he said I had got something wrong. I checked my work and argued that I was right. I was hit on the hands with a ruler. I knew I was right. Later it turned out that I was right, but I never could get on with maths after this. This problem was not helped by spells in hospital after the war which meant that I could not keep up with algebra etc. because of gaps in my teaching. However, this is jumping years forward.

Life was pleasant at the Schuurman farm most of the time. We did not have many scares, but had some. During the day in summer we used to be allowed out into the cornfields. One day we were in a neighbour's field when they started their harvest. Would they find us in the middle of their field, or would darkness come first? The night won! On another occasion we were out in the house when some Germans were advancing towards it. We dived under the beds, but the soldiers were on manoeuvres and nothing happened: no search or anything.

Time passed, and the Battle of Arnhem, Operation Market Garden, took place. All we knew was that the Allies had landed at Arnhem, the nearest big town. We heard machine gun fire and explosions. Our liberation had not yet arrived.

I think it was also about this time (the second half of 1944), that a doodlebug went 'round in circles one night. It finally crashed with a bang. I have often fantasized that it crashed on some German. It probably landed harmlessly in a farmer's field.

Then there was the low flying aircraft that machine-gunned something on the main road we could see from our farm. The story was that a German car had drawn its attention....

One day, old Mrs Schuurman was taken ill and was taken to hospital in a horse drawn cart. There was no petrol for the ambulance anymore. On another occasion an Allied aircraft dropped its wing tanks near our farm. The Germans came to see whether there was any petrol, but the resistance boys had beaten them to it.

Then, at last, came the liberation! It happened like this. I was in the pigpen when two or three Germans burst into the farm. They sat on the stairs leading to the loft above the cattle stalls. Mr Schuurman told me to stay with the pigs. The Schuurman boys went to get some help, and came back with some British or Canadian soldiers. They rushed the Germans and captured them. Ruth and Inge went wild with joy! At last we were free and at liberty again, and didn't need to fear the Germans any longer – so we thought! The Schuurman boys were kitted out in resistance uniforms now; great!

No sooner had the Germans been taken away, when from the farm at the back of our's, loads of Germans started ever so slowly coming towards our farm. The Schuurman lads were off on their bikes again, and within minutes some Allied tanks appeared on the road. They pointed their guns in the direction of the Germans – and that was it: all German hands went up! I tried to tell one of the tank crews that if they fired, they would hit our barn. They could not understand me, of course, but no shooting took place. The Germans were lined up on a farm track, and were led away.

The end of the war for me? Not quite. There was another farm on the other side of the road. I had never been there, so I went for a walk. Suddenly the ground developed little puffs and bangs. I tried to kick the puffs and Ruth screamed at me to come back inside. Was I being shelled or what? I don't know to this day, but until Ruth shouted I was not frightened at all.

One thing that struck me about the tank crews that had liberated us, was how white their bread was. They were having a meal while the Germans were led away.

The following few days were filled with great glee for the children. At the end of our road was the main road. Troops had been dug in on either side, in foxholes. There was a continuous line of transport passing: lorries and more lorries, with soldiers. Us kids were sitting on the fence, singing our hearts out and being bombarded with sweets! After a while things quieted down and, as far as I, a small boy, was concerned, went back to normal. The grown ups must have had many discussions about what to do with me. Mrs Schuurman was dead, Ruth was too young to take responsibility for me. Almost certainly, my parents were dead.

One day, I was taken back to the 'Huisstede'. Some time earlier, Uncle Johan had been released from the concentration camp, to bring in the harvest. So, once again I was with Uncle Johan and Auntie Dina at the 'Huisstede', but now as one of the family. For all we knew, my real family was dead. Communications were in chaos, and the Te Linderts had come to my rescue again. Then, one day Ruth and Bennie came, the coach was pulled out of the barn, the horse was hitched and we went for a long drive to a gathering. I guess it was a meeting of Jewish survivors in that part of the country.

Things were improving all the time, and finally I started going to school in Varsseveld. There was no noticeable difference between me and the other children. I was Dutch Reformed Church and spoke the local dialect by now, like the others.

One thing that I have always remembered from life at the 'Huisstede', was a foal being born to our mare. It was like in a bag when it came out, and as soon as it was cut out of this, got on its feet. I also remember the mare being taken to another farm, and being serviced by the stallion. So, like most farm children, I knew things that town children have to be taught in class.

As communication improved, Uncle Gilles and Auntie Lieze traced me. He was my father's best friend, and married to Lieze, a cousin on my father's side. So, one day Ruth came for me and we started our journey to Rotteredam. I can't remember how I felt about this move, but I do remember the journey.

We travelled to Arnhem in an army lorry converted into a bus by fitting some long benches. I think we changed at least once. At Arnhem we caught a train and were met at Rotterdam Station by Gilles who had a car. From there, we went to IJselmonde. On the way Gilles asked whether I could swim. At last, we arrived at Kreeksehaven and another episode in my life began.

The house seemed familiar to me; I must have stayed there at some time before the war. I met Auntie Lieze, and their daughter Liesje. Going there was another uprooting experience, as I had to cope with new circumstances. Liesje was not very kind to me; we just didn't get on. She probably resented my presence. I went to school in IJselmonde almost immediately after my arrival.

It is during this time that I had the first holiday that I can remember. Gilles had bought a gypsy caravan. The workman on his wharf got it ready, and one day Lieze, Liesje and I got in it, and off we went. The caravan was pulled by one of Gilles's lorries. As I remember, progress was peacefully slow, partly because the caravan could not be pulled fast, and also because of vast convoys of military vehicles. (Was this the big trek home for the Allies?) We had to stop several times as one of the axels overheated. Eventually, we arrived at the campsite and some happy days were spent there.

Unfortunately, it was not a happy household. Gilles wanted a homebody to come home to. Lieze was a professional violinist and got a job with an orchestra in Amsterdam. There were many rows about the cooking, the house, etc. They often ended by Gilles saying that Lieze was welcome to Liesje, but he would take me.

Gilles insisted that I started swimming lessons almost immediately on my arrival. This was not surprising: he owned a wharf, and on the other side of the road where we lived, was the river (or creek). We were surrounded by water. The swimming bath was located in the North of Rotterdam. My journey was by bus from IJselmonde to Rotterdam Central Station, then by tram to the swimming bath. What struck me was the utter desolation in the centre of Rotterdam. For a vast distance no building stood: it was as flat as a pancake. This was the work of the Luftwaffe, and the reason for the Dutch surrender. The Germans had threatened to take out one town at a time – the Dutch had nothing to stop them. It did not take me long to learn to swim.

One day Lieze took me to Amsterdam, to see Professor H. who had performed two operations for fistulas on my water works. We turned up early and were sent away. When we returned an older secretary was there, and she recognised me. The professor agreed to a further operation, gratis. After a few weeks I was again in the Juliana Kinderziekenhuis (children's hospital). Again, I had to climb on the operating table, and again the ether was administered by Sister W.

These experiences of operations in Holland have left me with an undying dread of hospitals. The operation was not successful.

At about this time Lieze started taking me to some strange adults who played with toys with me. One remark made to me by one of the ladies, was that I was self-centred. Hardly surprising. This must have been at the Dutch Child Guidance organisation. They probably had no idea what lay behind me.

The rows between Gilles and Lieze continued. Letters started arriving from Auntie Lilli, from England. One day I was told that I would be going to England. Poor Auntie Lilli. I don't think that she had any idea what she was taking on.

Then the day came for me to go. Lieze had stitched a container of halibut liver oil into the vest I was wearing. (strange, how one remembers trivia!) I was taken to the airport, and off to England I went, on my own! On the plane, there were some forms to be filled in. I asked the man sitting next to me, to help me fill them in. He took my documents, I thought to help me, but his motives were different! He was stopped at Northolt Airport and my documents were retrieved.

After the aircraft had stopped, we got out. As I walked towards the building, someone was calling my name. I looked – Auntie Lilli must have looked very much like my mother – I thought it was mother, but of course, it wasn't. Once we got out of the airport building, David's father drove us in his car to Ruislip. In the car I told Lilli about the halibut liver oil. On arrival I met Elli, Derek and David. Both Derek and David were playing with children's trikes. I could not communicate with them as I didn't speak English. I wonder whether David or Derek remember.

I could finish here. However, there is rather more to tell. That evening auntie took me home, in Clapham South. I was fascinated by the tube journey. Eventually, we got home, and auntie tried to cuddle me as she opened the door. I tried to withdraw.

After a week or so I started school. I was desperately unhappy. No one at school could speak Dutch or German. At home, auntie spoke to me in German, a language I hated. I replied in Dutch. Things were extremely difficult for me (and, no doubt, for Lilli too). At school, two children were put in charge of me, and whatever I touched, they told me the English word for it. Crude it might have been, but it worked: I rapidly learned English, but not without a great deal of unhappiness. I remember one day I cried bitterly on the school steps.

Auntie Lilli worked in the kindergarten near the school at this time (in Coldharbour Lane, Brixton). One of the biggest shocks Lilli must have had, was my kneeling before my bed every night, to say my prayers in Dutch. Poor Lilli took me to the Rabbi in Brixton shul, but what could he do?

One of the conditions the Dutch Authorities had laid down, was that I attended Child Guidance. Until I spoke English, nothing could be done. When I eventually went to them, I had begun to think in English. My previous life, as far as I was concerned, was a closed chapter. I didn't and wouldn't talk about it. Possibly also my training during the war of 'don't talk', was still with me. They gently probed, but got nowhere. I wouldn't talk. (Strange, I am quite a good communicator now.) Their last shot was to put me with a man who made me do needle work. I got bored – but nothing. The next visit was to the lady who told Auntie Lilli they could do nothing. But I seemed o.k. So much for that.

When I was seventeen I went back to Holland for a two-week holiday. I stayed with Lieze in IJselmonde, and went to the farm, and to my Aunt Herta. I also made a disastrous trip to Amsterdam. It was supposed to be a day trip, but I was back with Lieze by 2 p.m.

I arrived in Amsterdam Central Station, and started walking. I don't know how (after all, I was only six when I left Amsterdam), but I found myself outside the flats where my parents lived, Scheldeplein 6 II. Underneath the flat was a café. I went in and ordered a coffee. I then asked after the dog I had played with as a small child, eleven years earlier. Despite my broken Dutch, I was recognised. The people in the café looked at me as if I had returned from Mars, and started remarking who I was. I couldn't stand it. I left my coffee, went outside and burst into tears. I caught the tram to Central Station and went straight to Rotterdam. I didn't return to Amsterdam until the mid 70's.

In 1979 I went to visit Ruth in Israel. We went to Jerusalem, where Ruth took me to Yad Vashem, the memorial to the people murdered during the war. Like most tourists, I went with Ruth and Israel, her husband, through the exhibition, the pictures we all have seen on films and TV, and like most people, I regarded it as history. At the end of this hall, just before the exit, there are some stairs, draped in black, going up. Ruth said, let us go up and check whether your parents' names are recorded. We went up, and Ruth filled in a slip with my parents' details on it. There were some youngsters – too young to have been born before the end of the war – doing research. And then it struck me that the whole place was draped in black. There were rows upon rows of books, the whole length of the exhibition hall downstairs recording the names of our people who were murdered during the war. How many? 6 million, 6½ million. Eventually, the clerk returned with the books recording the names of my parents and their place of death. This is the only memorial they have, like the rest of the souls recorded. No grave, just the Yad Vashem. It is the nearest thing I will ever have to a grave for my parents.

As I left the hall, I tried to keep back my tears, but I couldn't. Ruth must have seen that I was upset, but we didn't talk about it. Like the tourists, we went past the memorial to the Concentration Camps, with their eternal flame. But it wasn't just interesting anymore. It meant, and still does mean to me, something personal.

I have never had any real, personal friends; I always hold back. With good reason, I think. Perhaps I have explained what lies behind my pathological hatred of the older generation of Germans. The youngsters I don't trust.

The granddaughter of Mr P., our family dentist in Floss, Bavaria, came to England in the 60's or early 70's. Her grandfather had risked being send to a concentration camp, by treating Lilli before she came to England. This young lady was told by her mother to visit Auntie while the rest of her class were going up to town. So Auntie Lilli and

I took her to Chartwell. She said that it was a very nice house, but who had lived here? It told her it had been the Churchills to which the girl replied: 'The bad man as bad as Hitler.' I went bananas at her. Afterwards, she admitted to Lilli that she knew what had happened during the war, as her grandfather had told her. However, what she said she had been *taught at school*. She talked about Dresden; I told her, what the Germans started, the Allies finished. What about London, Rotterdam, etc., etc.?

Perhaps you can understand how I feel about these things.

The Complexity of Survival

The small dormitory room was empty but for a young woman, a boy aged six years and his tiny sister, aged two. The young woman, Mrs de Jong, was in mental agony. The room had been crowded with children. From time to time a man with a clipboard entered and read out the names of children who were to board the train waiting in the street, into which the railway line ran. It was strange that our names (I was the boy) had not been called. If she had failed to hear our names, her life was in danger. But if she left the room to enquire, she risked her life for leaving without an order. Unlike many women left in concentration camp Theresienstadt, she correctly believed that the trains took people to their deaths, not just into forced labour. She had decided to accompany us all the same.

Eventually she did go outside. The train had left. Our names had not been called. We could return to the women's dormitory where she had kept us before. The train went to Auschwitz. My sister Erica and I are two of the 150 survivors out of 15000 children who entered Theresienstadt.

However, let me sketch our background first. My father, Rudolf Bernhard Stern, was a young Jewish architect from a well-to-do family in Berlin who stayed in Germany to combat the Nazis as long as he could, until 1938. Though raised in a privileged home, his ideal in architecture was to design good quality housing for working-class people. Though not physically imposing, having been hospitalised for pulmonary tuberculosis, he walked about Berlin with a length of steel wire down his trouser leg, to defend himself against Nazi thugs. During a search of his parents' house the Nazis failed to find his pistol in his untidy room. A young non-Jewish German woman fled with him and married him in Belgium. They moved to Hilversum in the Netherlands where I was born.

My mother had also been actively anti-Nazi. Once she was walking up the aisle of a crowded German train when her little suitcase opened. Its content of anti-Nazi leaflets spilled out, next to a Nazi Brownshirt. She was a pretty girl and the Brownshirt helped her to put the leaflets back into the case.

From Holland my father travelled to England, intending my mother and I to follow. He was sent back by Customs because of a communist book in his luggage. I seem to have a few snapshot memories of life with my parents in Hilversum though I was still two years old when we moved to Amsterdam. We led a reasonably comfortable life in a modern flat, no doubt because my grandparents could still afford to support my parents.

In Amsterdam, life at first seemed quite pleasant to me which means that my parents insulated me from their troubles. We lived overlooking the beautiful Vondelpark and I played with children in the street. There were plenty of them and I enjoyed it. Eventually my mother had to keep me away from them to avoid my being noticed too much, though I still went to nursery school. I enjoyed the ducks in the park and the walks there.

My third birthday was a memorable occasion. A great fuss was made of me, but the birthday party was more an occasion for the many adults who came. It was a sunny day and life still had much normality to it.

Soon Nazi laws made it impossible for my father to work as an architect. So he started making wooden toys. One day my father came home with black eyes. My parents said he had been boxing, but I wonder whether he had been beaten up by Nazis or their sympathisers.

Occasionally we visited my father's parents, Albert and Marie

Stern. They had also fled from Berlin after a Nazi official walked into my grandfather's central Berlin women's clothing business and expropriated it. They now lived in a quite impressive house, also near the Vondelpark, with their collection of Chinese antiques and some fine paintings which included an orchard scene by Van Gogh and an Odalisque by Matisse. Marie was the niece of a famous Dr Ebstein, known to every doctor in the names of a common form of 'hole in the heart' called Ebstein's anomaly, and Pel-Ebstein fever characteristic of Hodgkin's disease.

One of my grandfather's brothers, Isidore, had developed his employers' firm, a manufacturer of German brandy, into a major supplier of industrial alcohol. At that time anyone could walk into a pharmacy and buy this cheap drinkable product. Isidore Stern fought a long and ultimately successful campaign to ensure that industrial alcohol could only be sold to the public as methylated spirits, a major contribution to tackling Germany's epidemic of alcoholism. Isidore became a prominent industrialist. Amongst regular guests at his house were members of the German government.

My grandfather had taken on a young man from a haberdashery shop in a small Dutch town and trained him in his business in Berlin, as he had done with two sons of the Dutch Brenninkmeyer family, the owners of the C&A fashion stores. The young man, Lieuwe Bangma, started his own business in Amsterdam with an initial investment from my grandfather. He had become very comfortably off, living in a villa with a huge garden in the shadow of a beautiful thatched windmill, with a fine view of the city of Haarlem on the horizon. This connection was to contribute to the saving of my life and that of my sister.

My father had to go into hiding, becoming friends with the Dutch artist H N Werkman and joining the Dutch Resistance. Accompanied on bicycles by a son of Lieuwe Bangma and a Resistance friend of his, he fled to a farm near Amsterdam where the farmer hid Jews and weapons. The postman who delivered to the farm, was not a Nazi but thought it his duty to report suspect activity. A lorry load of soldiers arrived. My father ran into a field with a pistol. Before he was captured he shot two of the pursuing soldiers dead. He was never to know that this was to save the lives of his two children.

Via the transit camp Westerbork in the Netherlands, he was sent in a cattle truck to Auschwitz and then, late in 1944 or early 1945, to Buchenwald concentration camp. I do not know whether he was in one of the notorious 'death marches'. He was murdered in Buchenwald on March 11, 1945.

In the early stages when my father was in hiding, he visited us from time to time. His last visit was on November 20, 1942, the night before my sister was born. My parents were agitated and my father banged on the wall to alert the neighbours that my mother had to go to hospital. I was taken to friends of my parents, Jo and Cathrien Rademakers. Visiting my mother in hospital I saw the beautiful new baby, my sister Erica. But my mother became terribly ill and died of childbed fever, an infection transmitted by hospital staff. Not knowing what death was, I could not understand why I would not be able to see her again. The young Rademakers couple were stuck with me.

My mother did have a funeral, but I did not know about it nor do I recall being involved in any mourning, though Cathrien Rademakers did talk with me about my mother's death.

Jo Rademakers, a young architect, and his wife Cathrien lived not far from us. Even though I was not a Jew according to Jewish law, Nazi law counted me as one. The Germans made it abundantly clear by posters, broadcasts and newspaper announcements that anyone concealing Jews, would be dealt with in an unspecified but sinister-sounding way. Their brutality to the Dutch population did not encourage a mild interpretation. Jo and Cathrien never gave me the slightest inkling of this, but treated me as their son and I was happy living with them. Jo went out to work, but Cathrien did not and I had her company all the time. I still have a vivid feeling for the enormous beneficial effect of this constant contact, mostly apparently trivial, with the woman who had replaced my mother in my life. Perhaps it was all the more important because of the disruption of my life later on.

One day the Rademakers took me from their flat on the Rozengracht near the Royal Palace, to the church next to the palace. It was full. People crowded near the door and in the aisle. My sister had also been brought. She and I were taken to the font near the altar and we were baptised. Everything was done hurriedly. Neither my parents nor the Rademakers were religious and my grandparents were not notably observant. The motive was clearly fear of the Nazis.

One day at my junior school, the teacher told my class to line up along the wall in the school hall for some activity whilst she was sitting at a desk on the stage. Two young Dutchmen, perhaps 17 years old and dressed in civilian raincoats, intruded. They asked the teacher: "Is Martin Stern here?" The teacher said that I was not, but in my ignorance I gave myself away. The look in the young woman teacher's face haunts me to this day. Adults, of course, had to be very careful in what they said to a child about the Nazis, so I was not adequately prepared.

They took me on the back of one of their bicycles to an interrogation centre in a school building where I was taken into a large office with a single imposing desk. Behind the desk sat a rather fat man in the uniform of the "Grüne Polizei", the SD in the Netherlands. His only concern, despite my protests, was to check who I was. Otherwise, his behaviour was that of any typical bureaucrat I have met since. I was taken to another room and from the landing I saw through a door Mr Rademakers standing with his back to me. In response to my question, I was told that he was going on a journey and that I was not allowed to call to him. I was transferred to a cellar in a theatre with a miscellany of men and women. One bucket served as latrine.

We were transported to Amsterdam's Central Station where a bunch of women and I were put aboard a passenger train. During this journey, or perhaps the later journey in Germany, the women and I were out of the train amongst the rail tracks near a station. The women started singing a defiant march-like song to keep up their morale. A German soldier immediately ordered them to stop.

Unauthorised singing was clearly considered dangerous to the German Reich.

We arrived at Westerbork, a prison camp of single-story wooden huts creosoted nearly black and surrounded by a high barbed wire fence with heath land outside. I was placed in a section of a hut with boys of about my age. The others introduced me to the routine. All I had was the clothes I stood up in and a toy whistle in my pocket. The highlight of the day was a sparse meal, mainly consisting of what the boys called 'barbed wire': a modest amount of old tough runner beans sliced and boiled with the stringy thread undisturbed, making them unpleasant to eat.

Mr Lieuwe Bangma, who had been trained by my grandfather in Berlin, had four sons. His wife wanted a daughter. They collected my baby sister from the maternity hospital and took her into their family. But the Nazis had forced them to hand her over despite resistance which could be described as extremely brave or foolhardy. She had also been transported to camp Westerbork and was kept in a hut for babies so that I did not get to see her. Here she had an operation, a mastoidectomy for a life-threatening middle ear infection. An inmate-doctor would have performed this operation.

My memory of Westerbork, like that of the whole war period, consists of isolated incidents, like clips of a motion film. Young youth leaders seemed to organise activities for the children including art and crafts. A trench had been dug in the sandy soil and they had evidently found clay. One boy, aged about eight years, had made a beautiful clay pot like a type of ginger pot then traditional in Holland. My impression was and is that there were some very gifted and civilised children amongst those in the camp.

A rail line ran into the camp. Once a week a train, usually of goods or cattle trucks, would be loaded with camp inmates. I watched this from the edge of the clear ground next to the rail siding. Even at the age of five I found it disturbing to see mostly ordinary-looking men in railway or military uniforms crushing other ordinary people, those with whom I was in the camp, into the wagons. The doors were then secured shut with steel wire. When the train left, soldiers with rifles stood on little steps at the ends of the wagons, obviously to shoot would-be escapers.

A young man in Chassidic dress, with a black hat and a black beard, gathered a few of us boys into a small room with a blackboard and white chalk. Thus the first letters which I learned, were those of the Hebrew alphabet. I later forgot all but the letter alef and the letter shin which our teacher described as three little birds sitting on three twigs of a branch.

An extraordinary memory is of being taken out of the camp for some hours, together with a few other children and a couple of young women, onto the surrounding heath land guarded by armed German soldiers. One day I was taken to a hut with a kind of clinical room where a young man asked me questions and gave me a medical examination. The very young doctor seemed to be pensive and I got the feeling that something important depended on the examination. Soon afterwards I was told to get on one of the departing trains. This, remarkably, turned out to be a nice-looking green passenger train. In one of the carriage compartments I found myself together with my little sister, cradled in the arms of a woman I did not know, and wrapped in a beautiful white knitted or crocheted woollen wrap. Because of the large holes in the pattern I thought she would be cold, but the woman assured me that this very feature would keep my sister warm. The journey started comfortably, though no-one would tell me where we were going, and there was nothing to eat. We were detrained at a large railway station in Germany and led into a hall on one of the platforms, separated from ordinary German folk going about their ordinary business, by large glass panels in the ornate doors. We had to sit on the floor and hand in any metal objects. A woman next to me told me not to hand in my whistle, but I thought her advice was dangerous. I got up, went to the counter, and lost my last possession other than my clothes. The perfectly ordinary-looking railway official took the whistle and wrote something in a book.

We were loaded into a cattle truck, tightly packed. A bucket was put in the truck as a latrine for all of us. The door was sealed and the train left. The passenger train had taken us only a short distance. Now we were on a typical transport to a concentration camp. I think that at one stage in a journey of several days, the door of the truck was hinged down a little way whilst the train stood still, and some water was passed into the truck. It may be that the latrine bucket was emptied. My memory is that at first it was impossible to sit and that we were squashed together and could only stand. Later in the journey there seemed to be more room and some people were able to lie down. An old man next to me lay on his back with his eyes wide open, perfectly motionless. I did not understand that he was dead.

The slow journey seemed like an endlessly repeating clickety-clack, extremely uncomfortable. We were hungry and thirsty. Fortunately my memory is fragmentary. It took the introduction of welded rails which make a different sound, to enable me to travel by train subsequently without thinking of that journey. Eventually, the train stopped and the door was lowered. We got out and blinked in the sunlight, bewildered, miserable and ravenous. After being moved around I started to take in the surroundings. There were large buildings of stone or brick, not in themselves looking unpleasant from the outside. Not all that far, at the end of a street, there was an embankment of earth surmounted by a wooden fence without gaps. I wanted to run to the fence but was sharply warned not to. I was told there was nothing to eat, but after I pleaded with a youth leader he told a boy of my age to take me indoors and make me some porridge. He got a very small aluminium pan and put about a teaspoonful of rolled oats in the bottom. With a small amount of water and using the iron stove in the middle of the room, he produced the most memorable meal of my life. I found myself in a ground floor room of a building called an 'orphanage', a dormitory for boys of my age group who were in Theresienstadt without parents. I had no idea where my sister was.

Mrs de Jong, the Dutch name by which I knew her in Theresienstadt, was actually Mrs Catharina Casoeto – de Jong. She was a young Dutch woman from a Catholic family who had married

Mr Casoeto, a Jewish market trader from Amsterdam. For this she was sent to Theresienstadt, the camp used by the Nazis for temporary storage of Jews not in the first wave for extermination. They also used it in a fraudulent charade to support a myth that deported Jews were treated humanely.

Mrs de Jong wanted to look after some children. A member of the 'Jewish Council' which ran the camp under Nazi orders, said: "There is a train coming tomorrow with two children whose father shot dead two German soldiers. Why don't you look after them?" I may not even have spent one night in the 'orphanage'. Mrs de Jong fetched me and took me to the place where she slept. She had collected my sister from another building. We slept on the floor of what had been a shop. Through the shop windows we could see people on the street, and they could see us. Both the shop and the streets were terribly crowded.

My uncle, Erich Stern, one of two half-brothers of my father, sought us out. He worked in an office for the camp administration, which may explain how he found us. He said he wanted to help Mrs de Jong, but in truth there was nothing useful he could do. He did bring some used typewriter ribbon bobbins and I attempted to make a toy train engine using these as wheels. However, I had next to no other materials.

Mrs de Jong worked in the kitchens and I now know that she stole food for us which she made us eat in the dormitory. I can't remember what we ate most of the time, or where we ate otherwise. At a later stage there was a period during which children were allowed to go to a particular building to receive a bread roll and a small pat of margarine. The Jewish leaders installed by the Germans, ensured children were favoured in food distribution. At some stage we received food parcels, probably from the Red Cross, in grey cardboard boxes containing delicacies otherwise unheard of in Theresienstadt. The contents did not last long. The death rate from infections was high and starvation caused deaths in adults. Though I was often very hungry, my sister and I did not starve.

Goods trains came into the street in Theresienstadt and men were packed into them by guards and soldiers, my uncle Erich among them. The Germans said the men were going 'to the east', to work. Postcards arrived for the women remaining in Theresienstadt, once from each man. Mrs de Jong told me that most of her women friends believed the story about the work and that she had not been able to persuade them that the men had probably been killed.

We did not stay in the shop, but moved at least three times to different dormitories. Theresienstadt had been the Czech garrison town Terezin and we moved to dormitories in army barracks, crowded with wooden bunk beds. One dormitory overlooked the street with the rail spur. This had been constructed with slave labour to avoid having to march prisoners outside the concentration camp. I often looked down from our first floor windows and watched men being squashed into cattle trains. Eventually, the camp was almost empty of men. Later, a dark green passenger train pulled up and women whose husbands had been deported, were invited to board this train to join them. Many thus went to their deaths. I remember debates amongst the women about whether they should accept the offer. Mrs de Jong did not waver. She urged others not to go, mostly unsuccessfully.

From this dormitory we moved to a small room off the back of a larger dormitory in the same building, the so-called 'Hamburg' barracks. At least two notable events occurred here. One morning we awoke to find that the people in the larger dormitory had been ordered out during the night for a roll call. They had been kept standing outdoors for hours and none of them knew the purpose of the inspection. They had concealed the presence of our small room from those who ordered them out. Mrs de Jong was furious and felt they had risked our lives, though they felt they had protected us. The second noteworthy event which I remember with some detail, was a notorious visit of International Red Cross inspectors to Terezin. From being horribly overcrowded, Theresienstadt had become sparsely populated as a result of transports to extermination camps and a by high death rate from starvation and disease. Shops which had not been in use, suddenly had window displays and looked open for business. Mrs de Jong took me into one, to see if there was something she could buy. I assume she had some means of payment or exchange, or perhaps the special camp money printed on German orders. A lady appeared from a door behind the counter, explaining that there was nothing to buy. She fetched a teddy bear from the area behind the door and gave it to Mrs de Jong for me. Later, an arm came off and we found some banknotes in the stuffing of the bear.

In preparation for the Red Cross visit, dormitories in the 'Hamburg' barracks were fumigated to kill the bedbugs, fleas and other vermin. The windows and doors were sealed with gummed brown paper tape and we were warned not to enter them. I have read that the fumigation was done with Zyklon B, the same granules releasing cyanide gas which the Nazis used in the extermination camps for mass murder.

We were told the Red Cross people would come to our little dormitory. Mrs de Jong and the other women told me very firmly not to say anything and not to touch the visitors. When they came, accompanied by German officers, the visitors were wearing uniforms with thick olive-green woollen overcoats. A small group of them stood within a yard of me, but I could not understand their conversation which was brief. I have read that the Red Cross team were impressed with the humane nature of our incarceration.

At one stage the women in our little dormitory got some milk and cloths and made cottage cheese. Later, we moved to a dormitory at the other end of the town, overlooking some kind of factory or timber yard. A remarkable sight was that of horse-drawn carts loaded high with wooden coffins, albeit crude ones, travelling towards the periphery of the camp. I was told these were people being buried; a remarkable contrast to the mass burial pits or mass cremation ovens of other camps. What a privilege! But perhaps they were just manufactured in the camp and exported empty.

There seemed to be few German soldiers in Theresienstadt and I don't remember Germans in SS uniform prominently. There were civilian guards with uniforms more reminiscent of continental post office workers or railway guard uniforms. The black caps had coloured piping which indicated the nationality of the wearer, Czech or otherwise. The different nationalities were said to differ in their harshness towards the inmates. But the only action I remember them taking, was blowing a whistle at people walking on the grass in one of the squares.

Though I had hardly any contact with other children, some boys I met in one of the grassy squares told me that a boy who had brushed past a German soldier on a path across the square, had been shot dead on the spot. They also told me there had been hangings. I think they said this had happened near a small swimming pool which I seem to remember being empty.

The inmates at Theresienstadt wore ordinary clothes. I certainly did not arrive with luggage and I'm not sure if I ever received any clothing other than that with which I had been picked up at the nursery school. I do not know whether adults had any changes of clothing. But I remember that the women in our dormitory for a time talked about getting corsets made or fitted by a woman inmate. It seems possible that some people arrived with suitcases and had some extra clothing, and that clothes of the many who died of disease were redistributed.

Mrs de Jong had an overwhelming memory of the terrible stench in which we lived in Theresienstadt, and of pervasive filthiness. I have no memory of the smell, nor of the filth which that description evokes, though the place must have been filthy, given our circumstances. There was a men's lavatory such as one would expect to find in barracks. This had a row of washbasins and I think the taps worked. I may have washed there. I do know that shortly after my return to Holland a woman who looked after me for a day was disgusted that I did not know what to do with lavatory paper: there had been none in Theresienstadt. I do not think it was possible to bathe or shower. Mrs de Jong told me that the only way she could do this was to stand under some source of running water outdoors, naked in public.

At the age of six I did not know about menstruation, but I did notice that the women got hold of tiny bits of cotton wool which they put in their underwear and which came out soiled with blood. It embarrassed them greatly that I saw this.

Bedbugs shared our life and our blood. The French and Dutch word for a drawing pin (punaise) is also the word for bedbug. The head of a drawing pin is reminiscent in shape and size of an 'empty' bedbug. In this flat state they can quickly disappear into tiny crevices which were plentiful in our wooden bunks. When they have sucked blood, they swell up and are easily squashed, leaving a bloodstain, but doing this made no noticeable difference to their number. Fleas were common and I had them repeatedly. Comedians in old silent films sometimes act out a joke in which they watch an imaginary flea jump from one hand to the other. This joke will mean little to most people now, but I was very familiar with the prodigious jumping ability of these itchy pests. I can't remember having lice, but although these are more secretive than bedbugs or fleas, that does not necessarily mean I did not have any. The conditions made them inevitable and they were the carriers of a typhus epidemic at the end of the camp's existence.

I became very ill, with yellow skin and urine the colour of black coffee. This is likely to have been infectious hepatitis. Mrs de Jong insisted I should not go to a doctor (there were of course doctors among the inmates), but keep out of view and leaving the small dormitory only to go to the washroom or toilet. She told me that if I was seen in that state I would probably be sent away and killed.

I was taken to at least one theatrical show, but recall little of it. I do not recall the children's show 'Brundibar' which was performed in Theresienstadt. Mrs de Jong persuaded a man to teach me reading and writing. He made me form letters by sticking strips of gummed paper to a sheet of paper, but this did not last long and I can only remember learning the letter 'm'. When I started school in Holland I had to start from scratch. I remember no manifestations of religion.

Terezin, or Theresienstadt, was a small garrison town of decent-looking large buildings of an appearance common in the Austro-

Hungarian Empire. The streets were reasonably broad and arranged mainly on a rectangular pattern. There were public squares with grass and trees. The outdoor appearance of the place was mostly quite pleasant. The town, or at least the part to which we were confined, was small in area and I quickly became familiar with it by wandering about. On my only visit there since the war, I had some difficulty in orientating myself because in my memory, part of the town had turned through a right angle. Once I reconciled myself to the fact that my memory was tricking me a bit, I found my way around to familiar sites quite easily. The buildings had also shrunk remarkably, compared to my memory of them.

I have read that among Jews elsewhere in the Nazi empire there was a rumour about the existence of a 'paradise ghetto' for Jews, which referred to Theresienstadt. This may have been due to Nazi attempts to use Terezin as part of a cover-up for their atrocities, spreading this rumour themselves. Though nearer to a hell compared to normal free life, in comparison to the extermination camps Theresienstadt was relatively a paradise for some, including my sister and myself.

Loudspeakers in the squares played popular classical music at least some of the time, perhaps for the Red Cross visit. Long after the war Mrs de Jong once started humming one of the melodies, a waltz which featured a lot. She had not said anything, but I instantly recognised her referral to this loudspeaker music and she realised that I remembered it.

As far as I recall, I spent my time in whichever dormitory we occupied, or wandering about the streets of the little town. There were no toys or books and I had next to no contact with other children. During the day Mrs de Jong and the other women were absent. Mrs de Jong worked in the kitchens and some of the other women split mica. Once they brought a lump of mica to the dormitory to show me how such a piece could be split into transparent sheets.

One day a film was being made in the street outside the 'Hamburg' barracks. A curved line of adult inmates was arranged from one side of the street to the other and a tripod-mounted cine camera panned across the arc. I approached the scene from behind the people being filmed and tried to get into the picture but don't think I succeeded.

During our last period there, Theresienstadt was sparsely populated. Virtually all its men and children were dead or had been deported to death camps. The Germans only just failed to massacre the last of us, in trenches they forced inmates to dig for the purpose. Living skeletons of diseased human beings appeared from other concentration camps. Unlike our threadbare but normal clothes, they wore the well-known striped concentration camp uniforms. We were told to keep away from them because they had typhus and other lethal infections. There were times when we were told to shelter in cellars because of a danger of bombing. Water had to be boiled before drinking. Canon fire was sometimes audible in the distance.

One morning I woke to find Mrs de Jong excited and overjoyed . The Red Army had entered Terezin during the night and she had been up to welcome its soldiers. A tank crew member had given her a smashed compass from a vehicle, quite a large object. This was for me. I was disappointed that she had not woken me, but evidently she had wanted to enjoy this moment unencumbered by children. I can't blame her. Life in Theresienstadt was constant fear of death. She knew that her husband had been sent to a concentration camp and did not know that he had survived. The moment of liberation cannot be fully described to someone who has not been in that situation.

The Red Army moved on. We stayed in Terezin until army lorries arrived, for the start of our journey home. I remember being alarmed by the height to which we had to climb to get in, but the journey did not feel that bad. I guess our food must have improved. Mrs de Jong was allowed to sit in the cab next to the driver with my still two-year-old sister whilst the lorries continued at night and Mrs de Jong fell asleep. Suddenly, the door flew open and my little sister fell from the high driver's cab of the moving lorry. Erica was practically unscathed.

The convoy stopped at a little town and we were told to take showers as part of a delousing process. At this, the women became agitated. By now they had heard of gas chambers and absolutely refused to shower or to let me do so. Delousing was done by dusting DDT into our clothes. We continued our journey. One night was spent in an impressive chateau near some mountains. Its gardens had some sweet williams, the first flowers I had seen since before Theresienstadt. They still have this special meaning for me.

Part of our journey was by train and one overnight stop seems to have been at a railway station in a building overlooking a marshalling yard. We were warned to boil water before drinking it. Another overnight stop was in some sort of camp of wooden huts surrounded by a tall barbed wire fence, though we were free to wander out. While exploring the outside of this fence I came across an intriguing object, black and shaped like a thick disc. I was about to pick it up when some other boys hurried up to me and explained what a landmine was.

The last stage of our journey to the Netherlands was in the bottom of a large cargo barge of the type common on the Rhine. This was uncomfortable, with limited access to the hatch for a breath of fresh air. When the barge arrived in Holland, members of the Bangma family were waiting for us. Mrs Bangma had a friend in the Netherlands Red Cross and had asked him to look out for our names on lists of returnees.

We went to Mrs de Jong's flat in the 'Jordaan' district of Amsterdam, fronting onto one of the canals. Her husband was not there, but there was another woman in the flat. On perhaps the second day members of the Bangma family appeared and took us from her. This distressed me a great deal. Although I had been taken to their house during the war, I hardly knew them and I loved Mrs de Jong. Of course I knew my mother had died and I did not know what had happened to my father. More than forty years later I learned that Mrs Bangma, a forceful woman, had engaged a lawyer to compel Mrs de Jong to give us up. Mrs de Jong, traumatised, working-class and still unaware that her husband had survived, was unable to keep the two children for which she had repeatedly and knowingly risked her life. As I was being driven away from her flat I waved to her with a little triangular red and yellow bicycle flag which she had allowed me to take from her house.

We were only permitted to see her once more. She was allowed to visit, but was treated so unpleasantly that she could not face repeating the experience. Decades later I re-established contact. By this time she had breast cancer, from which she died not much later. Her husband had returned from his concentration camp, but had died before I found her again. He always regretted not being able to see us. They remained unable to have children of their own, but adopted a boy. The relationship proved difficult. She remained a wonderful woman, a thoroughly decent person, with whom I had a perfectly natural affinity.

The Bangma family was able to house my sister, but returned me to Mrs Cathrien Rademakers. She had been arrested and forced to leave her baby son in the flat. Her protest at this in the interrogation centre had been answered with a slap and she was told to shut up. Neighbours rescued the baby; Cathrien was released after some days. She had then used contacts to speak to a German army officer regarded as helpful by Dutch friends, trying to get her husband released from the notorious concentration camp at Vught in the Netherlands. The officer agreed and made a phone call. However, German administration was becoming chaotic and the camp had received instructions to transfer inmates to Germany. Her husband was put arbitrarily on a train and sent to Neuengamme concentration camp where he was murdered. Cathrien received a parcel containing his spectacles.

She treated me as normally as she had before. I had my seventh birthday at her flat and she enrolled me at a primary school within sight of the Royal Palace in Amsterdam. The walk to school took me close to the Anne Frank house. Her story was not known at that time. Close to that point is a beautiful church with a lovely carillon, the tunes of which cheered the many pedestrians, myself included. One morning I crossed a side street without looking; there had hardly been any cars in Theresienstadt. A man saved my life by grabbing my collar and dragging me out of the path of a van. Another morning, on the same route, I fell into conversation with a man walking to work. Soon he had my story out of me. He reacted with obvious pity. I found this difficult. This single incident resolved me not to speak about my past to strangers, a decision I did not change until recent years.

At the school I had a distinct feeling that there was the class of other pupils and there was me, floating around as a separate entity. Since the age of three I had had little contact with other children with the exception of my tiny sister. Learning to interact more normally with the others and to feel part of the class, took me longer than my short time at that school.

During the next five years I was housed with three further families in two countries. I went to seven schools. Each of the families was very different, and mutual adaptation was harder with each successive move. Moreover, the moves were not those I would have chosen. In two of the households there was clearly no unanimity about wanting me in the family though in both cases warm relations eventually developed. I would have been happier staying with Mrs de Jong or Cathrien Rademakers, because I felt very close to both, or with my Israeli family who wanted to take us and whom I knew and loved. It was a difficult time. The last two Dutch families were horrified by my wish to be brought up as a Jew. They brought me up as a Christian and then transferred me to my Jewish family in the U.K., where this was resented.

Attending an English boarding school, decided upon against my wishes before I moved to England, was a disaster. It separated me from even problematic family support. Anti-Semitism among the pupils was a problem. Though considering myself Christian then, I could not bring myself to say I was not a Jew and accepted the consequences. Good fresh air came with a move to the Manchester Grammar School where intellectual and educational effort made prior status and background irrelevant. Brasenose College and the University of Oxford provided copious opportunity to develop whatever ability or interest its students had.

Of course I am grateful to those who brought me up and I learned valuable things from each of them individually, but repeated upheaval, trauma and insecurity followed from the wartime events. Problems inevitably arise from disrupted family relationships and care of traumatised children by traumatised adults, in addition to the problems which can arise in any life. I fervently hope that in other cases of genocide and atrocity, the interests and wishes of each child will be taken into account much more seriously, as they are supposed to be in family law, difficult as this is to achieve in the disruption following such events.

One piece of luck was nowhere near enough in order to survive the methodical, industrialised extermination plans of the Germans and their collaborators. But luck can also be bad luck, as in my father's betrayal by an idiot.

The Rademakers hid me at the cost of a good man's life and the Bangmas hid my sister, risking theirs. Thus we entered the concentration camp system late, a great help to survival. My non-Jewish mother reduced, in Nazi eyes, our priority for being killed. Efforts by the Bangmas to influence Nazi officials may have contributed to us being sent to Theresienstadt, not Auschwitz. Surely, Germans were responsible for the fact that a member of the 'Judenrat' (Jewish Council) in Theresienstadt knew that our father had killed two German soldiers, causing Mrs de Jong to choose us from amongst the other children. Perhaps it was because we were not housed with the other children that the Nazi machine slipped up and our names were not on the list for Auschwitz. Mrs de Jong was intelligent, brave, resourceful and motherly. She stole food for us. She kept me hidden when I was ill. Boys I met warned me not to brush past German soldiers. Towards the end, the Red Army foiled German plans to murder us en masse. Even on the way back, my sister survived a fall from a lorry and other children saved me from a landmine. We escaped death from diseases which were rife. Apart from the courage, sacrifice and help of others, sheer random chance was important.

Westerbork and Theresienstadt contained countless children who were better than I, but perished. We don't have their stories. I was lucky. I survived. I was in a concentration camp which was a paradise compared to the extermination camps, though a lethal hell or its antechamber to most when compared to normal life.

Even as a child, ignorant of the full extent of the holocaust, it appeared monstrous to me that German officials and soldiers, railway workers and Dutch collaborators worked at our destruction as a matter of normality and routine, no matter what the resulting horror.

I survived and so did enough friends and members of my family to provide a home and education. I have a wife, three children and two beautiful little granddaughters. I have retired from a medical career which gave me the wonderful opportunity to tackle illness with skills gained from great teachers and patient patients.

I am proud of and grateful for the friendship of other holocaust survivors. It often seems to me that for us, other people can be divided into those to whom one can't explain, and those to whom there is no need to explain.

I was once asked by a non-Jewish friend, the son of my grandparents' neighbours, non-Jewish Germans who fled Germany rather than live under Nazism, whether all these events were now safely in the past and 'behind me'. Any hesitation was due to the unexpectedness of the question, but I answered that every second of every day of my life is influenced by those events. Giving this answer made me question it. I have made a point of asking the opinion of other holocaust survivors about this answer. None so far has disagreed with what I was trying to say. Surely the same applies to any other human being who has suffered comparable events.

LILI STERN-POHLMANN

The Unsung Heroes to Whom My Mother and I Owe Our Lives

I made my escape from the Lvov (Poland; now Lviv in the Ukraine) Ghetto on a particularly cold November night of 1942. I was ten years old. My grandparents, a few neighbours and I were hiding under the floorboards of our one-room 'apartment' in the Ghetto. My mother, Cecylia (Cesia) Stern–Abraham, née Brück, was not with us that night: at the special request of some non-Jewish friends who needed her help, she was spending the night with them 'on the other side'. The penalty for that was death for all concerned. On that very night the news spread within the Ghetto that a 'specific selection' was due to start in the early hours of the morning. All those not 'usefully' employed by the military and/or the heavy industry would be rounded up at the points of entrance to the Ghetto and subsequently sent to extermination camps. My mother was not employed by either: she worked for the German Civil Service Authority (slave labour). I knew that she would be desperate to get back to the Ghetto, to us – her daughter (myself) and her parents. By then she had already lost her husband (my father), and her five-year-old son (my brother).

At three o'clock in the morning, in my pyjamas, a pair of galoshes and a light cardigan on top – having made sure that everyone around me was deep asleep – I crept up the ladder, lifted the two floorboards and squeezed through. Nobody heard me, nobody saw me, I was out.

The night was beautiful. The virgin, powder-fresh snow was lying deep, the moon was full. To get to the 'other side' I would have to climb over the railway embankment which was not an easy procedure, particularly in full moonlight … I just about managed to get myself to the top of the embankment when, suddenly, there were machine-gun shots all around me. I fell flat, deep into the fresh snow, and lay there, motionless. The shots continued for a while, and then silence … Was I wounded? Were they looking for me? Would they find me?

Silence … silence … Realising that I was unscathed, I knew that with the full moonlight above and the dazzling white snow all around, it would not be easy to get over the embankment without being clearly seen by the guards. I put as much snow over me as possible and slowly, began to 'snowball' over the rail tracks and down the other side. It was quiet, uncannily so. For another while I lay in the snow – a snowball myself – and waited; then slowly, very slowly, I began my unforgettable journey to town, to my mother. I walked along one of the longest streets in town, the only way of getting there. I knew that on each side were enormous military barracks – once Polish, now German – in front of which, day and night, there were soldiers standing guard. I had no other way. I had to keep walking to get past them. There was not a soul in the street at four a.m., just me, in my pyjamas, so obviously from the Ghetto. 'They are bound to stop me', I thought, but I kept on walking, passing one guard, then the next, on the other side of the street. 'Now they'll shoot me, in the back' … but nothing … quiet … only the sound of my own footsteps in the crisp, fresh snow that made me feel that the whole town could hear me.

These two soldiers on guard are my first two, unknown, 'Unsung Heroes'. I wish I could have said 'Thank you' to them.

As I reached the tram depot, I managed to creep inside and hide under a bench – at least I was out of the bitter cold! After some time (which seemed more like an eternity), the first workers began to show up, then the conductors, the drivers, and slowly, slowly the tram began to fill up with people going to work. I decided to squeeze into a corner and make myself 'invisible'– what a silly thought! I prayed that no-one would denounce me. I hadn't much hope of that, but still, somehow I *knew* I would reach my destination – my mother's life depended on me. The conductor passed me by countless times, pretending not to notice my presence. By now the tram was well on its way and full to capacity. I was seen by many and looked at in silent curiosity, yet no-one approached me, no-one said a word to me, no-one pointed a finger at this, quite obviously, Jewish child on the run – everyone looked the other way …

These special people are next on the list of my 'Unsung Heroes' who, by their silent conspiracy, helped to spare not only my life, but also that of my mother whom I reached *just* in time to prevent her from going back to the Ghetto and to certain death.

Our subsequent saviours were three total strangers, namely Frau Irmgard Wieth, a German civil servant, employed as a secretary by the Nazi local government; Herr Max Kohl, a German leather-tanning specialist; and the Metropolitan Count Andrej Szeptyckyj, head of the Ukrainian Orthodox Church.

Frau Wieth was a remarkable human being who saved not only my life, but also that of my mother and two more people – a husband and wife. There was no question of any kind of payment or reward – on the contrary, she shared her own rations with me. She was highly intelligent, shy, and rather eccentric. Among her eccentricities, first and foremost, was her absolute obsession with garlic! A firm believer in its medicinal properties, she would consume large quantities of it daily, as a prophylactic. Needles to say, this habit did not endear her to her friends, suitors and immediate colleagues at work: yet she would rather do without people than without her garlic, and so, slowly slowly, she became a complete recluse, a loner. Did G-d will it that this strange fetish of hers should become our salvation?

Frau Wieth occupied a rather luxurious two-room apartment in a four-storey building requisitioned for high ranking SS-officers and their families, within the SS- and the Police District of Lvov. This apartment was originally allocated to her friend, an SS-Obersturmführer. However, he was soon transferred for other 'duties' to a Jewish Concentration Camp in Holland and, before leaving, recommended that she should stay in the apartment.

At one point, while the four of us were being hidden by Frau Wieth, this – by now, long forgotten – friend suddenly decided to pay her an unannounced visit. This turned out to be two weeks' leave! A fortnight under the same roof with a henchman who, had he found us, would have shot us on the spot, Frau Wieth included … yet, she did not dispose of us during this fateful visit, but – inexplicably and miraculously – managed to keep us hidden from sight in the tiny kitchen larder. It is indeed nothing short of a miracle from G-d that she and we four survived that visit.

Earlier on, while I was still alone with her, she was quite unexpectedly called back to Germany for two weeks. Nothing would induce her to let me go to my mother, to the Ghetto. Instead, she decided she would take me with her to Germany. 'But how?', I asked. 'Simple', she said, "we shall cut your hair very short, I shall get you a 'Lederhosen' outfit, and you'll be a boy.' By then I spoke German fluently, without a trace of an accent. We travelled to Germany as mother and son, and came back to Lvov after two weeks. During that journey countless 'miracles' occurred, as indeed, they did during our stay with Frau Wieth.

Our ways parted only after Frau Wieth was ordered back to Germany, towards the end of 1943. After the war I looked and finally found Ms Wieth in a Russian camp in Czechoslovakia, in a pitiful condition. By that time (1947), my mother and I were already in London, and within two years we were able to bring her over here. In 1949 Ms Wieth left London for the USA. She subsequently became an American citizen, living and working happily in New York, refusing *ever* again to speak or write in German. (I also lived in New York, from 1954 till 1964.) She spent her last days close to us, in England, a country and people she always loved and revered. She died in 1981.

Despite her many protestations ('I have done nothing to deserve it.'), Ms Wieth received the highest Israeli honour – the Medal of the Righteous – in the 1960s. She bore a remarkable resemblance to

Katharine Hepburn. A photograph of the ceremony where she was surrounded by Israeli officials, in the Israeli Consulate in New York, is and will remain one of my most precious possessions. She also planted a tree in the Avenue of the Just in Yad Vashem, Jerusalem.

Herr Max Kohl (from Stuttgart where his family still live) was brought over by the German occupation authorities to Lvov, to open and run a leather-coat factory for the Gestapo. Having arrived in Lvov, he insisted that the factory be sited within the walls of the Ghetto. He then employed approximately fifty Jews – including my Mother – as 'specialists'. Time and again, he risked his life, bribing high-ranking Gestapo officials with free, high-quality leather coats so that they would spare 'his' Jews. This man was by any standard, a 'mini–Schindler'. He, too, was honoured by the State of Israel in the same manner as Ms Wieth, both on our testimony and recommendation.

When Frau Wieth had been recalled to Germany, she did not leave Lvov before making sure that we had some other safe place to go to. This time it was His Holiness, The Metropolitan Count Andrei Szeptyckyj, who gave us (and many others, in particular, Jewish children) shelter. Risking his life, he first took us into his own palace, adjacent to the cathedral in Lvov. After a while he moved us to various convents and orphanages within convents. We were kept and sheltered there until we were liberated by the Russians in 1944. This brave and compassionate man saved approximately 200 Jewish lives – 'his' Jews are scattered all over the world, and those still alive today can pay testimony to his heroism.

Lvov was liberated by the Russians in July 1944. A year later my mother and I left for Krakow. It took us seven days to reach that city. There, Rabbi Dr Kahane, by then the Chief Rabbi of the Polish forces, was attempting to trace displaced Jewish children throughout the country, in order to either reunite them with their families, if any of those had survived, or to find new lives for them. He worked in close co-operation with Rabbi Dr Solomon Schonfeld of London. In 1946 I was fortunate to be brought over to London by Rabbi Dr

Schonfeld, in the first of the three transports of Jewish children from Poland. My dear mother joined me one year later. She died, aged 94, in London in October 2001. We were the *only* survivors of an extended family of more than 300 … I do not know 'why we two?', but what I do know is *to whom* we owe our lives, and to whom our gratitude is eternal. They are our 'Unsung Heroes': in their humanity and compassion, and through their selfless, heroic deeds, they all merit to join the ranks of 'whosoever saves one life, saves the world entire'.

Both Frau Wieth and Herr Max Kohl were thus honoured – but, as yet, to our great sadness and dismay, not so the Metropolitan Szeptyckyj …

JANINE WEBBER (PREVIOUSLY GALLOWAY)

Of Many Encounters

I was born in Lwow (in Poland, now Lviv in the Ukraine) in 1932. It was then the third largest town of the country, with beautiful renaissance-style buildings and a well-known opera house. My mother, Lipka Monat née Hochberg, came from a large orthodox Jewish family. She had nine brothers and sisters; not all of them were religious. My father, Alfred Monat, was an only child. He was an accountant by profession. My parents had opened a grocer's shop and seemed quite successful. I was called Niunia, and my life was that of a normal, happy child.

In 1939 the Russians unexpectedly marched through the streets of Lwow. To my parents it must have been very worrying to see these dreaded invaders wrecking their peaceful existence. They had good reason to believe the worst. The rumour quickly spread that all those who owned property would be sent to Siberia. My parents who owned a shop and half a house, immediately tried to find a solution to this daunting prospect.

My mother had befriended a Russian woman. Together with their children, they would go for picnics in the local park. To me, this park was like a forest, thick with bushes and trees, wild flowers, dark corners and perhaps animals. Here and there, a sunny glade with a bench or two, dispelled its mystery. However, I had a strong feeling that if I lost sight of my mother, I would disappear in its evergreen density. So I kept close to her. The two women sat on a wooden bench and chatted, and we, the children, ran around and ate our

237

sandwiches. Occasionally, I would glance at my mother, just to see her peacefully sitting there, quietly smiling, so lovely. I see her black eyes, her gentle gaze, her beautiful pale yellow dress, and warmth envelops me. I do not see anybody else; nobody else matters. She is there, and it is enough to comfort me, to fill me with happiness.

On a clear, sunny day, the workers celebrated the 1st of May. Through the window of our bedroom I saw the groups of men and women walking in the street, each group carrying objects, symbols of their product: a huge spoon for the cutlery makers, a big shoe for the shoemakers, and many flags and tanks. Women wore colourful dresses, and many had multicoloured ribbons floating in their hair. It all seemed so guileless, so cheerful, a genuine celebration, far removed from the fear my parents felt at that time.

Somehow, they managed to remain in Lwow. Whether it was through the friendship with the Russian woman, as I assumed at the time, or simply that, in fact, they were not rich, I do not know, but their fear was dispelled and the calm returned. I started going to the kindergarten, at first a little intimidated by all these children and the mistresses, as I was quite shy, then gaining confidence. However, it was with my mother that I learned to read and write, it seems in quite a short time. When I was nine years old my education stopped. The Germans were coming.

Sometimes I wonder what would have happened, had my parents been sent to Siberia rather than remaining in Lwow. Maybe they would have been still alive.

In 1941 the bombardments started. The bombs started falling all around us. My mother would take me by the hand and we would run down the three floors to the cellar. She was sometimes sick down there. I could guess her nervousness, I could see her terror stricken face and feel her trembling body. But I was not frightened of the bombs. I was not aware of the danger. I found the noise upsetting, and above all, seeing my mother's face so pale, was very unusual. I held tightly on to her, unable to grasp fully what was going on.

The bombardments did not last long, but the pink and grey façade of our house had been badly damaged. Soon the Russians left, and in June 1941 the Germans arrived. For the first few days we hardly went out. We stayed in the apartment, while my father was trying to make a living. One day, as we were waiting for my father, we heard a terrifying screaming and the sound of running steps on the stairs. My father burst in shouting: 'The Germans are rounding up the Jewish men!' It seems that the caretaker of our building, a Gentile, had pointed out to the Germans that there were some Jewish families in that building. Immediately my mother locked the door and pushed a table and a bed towards it, to stop the Germans coming in. With all my strength I, too, was pushing the furniture. They banged angrily on the door, shouting in German, but somehow left after a while. Meanwhile, my father had run to the window and jumped onto the first floor balcony. From there, he managed to escape on to the roof nearby. When all was quiet, he came back, limping and in great pain. He had fractured his leg, and had to have it in plaster for a while. The tension this first rounding-up produced, the frightened expressions on my parents' faces and my father's escape, left me with a feeling of bewilderment and insecurity. From then on I was always frightened. However, for my parents, as I can now imagine, it must have been extremely distressing.

The persecution of the Jews escalated at a fast pace. We were told to leave our apartment and all our belongings, and to move out to an area outside Lwow. This was in preparation for sending us to the ghetto.

We left in haste, only taking with us a small suitcase, and went to live in a small house where we were allocated a tiny room for all five of us. Two families were already there, as well as my cousin Nina (the daughter of my mother's sister Regina), her parents and her brother. In our room there were two beds, one for my parents and one for the children. There was also a small cooker with two rings, and a small table. There was hardly any room to move. My grandmother had a bed in another room where there was a wardrobe of which I will tell more below. We did not have much food, and the money must have run out quickly. I remember my mother giving us some potatoes, and cooking the peelings as well. She only ate some peelings. After a while her body started to swell, from what I assume was the lack of proper food. It was especially difficult after my father had been caught. My aunt Rouja (also a sister of my mother) sold some clothes and helped my mother and Nina's mother to buy some food. In this overcrowded house we stayed just a short while.

My parents dug a hole under a wardrobe. Three people could get into it by lifting the bottom shelf. The day my parents learned that a German raid was coming, my mother, my brother and I hid in the hole. I knew by now that it was not a hide-and-seek game. I could suddenly hear my grandmother's screams. However, we all kept quiet; there was just the noise of my heart pounding. They discovered my family in the loft. They pushed my grandmother downstairs and took my family away. We learned later that my father had been shot, while Nina's father and her ten-year-old brother had been transported to a concentration camp.

A few days later, we learned that there was going to be another raid. We could hear the Germans down the road screaming and swearing at the Jews. This time we quickly ran to a small wooden shed in the courtyard. In addition to us, there was my aunt Regina with Nina, and another family. We heard the SS approaching and their dogs barking. I saw the soldiers through the wooden slats and noticed their shiny black boots. The image of those well-polished boots and their pounding on the paved courtyard would often haunt me in my dreams and continued to terrify me.

Suddenly Nina who was hardly four, started to cry. Her mother tried to pacify her, but she continued all the louder. The woman with us grabbed a pillow and covered Nina's face. I remember the anxiety in the eyes of my aunt and my mother, but nobody stopped the woman pressing the pillow on Nina's face. We sat there, huddled together in complete silence, while outside the cries went on. It seemed to last for ever. At last the Germans left. When the pillow was removed, Nina was fast asleep and breathing normally.

Slowly we emerged from the wooden shed and silently returned to our rooms. For a week or two we continued with a semblance of a normal life. The children played quietly in the courtyard, and the adults whispered among themselves.

My mother. She does not laugh, she does not smile, she hardly speaks. My mother. She looks sad, pale and distant. In my mind there is a rush of questions. Where is my father? What happened to my grandmother? These words are never uttered. I remain silent and my mother does not speak. I want to show her that I care, but I do not know how. I cannot cry any more and my feelings are now numb.

We were told to move out. The ghetto was ready for us. A big area was surrounded by a high fence, and we moved into a room on the first floor of a big building. The greyness of that room, the bareness of the surroundings, a lack of food, of clothes, is what we found there. Looking through the window I saw people in rags rushing about and begging. 'Who was still left?' I wanted to ask, but never did. Of the members of our big family, just three adults were left with us. I learned after the war that two of my cousins had survived. One of them, Nusia, had jumped from the train going to Auschwitz.

The raids continued. At first, they came for the adults. Rudi, Rouja's friend who spoke German, would be warned of the raids by a member of the SS who seemed to like him. My mother hid in the cellar of the building. It was a dark, dank tunnel, infested with rats. Petrified, I saw them running around. In that hole she caught typhus. Hoping to relieve her discomfort, my uncle carried her to our room. One day, when she was lying in bed, we heard the usual screams of the Germans running upstairs. My uncle hid, and we completely covered my mother with the duvet. They kicked the door open, and looked around for adults. Nina, my brother and I, kept quiet. They left, not having found anyone.

My uncle Zelig prepared a bed for my mother in the cellar. It was safer to be there, as anybody found sick would have been thrown into a wheelbarrow, then pushed into a ditch, dead or alive. That is what happened to Nina's mother. Zelig washed and fed my mother. When

I went to see her, she was lying in this narrow bed, covered with sores, unable to move. Very soon, she became delirious and did not recognise me. I ran out, unable to bear it.

I was nearly nine when my uncle found a Polish family of farmers, whom he paid to hide my aunt and myself. We went to a remote village where there seemed to be one big farm with some stables surrounded by fields. The farmer led us to a stable filled with straw, where we slept, and the farmer's wife brought us some food.

One day the farmer appeared, alone. He went up to my aunt, almost touching her, and started whispering to her. Although I did not know what was going on, I could guess by my aunt's distressed looks that something unpleasant was happening. When he started molesting her, she looked very frightened, knelt in front of him and begged him to leave her alone. She went on begging him in a plaintive voice, and tried to kiss his hand. He continued pressing her. Suddenly, she got up and ran out. I was left alone with the farmer. He hesitated for a while, then went out.

The next evening they called me in and told me to share the bed with their son who was about 15. As I lay down, I could feel him coming closer to me. I pushed him away and quietly told him to leave me alone. He continued nevertheless. So I got up and found a big stick which I put between us and warned him that if he came closer, I would hit him. He stopped, and soon fell asleep. I tried to keep awake, still unsure what to do. However, soon sleep overcame me. In the morning, the farmer's wife locked me up in a tiny room, where there was a bed and a bucket. I stayed there for a few weeks, lying in bed covered with a big black coat. The bed and the coat were infested with lice. I could see them crawling around, and as I had nothing to do and no one to talk to, I spent my time killing the lice and looking at the whitewashed walls. After a while, I started seeing bulls, rabbits and lion-type animals with horns as well as people grinning, open-mouthed as if screaming and one-legged monsters with guns and knives in the cracks of the walls. Everything seemed to be moving and looked very real to me. I do not remember being frightened, but only wanting to speak to someone and tell him what I was seeing. The woman who brought me some food, never spoke to me. One day, she unlocked the door and told me to leave.

I do not remember how soon or in which way I found myself with another Polish family, this time with my brother. He was about six or seven. We were kept indoors all the time. I had a dress, in the hem of which my uncle had put some money for us. A soon as we arrived, the mother of the family took my dress away and gave me some old clothes. I never saw that money again.

One day, the daughter of the family, an attractive 20-year old woman, brought in an armed SS-man. They called me outside and the German soldier looked at me and said 'Go!' pointing into the distance. I started walking, thinking that perhaps he would shoot me. I continued walking, not knowing where to go.

I walked in the fields for a long time. The evening was approaching and I was hungry. I saw a woman working in the fields. She seemed an ordinary, kindly person. I asked her for some bread. She wanted to know who I was and where I came from. I made up a story about the Ukrainians who had killed my family and gave a name of a village. She seemed to believe me and invited me to her house. There she gave me some food and said: 'You can stay with us and help us with the cows.' That is how I became a shepherdess. I stayed there for a few months and was well treated.

I was in the fields with the cows when I saw in the distance a woman coming towards me. As she came closer, I recognised the daughter of the Polish family who had looked after my brother and myself for a while. She said with a smile: 'The SS-man buried your brother alive.' I just looked at her and remained silent. She brought the SS-man, she killed my brother, I kept thinking. I did not cry. I could not cry any more. At the time I was numb and felt no emotions. Now, when I remember her sadistic expression, I am filled with anger and pain. Murderous fantasies cross my mind. My dreams are haunted by violent deeds. I wake up exhausted by so much aggression, aghast with such bellicosity. I am a mild, passive person. It surprised me that, after so many years, I still harbour these strong feelings.

Later, as I was walking through some wheat fields, I saw a family hiding there. There was an older woman with three teenage children. She looked at me in a puzzled, but silent way. I immediately guessed that they were Jewish and frightened. To reassure them, I said: 'I, too, am Jewish.' We talked for a while and soon I left them.

My Polish family told me to leave. They had learned that I was Jewish, and it was too dangerous to keep me. They bought me a train ticket, and I went back to Lwow. For a long time I thought that it was this Jewish family which had betrayed me by telling my Polish family that I was Jewish. Now, I am sure that it had been the Polish woman who had called in the SS-man.

I had been given by my aunt Rouja the name and address of a Polish man, Edek, the caretaker of a convent. By sheer luck I managed to find his address. He was sitting in his office alone. I told him who I was. He just looked at me without saying a word. Then he got up and said, "Follow me at a good distance." I wondered if he was going to give me away to the SS and decided that if I saw Germans, I would run in the opposite direction. Eventually, we arrived in the grounds of a big building. He told me to wait by a small building. When he came back carrying a ladder, he told me to climb the ladder and go through the door to the loft. When I opened that door I saw a group of people sitting or lying on the floor of the loft. Aunt Rouja was there as were my uncle Zelig and Rouja's boy friend; altogether 14 people. After a month or two we moved to a bunker under the stable floor, which they had dug out, working at night.

I stayed there for nearly a year. The conditions were poor. We would take it in turns to lie on the planks or sit. There was no room for walking, there was no air and the sanitary conditions were minimal. There was very little food; I remember eating bread with chopped raw onions mixed with a few drops of oil. Also, it was very hot because we had no fresh air, and I wore only my knickers. After a year my aunt and uncle decided that I would not be able to survive in this hole much longer. She managed to get me false identity papers and I had to learn all my new personal details by heart. My story was that I was a survivor of a village whose inhabitants had been killed by the Ukrainians.

One day we left the bunker. I had difficulty in walking because I had not walked for a year, and I was very pale and thin. My aunt took me to a Polish Committee that was set up to help Poles who had been persecuted by the Ukrainians. They did not believe my story straight away, and went to look for someone from the village. Eventually, they came back and said they could find no one, and gave me papers to go to a convent. My aunt took me there, and was asked again if I were not Jewish as I looked so sickly. She convinced them that I was not Jewish. I spent one night there, and was sent on to a different convent, in Krakow.

There were perhaps 30 children there. We all slept on blankets on the floor. While the children were playing and running, I had to sit because my legs ached so much when I walked. I went one day to the Mother Superior and asked why I could not run. She looked at me and said: "You have to accept that you will never walk properly." I was also worried because I did not know the Catholic prayers; I tried to mouth them.

One day a priest arrived. He wanted to take four children to give them shelter in his house. He looked kind and smiled at me. I asked him if I could go with him. He had a small house and a garden. I used to sit in his garden and tried to walk. Little by little my muscles strengthened. The priest was a nice man. I slept in the lower part of a bunk bed. The girl on top used to wet the bed. As the mattress was thin, it would occasionally run onto me. I did not want to complain, so when one day an elderly couple came and asked if one of us would like to go to live with them in their village and help them in the house, I said I would. And that is how, at the age of 11, I became a maid and a cowgirl. I never told anyone I was Jewish; I was too frightened. I went to church every Sunday, learnt the catechism, went to confession and did my first communion. I found the confession difficult, because I could not think of anything that I had done wrong. But I liked the priest and wanted to please him, so I invented a few minor incidents. I tried to repress my Jewishness and thought that all my family had been killed.

When I arrived in that village, I wrote to Edek, the young man who was the caretaker of the convent and who had hidden the 14 of us, and gave him my address. Six months after the war, my aunt came to fetch me. I was in the fields and saw her coming. She said, "Do you know who I am?" "Yes," I replied. "Do you know you are Jewish?" I did not know who I was anymore, and was frightened to answer.

She put me in a children's home in Poland but there was still a lot of anti-Semitism. In fact stones were thrown at our home, and very soon we left for France. I went to school in France, passed a few exams, and worked for a year.

At the end of 1956 I went to England to improve my English. I met an Englishman and eventually settled here. I have two sons and two grandsons, and I love them very much. I tried to teach them tolerance, to accept people whatever their religion or colour of skin, so that we do not persecute those who are different.

SIMON WINSTON

Born in Radzivilov

I was born in 1938 in Poland, in a town called Radzivilov, now in the Ukraine. Many Jews in the town worked in the grain industry and my grandfather part owned a flour mill. The Jewish population was extensive and they had their own synagogues and schools.

I was a small child when my life, that of my family and thousands of other local Jews began to change forever. I don't remember the trauma of my early childhood, but I can describe accurately the events that unfolded thanks to a manuscript my father wrote after the war and by remembering stories my father told me.

In 1939 Germany invaded Poland, but it wasn't until June 1941 that the Nazis entered Radzivilov. They were brutal to Jews right from the start and very soon issued some 'Jewish' laws': Jews could not own radios; Jews could not walk on the pavements; Jews had to wear yellow patches to identify them; and Jews were not allowed to leave town. The penalty for disobeying these 'Jewish' laws was death.

On 15th August 1941 all 7000 Jews were ordered into the Market Square where SS machine-gunners pointed their machine guns at them and they feared the worst. After being intimidated and held like frightened rabbits for two to three hours, the machine-gunners left and the Jews were ordered to go back to their homes. When they got home they found their homes were empty. The Germans had stolen all their possessions.

On 9th April 1942, a ghetto (prison) was constructed for the Jews. It was in the slummy part of town and conditions were dire. Living conditions were very cramped and lacked proper sanitation. The ghetto was surrounded by brick walls and barbed wire. German soldiers guarded the outside perimeter of the ghetto and Ukrainian Nazis patrolled inside.

The ghetto was divided into two parts, with a road passing through the middle. Ghetto One was for the 'useful' Jews – the young, the strong and those who could work. About 1000 Jews lived in Ghetto One, including my parents. They were sent out to work for twelve hours a day and they were rewarded with a reasonable amount of food to eat. Ghetto Two was for the 'useless Jews' – the old, the weak, the ill and children who had lost their parents – about 5000 of them, including my grandparents. They were not given any food at all. They were starving to death – and that was the intention!

On 1st July 1942, when there were only 2000 Jews left in Ghetto Two, the Germans decided that they weren't dying fast enough, so they gave them a push. All 2000 were ordered into The Great Synagogue Yard. The men were separated from the women and force-marched about five kilometres to a clearing in the nearby woods. When they got there they found two large, newly-dug pits covered in lime. The men were then ordered to take off their clothes, put them in a pile and stand around the first pit. Like zombies, they did as they were told and very quickly they were all shot dead. They fell into the pit and soon their bodies were covered over. The same fate awaited the women who were buried in the second pit. That day 2000 innocent Jews were brutally murdered by the Nazis.

Soon the situation in Ghetto One was becoming desperate because there were less work duties and therefore much less food. People feared the worst and started to make plans to escape, including my parents. My father had foreseen such a situation, even before the ghetto was created. To prepare himself, he sold most of his valuables and converted the money into gold ingots which he hid in various personal possessions – such as in clothing and in false bottoms of shoes and brushes. These gold ingots would be used later to purchase our escape and to pay for hiding places.

On 29th September 1942, my parents made their escape, taking me and my older brother, Joseph, with them. My family spent the next two years in hiding, moving from one hiding place to another as danger threatened. I remember my time in hiding fairly well and have many fascinating stories to tell students and adults when I give talks about my experiences. One story tells how, immediately after escaping from the ghetto, the family had to cross a river to get to their first hiding place and my father had to carry each of the family on his back, the water reaching his neck. I also tell a scary story of how I was caught by a group of Ukrainian soldiers but was able to talk my way out of trouble. There are many other stories I remember, mostly sad, but some funny.

Late in 1944, in our last hiding place in the cellar of a barn, I remember the farmer, in broad daylight, opening the trap door and telling us that we were free. He said that the Russians had defeated the Germans in battle and the Germans had run away. This was great news and my family were no longer fugitives. Sadly, this did not mean that we could go back to our home because this was now occupied by a Russian family and no way would they give back this home to its rightful owners. In fact, some other Jews who had survived in hiding and tried to reclaim their properties, were actually killed for trying to do so. So my family and I became refugees: homeless and all the time looking for somewhere to live.

For two years my family wandered from one D.P. (Displaced Persons) Camp to another, all the time looking for a permanent home. Eventually, in 1947, my mother discovered that she had a brother living in Nottingham. How he got to England before the war is another story, but he did everything possible to bring my family to Nottingham; first ensuring that we had a home to live in and then securing a job for my father.

I very quickly tried to make up for my lost childhood. I made friends, took part in sports and games, went to school and made a serious effort in learning a new language. In fact I did well at school, passed exams to enable me to go to a Grammar School and just failed going to University. National Service intervened so I had to do two years in the Army. After the Army I worked for five years as a civil engineer, then as a teacher, from which job I retired three to four years ago.

All this time in England, I never talked about my bitter experiences during World War II, not even to my Jewish friends. Then, about thirteen years ago, I read an article in my local newspaper about a Holocaust Centre, not far from where I still live – Beth Shalom. My curiosity quickly propelled me to visit the place and I was amazed at what I discovered: The Exhibition, the Memorial Hall and the Rose Garden. I am now very involved with the Centre and regularly give talks there. I am particularly anxious to let people know what happened to Jews in what is known as The Holocaust. My purpose is to enable people to learn lessons from the past and to commit them to do everything possible to make sure that such evil doesn't happen again.

GISÈLE WINTON

Childhood Memories

I am a French Jewess and was born in Paris. In 1939 the war with Germany was declared. They occupied France in May 1940. I was a little girl at the time and remember that all my family, aunties, uncles, cousins and my parents, went to Royan, a seaside resort situated in the west of France. I was told later, that we stayed there for three months. We then returned to Paris.

I used to read the newspapers at a very early age and would ask my parents about these people who were called "dirty Jews". They did hide the truth from me, in case I would tell people about our identity. I felt sad for those persecuted people and never wanted to be one of them. At the age of seven, one of my mother's cousins decided to tell me that I was also Jewish. This news did upset me very much. Besides having a shock, I felt now that I was different from the other children I knew. I therefore sensed that my ordeal would last a lifetime!

My grandfather, uncle, and cousin were interned in Drancy in a large place, like a warehouse, used as a prison. Fortunately, the family approached the Germans and told them that we were not Jewish and that it was a mistake! They did let them go. All the family, including my parents, held false passports, pretending that we were Persians of Muslim origin. This was organised by a friend of the family who was born in Boukhara, like us. This region is situated in the south of Russia. He was a doctor who helped all our families as one of our great-grandfathers had performed a great kindness to his family in the past; the favour was returned!

I do remember when I was six years' old, my father was knocked down by a German lorry while crossing the road and could not move at all for the next two weeks. The German did apologise and used to visit my dad, but never knew that we were Jewish. We had no mezouzas in the flat. It must have been quite frightening for my parents to have the "enemy" in the flat. I think that we were the only Jewish family amongst the French people in our area. Maybe there were others, but they would not admit it.

I learned later on that my mother was pregnant when I was four years' old and unfortunately, she had an abortion due to the war – it was a little boy. My parents lived to regret it all their lives, as my mother was unable to conceive again.

I was very frightened by all the planes flying night and day. It seemed like hell on earth. When I asked my mother if there was a more silent world and she answered in the affirmative, I thought that that time would be the happiest day of my life. I knew only this world where after all the siren calls our neighbours would rush into the basement of our flat and huddled together. It was only fear and terror everywhere. The Germans sent bombs that were called V1s and V2s.

One day this horrible war ended and all the noises from the planes stopped. Life started with a wonderful silence. It was beautiful! It was bliss!

Then it was the turn of the American soldiers to enter Paris, with great triumph and with their enormous tanks. Everybody received them with great honour which they deserved. Many French women jumped on their tanks to give them big kisses. They distributed colourful sweets, cigarettes, chewing gum, oranges, and ballpoint pens to the grownups and children. Today the Americans can do no wrong – I absolutely adore them!

REMEMBER

זכור

We remember the following members who died since the Child Survivors' Association of Great Britain was established. They are sadly missed.

Agnes Spinner

Dennis Goodman

Edyta Klein Smith

Halina Sand

Harvey Millan

Helena Pelc

Henry Abraham

Liliane Nisenbaum

Lusia Wineberg

Manfred Friedmann

Margot Reich

Nathan Breskin

Paul Oppenheimer

Pieter Steinhardt

Rosalind Bild

Ruth Edwards

Tom Sinclair

Ludwik Finkelstein

Dorrith M. Sim

Edgar Lax

Peter Eden

Susanne Ullmann

Abraham Pollack

Kurt Knopf

Edward Webber

Adam Sobey

Bettine LeBeau

Helga Ederer

In memory of my grandmothers who perished during the Shoah:

Maternal grandmother, Mrs Margarete Schwarzstein, Berlin, 1942
Paternal grandmother, Mrs Fanny Ochs Abraham, Theresienstadt, 1942

Henry Abraham

In Loving Memory of

Our father, Josef Ben Jacov Schütz who died in Bergen Belsen in January 1945,

Our grandmother Perla Schütz (Zimmetbaum),

And our many aunts, uncles, cousins and friends who perished in the Holocaust.

May they never be forgotten and may they rest in peace.

Ruth Usrad
Betty Bloom
Bronia Veitch

In Memoriam

My father Leonard David Frank
died Auschwitz, January 1943, aged 39. Lawyer

My grandmother Flora van Lier
died Auschwitz, August 1942, aged 65. Violinist

My aunt and uncle, Felicia and Machiel Wolff
died Auschwitz, August 1943, aged 40 and 39.

My uncle Herman Frijda.
died Auschwitz, October 1944, aged 57. Professor.
He refused to serve on the Jewish Council

My cousin Leo Frijda.
shot in Bloemendaal, October 1943, aged 20. Resistance leader.

My cousin 'Jops' Jacobsen.
killed whilst attempting to row across the North Sea, November 1942, aged 26.

and so many others in the family.

and finally,
my dear friend, Zeeg (Ze'ew) Frenkel
fatally shot in Westerbork during an air raid by the RAF, summer 1944, in his 60's. Anglophile.

Steven Frank.

The following people perished in Auschwitz on June 14th 1944:

My mother Rozsi Fischer née Herzteld	aged 39 ½
My sisters Judit Fischer	aged 13
Mädi Györgyi Fischer	aged 5
My brother Shloime Andor Fischer	aged 12

and many aunts, uncles and cousins.

Hedi Fischer Frankl

In memory of my family, those I knew and those many more I did not even get to know

My father Samuel Fransman, died Belsen 31/10/1944 age 40

My mother Anna Fransman-Rabbie, survived Belsen, died London 4/4/1980 age 80

My grandmother Rebecca Fransman-Appelboom, died 13/3/1943 Sobibor age 82

My aunt Sophie (Sippora) Fransman, died 30/9/42 Auschwitz age 40

My aunt Leentje Fransman, died 28/5/1943 Sobibor age 51

My aunt Grietje Fransman, died 28/5/1943 Sobibor age 49

My aunt Deborah Peper-Fransman died 3/12/42 Auschwitz age 58

My uncle Max Peper died 13/11/42 Auschwitz age 59

Their son-in-law Barend Italiaander died Sobibor, 4 June 1943 age 31

His wife Schoontje Jeanette Italiaander-Peper died Sobibor, 4 June 1943 age 36 and son Rudolf Abraham Italiaander Amsterdam, died Sobibor, 4 June 1943 age 4, and daughter Nora Italiaander Haarlem, died Sobibor, 4 June 1943 age 2

Max and Deborah's first son, Juda Peper died Sobibor age 32

His wife Anna Peper-Noach died Sobibor age 36

Max and Deborah's second son, Joseph Peper died Midden-Europa, 31/ 10/1943 age 29

His wife Sientje Greta Peper-Italiaander died Auschwitz, 5/10/1942 age 24 and their only son Ido Peper died 5 October 1942 Auschwitz, age 1

Their son-in-law Benjamin Zilverberg died in Auschwitz, January 1944 age 27

His wife Miriam (Jannie) Zilverberg-Peper survived Auschwitz and Ravensbruck died Amsterdam, August 2010 age 94

Max and Deborah's third son Mauritz Peper died August 1942 Auschwitz, age 18

My uncle Samuel Blom died 14 September 1942 Auschwitz, age 55

His wife Eva Blom-Fransman died 14 September 1942 Auschwitz, age 53

Their son Joseph Blom died 30 September 1942 Auschwitz, age 26

My uncle Hyman Fransman died 28/1/44 Auschwitz, age 47

And my mother's extensive Rabbie family, victims of the Holocaust:

Abraham Marcus Beffie 10-Aug-1942 Auschwitz age 34. Laura Hendrika Beffie-vaz Diaz 30-Sep-1942 Auschwitz age 32. Hadassa Bino-Rabbie 7-Dec-1942 Auschwitz age 65. Clara Boas-Rabbie 4-Jun-1943 Sobibor age 67. Nathan Bouwman 28-May-1943 Sobibor age 55. Rebecca Bouwman-Rebie 3-Dec-1942 Auschwitz age 57. Hartog Brilleman 2-Apr-1943 Sobibor age 64. Rebecca Brilleman-Rabbie 2-Apr-1943 Sobibor age 64. Eliazer Davids 9-Apr-1943 Sobibor age 64. Henriette Davids-Rabbie 9-Apr-1943 Sobibor age 66. Gerrit Mozes de Vries 10-Feb-1944 Monowitz age 20. Simon David de Vries 31-Mar-1944 Poland age 47. Hadassa Dresden-Rabbie 5-Feb-1943 Auschwitz age 63. Henk Fransman 8-Apr-1944 Auschwitz age 1 month. Samuel (Sam) Fransman 31-Oct-1944 Bergen-Belsen age 41. Wilhelm Fransman 21-Jan-1945 Central Europe age 31. Eva Fransman-Rabbie 8-Apr-1944 Auschwitz age 31. Hartog Geleerd 9-Jul-1943 Sobibor age 39. Branca Geleerd-Rabbie 9-Jul-1943 Sobibor age 37. Benjamin Goudeket 21-Sep-1942 Auschwitz age 68. Regina (Gien) Goudeket-Rabbie 21-Sep-1942 Auschwitz age 62. Rebecca Hondsregt-Rabbie 5-Mar-1943 Sobibor age 71. Samuel Koster 16-Feb-1944 Masselwitz age 48. Elisabeth (Liesje) Leeuwin-Rabbie 26-Mar-1943 Sobibor age 69. Salomon Loetè 28-May-1943 Sobibor age 56. Rebecca Loetè-Rabbie 28-May-1943 Sobibor age 58. Jacob Maijkels 5-Mar-1943 Sobibor age 72. Joseph Pam 17-Sep-1943 Auschwitz age 67. Rachel Pam-Rabbie 17-Sep-1943 Auschwitz age 72. Gerrit Polak 31-Aug-1944 Central Europe age 48. Levie Polak 4-Nov-1942 Auschwitz age 47. Mirjam Polak-Rabbie 12-Feb-1943 Auschwitz age 73. Roosje Polak-Rabbie 26-Mar-1944 Auschwitz age 52. Mozes Polk 21-May-1943 Sobibor age 40. Helena Polk-Rebi 21-May-1943 Sobibor age 37. Abraham Rabbie 31-Mar-1943 Central Europe age 48. Abraham (Bram) Rabbie 31-May-1945 Bergen-Belsen age 43. Benjamin Rabbie 30-Sep-1942 Auschwitz age 22. David Rabbie 16-Jul-1943 Sobibor age 42. Esther Rabbie 2-Jul-1943 Sobibor age 15. Eva Rabbie 28-May-1943 Sobibor age 20. Eva Rabbie 31-Jan-1944 Auschwitz age 21. Eveline Rabbie 16-Jul-1943 Sobibor age 7. Frederik Rabbie 28-Feb-1943 Auschwitz age 25.

Frederik (Frits) Rabbie 21-May-1943 Sobibor age 46. Frits Jacob Rabbie 9-Oct-1941 Mauthausen age 22. Gompel Rabbie 19-Sep-1941 Mauthausen age 25. Helena Rabbie 24-Apr-1945 Bergen-Belsen age 12. Herman Abraham Rabbie 30-Sep-1942 Auschwitz age 36. Hermanus Rabbie 5-Mar-1943 Sobibor age 69. Isaac Rabbie 16-Jul-1943 Sobibor age 39. Isaac (Ies) Rabbie 1-Feb-1945 Bergen-Belsen age 40. Jacob Rabbie 3-Dec-1942 Auschwitz age 75. Jacob Rabbie 16-Apr-1943 Sobibor age 58. Jacob Rabbie 28-May-1943 Sobibor age 53. Jacob Rabbie 21-May-1943 Sobibor age 23. Jacob (Jaap) Rabbie 19-Nov-1942 Auschwitz age 65. Jacques Rabbie 7-Dec-1942 Auschwitz age 75. Jesaias Rabbie 31-Jan-1944 Auschwitz age 29. Joel Rabbie 9-Apr-1943 Sobibor age 71. Joseph Rabbie 16-Apr-1943 Sobibor age 69. Joseph Rabbie 2-Jul-1943 Sobibor age 44. Klara Rabbie 31-Jan-1944 Auschwitz age 17. Lena Rabbie 28-May-1943 Sobibor age 16. Levie Rabbie 12-Oct-1942 Auschwitz age 67. Levie Rabbie 31-Jan-1943 Blechhammer age 39. Marianne Rabbie 3-Dec-1942 Auschwitz age 60. Mozes Rabbie 28-May-1943 Sobibor age 89. Mozes Rabbie 31-Mar-1944 Poland age 27. Mozes Rabbie 30-Sep-1942 Auschwitz age 24. Mozes Rabbie 28-May-1943 Sobibor age 15. Mozes (Dikke Max) Rabbic 23-Jul-1943 Sobibor age 45. Naatje Rabbie 31-Oct-1944 Auschwitz age 40. Rika Rabbie 28-May-1943 Sobibor age 12. Rudolf Rabbie 29-Sep-1941 Mauthausen age 19. Salomon Rabbie 3-Dec-1942 Auschwitz age 55. Salomon (Sam) Rabbie 31-Jul-1942 Auschwitz age 43. Samuel Rabbie 26-Mar-1943 Sobibor age 63. Samuel Rabbie 2-Jul-1943 Sobibor age 47. Samuel Rabbie 30-Apr-1943 Sobibor age 39. Sara Rabbie 3-Jul-1943 Sobibor age 19. Sara Rabbie 2-Jul-1943 Sobibor age 9. Serah Rabbie 16-Jul-1943 Sobibor age 11. Simon Rabbie 11-Oct-1944 Auschwitz age 59. Simon Rabbie 31-Aug-1943 Central Europe age 47. Simon Rabbie 28-Feb-1943 Auschwitz age 43. Sonja Hadassa Rabbie 8-Oct-1942 Auschwitz age 11. Simcha Rabbie-Acohen 2-Jul-1943 Sobibor age 41. Mina Rabbie-Blitz 8-Aug-1942 Auschwitz age 48. Elisabeth Rabbie-Borstel 16-Jul-1943 Sobibor age 33. Henriette Rabbie-Dresden 5-Feb-1943 Auschwitz age 58. Mietje

Rabbie-Eijl 8-Oct-1942 Auschwitz age 50. Esther Rabbie-Elzas 15-Oct-1942 Auschwitz age 43. Rachel Rabbie-Elzas 28-May-1943 Sobibor age 51. Esther Rabbie-Groenteman 16-Jul-1943 Sobibor age 20. Hendrika Rabbie-Hamel 30-Sep-1942 Auschwitz age 39. Cornelia Rabbie-Kinsbergen 3-Dec-1942 Auschwitz age 56. Sara Rabbie-Kloot 10-Aug-1942 Auschwitz age 31. Lea Rabbie-Kraal 23-Jul-1943 Sobibor age 45. Betje Rabbie-Meijer 26-Mar-1943 Sobibor age 63. Marianne Rabbie-Polak 3-Dec-1942 Auschwitz age 69. Phoebe Rabbie-Pyper 19-Nov-1942 Auschwitz age 65. Leentje Rabbie-Rabbie 12-Oct-1942 Auschwitz age 6. Berendina Rabbie-Rood 6-Sep-1944 Auschwitz age 65. Rebecca Rabbie-Sluis 31-Jan-1944 Auschwitz age 25. Roosje Rabbie-Snoek 11-Oct-1944 Auschwitz age 58. Jansje Rabbie-van Staveren 5-Oct-1942 Auschwitz age 46. Hester (Hettie) Rabbie-Velleman 31-Jul-1942 Auschwitz age 39. Rosa David Rabbie-Versteeg 28-May-1943 Sobibor age 51. David Rebi 29-Aug-1942 Auschwitz age 53. Rachel Rebi-Lenson 29-Aug-1942 Auschwitz age 50. Isaac Rebie 29-Sep-1942 Auschwitz age 64. Roosje Rebie 3-Dec-1942 Auschwitz age 56. Dientje Rebie-van Dam 28-Sep-1942 Auschwitz age 63. Rebecca Reens-Rabbie 16-Apr-1943 Sobibor age 73. Elisabeth Roodveldt-Rabbie 11-Jun-1943 Sobibor age 44. Hartog Sak 30-Sep-1942 Auschwitz age 32. Suze Rebecca Sak-Beffie 10-Aug-1942 Auschwitz age 33. Verdona Stad 31-Jul-1942 Auschwitz. Helena (Lena) Stad-Rabbie 31-Jul-1942 Auschwitz age 17. Abraham Stodel Disappeared. Henderina Stodel-Rebi Disappeared. Hermanus Stork 7-Dec-1942 Auschwitz age 4. Jeannette Milly Stork 7-Dec-1942 Auschwitz age 7. Joseph Stork 28-Feb-1943 Auschwitz age 41. Louis Stork 7-Dec-1942 Auschwitz age 8. Meijer Stork 7-Dec-1942 Auschwitz age 10. Frederika Stork-Rabbie 7-Dec-1942 Auschwitz age 35. Martina van Aalst 4-Jun-1943 Sobibor age 18. Anna van Aalst-Rabbie 30-Apr-1943 Sobibor age 46. Emanuel van Thijn 4-Jun-1943 Sobibor age 44. Siegfried van Thijn 4-Jun-1943 Sobibor age 10. Henriette (Jet) van Thijn-Rabbie 4-Jun-1943 Sobibor age 40. Marcus Wolff 13-Mar-1943 Sobibor age 88. Rebecca Wolff-Rabbie 3-Dec-1942 Auschwitz age 65.

John Fransman

These are the members of my close family who died during the war:

Lipka, my mother, died in the ghetto
Alfred, my father, killed by the Germans
Tunio, my brother, buried alive
My grandmother Monat
Josyf Mayer, my uncle, killed in the ghetto
Rivka, my aunt, died in the ghetto
Izio, my cousin, died in a concentration camp
Aron, my uncle, his wife and child, killed in the ghetto
Dodel, my uncle, killed
Motel, my uncle
Jojny, my uncle, killed
Josif, my uncle, died in a concentration camp
Mania, my aunt, killed in the ghetto
An aunt, wife of uncle Zelig, and cousin Stella.

Janine Webber (formerly Galloway)

In Memoriam

My maternal grandmother, Chaya Ganz née Wirtenthal, aged 52 years
grandfather Nachum Ganz, aged 56 years
uncle Mundek Wirtenthal, aged 32 years
aunt Lolla Ganz, aged 27 years, and her unborn child.
uncle Abrumek Ganz, aged 18 years.
My paternal grandmother Gisa Garfinkle née Rottler, aged 50 years
aunt Rusa Garfinkle, aged 34 years
uncle Isu Garfinkle, aged 22 years
aunt Dora, her husband and five children
maternal great-uncle Liebish Wirtenthal, aged 45 years, his wife and child
my maternal great-uncle Shmuel Wirtenthal, aged 55 years, his wife

Machla and
daughter Pesca, son Mijorkal, aged 23 years, and younger son
Abramelu.
My Maternal second cousin Max Rupp
cousins Hayka Klein and Janek Klein.

In memory of all those of my family, named and unnamed, who were
murdered in the Holocaust.

Alfred Garwood

In memory of

My father Mendel Apelzon, born 25.8.1910 in Glowko, Poland,
died 10.2.1943 in Auschwitz – Birkenau

Paternal grandfather Isak Leib Apelzon, born 1883 Glowko, Poland;
killed 1943?

Maternal grandfather Henoch Pomocnik, born 1884?, Dzialoszyce
deported September 1942 to Betzec

Maternal step-grandmother Ester Weintraub, born 1890?,
deported September 1942 to Betzec

Paternal step-grandmother Necha Apelzon
killed 1943?

Maternal aunts Mania Pomocnik, born 1916?, Dzialoszyce;
deported 1942 to Belzec
Ester Pomocnik, born 1918, Dzialoszyce
deported 1942 to Belzec
Brocha Pomocnik, born 1921?, Dzialoszyce
deported 1942 to Belzec

Great Aunt Sara Reisel, born 1881?,
killed September 1942 in Dzialoszyce

Paternal Aunts and Uncles
Motl Apelzon, born 1931, Lodz;
killed 1942?

Moshe Apelzon, born 1916, Lodz;
killed 1942?

Chaid Apelzon, born 1933?, Lodz;
killed 1942?

Freida Apelzon, born 1935?, Lodz;
killed 1942

Lea Goodman

Relatives who died in the Holocaust:

my mother Hanna Hecht née Dub
my father Joseph Hecht
my brothers Israel Hecht and
Schmuel Avrum Hecht

Jacob Hecht

I wish to commemorate my family who perished in the Holocaust:

Mother Helena Husserlová,
born 16th August 1910 in Zdikov, Czechoslovakia
died Auschwitz 1944

Father Pavel Husserl,
born 12th July 1904 in Vienna, Austria
died Lodz, Poland, 1942

Grandparents, aunt, uncle, mother's sister and brother (dates unknown).

I also wish to commemorate Alice Goldberger who cared for me when I came to England, with her devoted helpers, Sophie Manna and Gertrud Suse.

Zdenka Husserl

In memory of

Salo Jacob and
Salka Jacob née Keins, both late of Gleiwitz

Hans Heumann, born 27.5.1896, Hertha Heumann née Jacob, born 8.9.1905, and their daughter Anita Heumann, born 29.5.1930, all of Gleiwitz and Berlin

Jacob Lax, born in Rzev, on 12.5.1880

Amalia Lax née Keins, born in Antonienhütte, Kreiz Kattowitz, on 15.9.1883 both formerly of Berlin.

Remembered by **Edgar Lax**
In Memory of

My maternal grandparents Felner,

My paternal grandparents Mandelbaum,

My husband's grandmother Lipski,

And many members of our family
who perished in Warsaw and Lodz, Poland,
during the War.

Mireille Lipski

In memory of my grandparents,

Selig Obstfeld (1865 – 1943),
his wife Esther Obstfeld née Obstfeld (1882 – 1943),
Joseph Vet (1877 – 1942), and
his wife Henriette Vet née Emmering (1878 – 1943),
uncle Loebel Obstfeld (1895 – 1943),
his wife Marguerite Obstfeld née Mahler (1903 – 1945),
uncle Izaak Obstfeld (1913 – 1943),
cousin Marco Obstfeld (1922 – 1941).
aunt Kitty Bed née Vet (1901 – 1943),
and her husband Meyer Bed (1900 – 1943),
cousin John Bed (1926 – 1942),
and cousin Henriette Bed (1930 – 1943).

as well as in memory of my wife Dorothy's

grandfather Hermann Philippsberg (1861 – 1942)
and his extended Philippsberg-family:
Amalia, Bianca, Herta, Margarethe née Meyer, Margarethe née
Rosenthal, Regine née Tischler, Salusch, and Simon,
uncle Leo Goldschmidt (1895 – 1942)
and cousin Werner Goldschmidt (1924 – 1942),
and great-uncle Max Kaufmann (1883 – 1942).

They all perished during the Holocaust.

Henri Obstfeld

In memoriam of relatives who perished during the Holocaust:

Our father, Dr Johann Felix Robert (Hans) Oppenheimer
born 18-06-1901 in Fürth, near Nuremberg
died 20-03-1945 in Bergen-Belsen

Our mother, Dr Friederike (Rita) Oppenheimer
born 23-01-1902 in Heidelberg
died 17-01-1945 in Bergen-Belsen

Our paternal grandfather, Josef Oppenheimer
born 19-10-1866 in Kleinwallstadt
died 23-07-1943 in Sobibor

Our paternal grandmother, Meta Oppenheimer née Baum
born 10-02-1876 in Nuremberg
died 23-07-1943 in Sobibor

Our maternal grandfather, Dr Rudolf Fürst
born 01-09-1865 in Heidelberg
died 26-03-1943 in Sobibor

Our maternal grandmother, Hedwig Fürst née Oppé
born 04-10-1875 in Muhlhausen
died 26-03-1943 in Sobibor

Eve Oppenheimer

In blessed and cherished memory of

My father Filip Stern, aged 38

My brother Uriel Stern, aged 6
Both perished in Lwow (now Lviv) in August 1942

My grandparents Aba and Hinda Brück

and an extended family of more than 300 persons.

Lili Stern-Pohlmann

In memory of my dear family, all perished in the Holocaust:

Father, Erno Blau
Mother, Gizella Blau née Kohn
Aunts and Uncles:
Kohn, Armin; son and daughter
Kaufman, Reszin; wife and three children
Kohn, Deszo; wife and five children
Kohn, Jeno; wife and baby
Kohn, Bela; wife and eight children

Susan Pollack

In memory of

my mother Fela Herclich Blit
grandparents Mordechai and Leah Herclich
grandparents Fela (née Winawer) and Wolf Blit
uncle Leon and aunt Niusia Herclich
aunt Bella Herclich and her fiancé Josef
aunt Gucia and uncle Jakub Felenbok
aunt Pola Blit

and cousin Gienia Herclich
together with so many other members of my extended family – old,
young, children – who perished during the annihilation of the Warsaw
Ghetto.

Wlodka Blit Robertson

In memory of

Auguste Schallmach – killed in Auschwitz
Else Rosenthal née Schallmach - died in Theresienstadt
Siegfried Rosenthal – killed in Auschwitz
Sally Studinski – died in Theresienstadt
Frieda Studinski née Lachman – died in Theresienstadt
Samuel Selmanson – died in Auschwitz
Adelhaid Nathan née Gluck – killed in Auschwitz
Bertha Lewy (née Braunchen Stensch) – died in Theresienstadt

My mother's cousins:
Theodor Herrmann - deported Auschwitz 4th March 1943
Bianca Herrmann née Sachs - deported Auschwitz 4th March 1943
Their son Heinz Herrmann - deported Auschwitz 19th February
1943

Bela Rosenthal

In Memory of:

My paternal Grandparents Moses & Perla; my uncles Samuel
Zimetbaum & Gerry Zimetbaum, their wives and children. They
lived in Tarnow, Poland, and are believed to have perished in Belzec
Death Camp in 1942

My maternal Grandparents, Bluma and Isaac Mendel Perleman, from Warsaw, Poland, all my mother's siblings, my seven aunts and uncles, their husbands, wives, children and grandchildren. Some lived in Warsaw and are believed to have perished in Treblinka, others lived in Paris and are believed to have perished in Auschwitz.

Some of my aunts gave us shelter in Paris and I played with my cousins there. Forgive me that your faces have vanished from my memory and that your names are forgotten. But the fact that you lived, and the manner of your deaths, I remember.

Joan Salter (born Fanny Zimetbaum)

In Loving Memory of my dear Parents

Hans Oppenheim, born April 16 1895 in Bad Sachsa,
Deported June 17 1943 to Teresienstadt and thence to Auschwitz, October 12 1944,

Trude Oppenheim née Lindenfeld, born May 3 1902 in Kassel,
Deported June 17 1943 to Teresienstadt and thence to Auschwitz, October 12 1944.

Dorrith M Sim

In memory of

my father Jeno Schwet
my mother Nusi Schwet
my uncle Gyula Schwet
my cousin Eva Schwet

Tom Sinclair

In loving memory of

my father Paul,
mother Rose,
and youngest brother Marcel, 13 years old.

They were murdered on arrival in Auschwitz, on the second of June 1944

Freda Wineman